D0484058

WITHDRAWN
UTSA LIBRARIES

MONK'S TALE

MONK'S TALE

The Pilgrimage Begins, 1941–1975

Edward A. Malloy, C.S.C.

University of Notre Dame Press   *Notre Dame, Indiana*

**Library
University of Texas
at San Antonio**

Copyright © 2009 by University of Notre Dame

Notre Dame, Indiana 46556

www.undpress.nd.edu

All Rights Reserved

Manufactured in the United States of America

Library of Congress Cataloging-in-Publication Data

Malloy, Edward A.

  Monk's tale / Edward A. Malloy.

    v. cm.

  Includes index.

  Contents: v. 1. The pilgrimage begins, 1941–1975.

  ISBN-13: 978-0-268-03516-7 (v. 1 : cloth : alk. paper)

  ISBN-10: 0-268-03516-4 (v. 1 : cloth : alk. paper)

  1. Malloy, Edward A. 2. Malloy, Edward A.—Childhood and youth.

3. University of Notre Dame—Presidents—Biography. 4. College presidents—

Indiana—Biography. 5. University of Notre Dame—Faculty—Biography.

6. Catholic universities and colleges—United States—Case studies. 7. Priests—

United States—Biography. 8. Catholic Church—Clergy—Biography.

9. Catholic Church—United States—History—20th century. I. Title.

  LD4112.7.M35A3   2009

  378.772'89—dc22

  [B]

                          2009022894

∞ *The paper in this book meets the guidelines for permanence and
durability of the Committee on Production Guidelines for Book Longevity of
the Council on Library Resources.*

CONTENTS

ACKNOWLEDGMENTS

To my mother and father, who welcomed me into the world, raised me in love, and provided a religious and educational foundation that has given me a privileged start in life.

To my sisters, Joanne and Mary, who helped to create a family where our individuality could be respected and fostered without losing our sense of solidarity and mutual responsibility.

To my teachers, coaches, and mentors, who believed in my potential and never allowed me to give up on my dreams.

To Joan Bradley, Walt Collins, and Carole Roos, and my student interns, Patrick Coleman, Brendan Ryan, Patrick Nugent, and Gregory O'Donnell, who have helped to bring this project to fulfillment.

PROLOGUE

I was fifty-five years old before I found time to explore Ireland, my ancestral homeland, at a leisurely pace. In November 1996, Notre Dame played a football game in Dublin against the U.S. Naval Academy. Over 10,000 Notre Dame fans and 5,000 Navy fans used the occasion to go to Ireland and visit the various tourist locations and, in some cases, to play golf on some of the legendary courses of the island. I knew that I would have many hosting functions during the game week, so I arranged with my two sisters, Joanne Rorapaugh and Mary Long, and Mary's husband, John, to spend the week before the game driving around to see the wonders of the south and west of Ireland, staying in inns, hotels, and even a castle or two. Five or six years earlier, I had gathered some genealogical information, and this was a chance to pursue that quest on native soil.

Mary slipped and fell a few months before our trip, breaking her elbow, but that was not enough to dissuade her from participating. Early on in our tour we stayed overnight in Westport, the capital city of County Mayo and an interesting port and cultural center. Our intention was to venture out from there to Castlebar, a close-by town which I knew was near our estimated ancestral area on my father's side.

In Castelbar we saw various spellings of our name (Malloy, Molloy, Mulloy) on some of the major establishments, including a pub, a grocery, and a hardware store. We ventured into a large Catholic cemetery where many of the tombstones had been reconstructed, presumably by American relatives. A genealogist back in the States had suggested to me that the village of Graffamore, near Castlebar, was most likely the center of the Malloy heritage in County Mayo. After some inquiry among the locals (famous for their circumspection and their delight in misdirecting tourists), we were able to locate Graffamore. But we did not know what to do next.

Unfortunately, my sister Joanne fell on one of our cemetery tours and needed medical attention. While she awaited treatment and Mary sat with her, John and I decided to go exploring. We stopped at the end of a country lane and allowed our creative imaginations to evoke a possible site where these relatives might have been living a century or two ago. Finally, we decided to stop for gas and were directed to the two-room Saint Patrick's National School in Cornanool, right next door to the gas station. Our informant suggested it might be a source of reliable information about families in the area.

And so it was. The school's two teachers and seven or eight grades of students were taking a recess as we drove up, so we were able to come inside the school and look through some old grade books going back into the late nineteenth century. There were, indeed, Malloys listed (with various spellings). The recurring pattern would be that they stayed in school through the fifth or sixth grade, and then quit to work on the farm or emigrate to the United States or Canada.

After Joanne had been attended to by the Irish doctor, all four of us returned to the school, where they graciously shared access once again to the old grade books. How impressive it was to feel this kind of connection across the decades with those who most probably had genetic links in common with Joanne, Mary, and me. It struck me at the time, and it still does, that not so long ago the Malloys were fortunate if they received any education at all. But then my grandfather finished grade school, my father completed high school, and now I had the good fortune to return to this primordial area as the recipient of a doctorate and as the president of a great Catholic university.

Who from the past would ever have believed it?

MONK'S TALE

CHAPTER 1

ROOTS

FAMILY TRADITION HAS IT THAT AT MY BIRTH ON May 3, 1941, in Georgetown University Hospital, my high school–educated father came into the birthing area, took me from my mother, and with great pride raised me into the air and proclaimed: "This is my son, my firstborn, and some day he is going to go to college. Even better, he is going to attend Georgetown University." In turn my Uncle John Malloy, who lived a few doors away from us and who at that time had no children of his own, took me from my father and offered an alternate prediction. "He is surely going to attend a fine university," he asserted, "but he is not bound for Georgetown. He is going to go to the University of Notre Dame and some day he will become president there." It is hard to say how accurate these reports are, but at the time of my presidential inauguration my Uncle John was present and took great pride in seeing his prophecy come true.

The year before my birth my parents had moved to Washington, D.C., from Scranton, their birthplace and hometown in the anthracite coal district of northeastern Pennsylvania. My father's side of the family was thoroughly Irish, even though my grandfather Malloy was probably born in Liverpool, England, where his parents had emigrated seeking work. My mother's side of the family had both Irish and English roots. Neither side had much in the way of financial resources, but in-laws on my mother's side ran a grocery store in a neighborhood of Scranton called Kaiser Valley. It was there that we went on summer vacations, taking over a couple of rooms in their family home. It was a bit crowded, but we made do. Trips to Scranton were times for visiting with relatives, being doted on, and enjoying a change of pace from the normal routines of D.C. The idea of staying in motels simply never came up. It was only later that I discovered from my parents how tight a budget we usually had on these excursions.

My aunt, Sister Elizabeth Malloy, Immaculate Heart of Mary (I.H.M.), was the only member of our extended family who had pursued a religious vocation. She became a nun at an early age and followed a ministerial career in primary education in various schools in Pennsylvania and Maryland. Although her life was relatively cloistered, especially in the era before the Second Vatican Council, my parents, my sisters Joanne and Mary, and I would visit her when possible during the school year, and even more enthusiastically in the summer because the sisters had a summer place near LaPlata, Maryland, on the Potomac River.

On our school visits we would be greeted at the entrance by a sister other than my aunt and escorted to one of the parlors where we would sit and wait while some student played "Heart and Soul" or "Blue Moon" on a piano down the corridor. Eventually, Sister Elizabeth would arrive. About halfway through our visit, one of the nuns would return and ask if we wanted milk and cookies. A few moments later we would receive our snack, and eventually it would be time to leave. Each convent had the same basic smell, a light touch of rose or lilac. We always felt warmly greeted, but my sisters and I were curious about many things, especially whether the nuns had a full head of hair under their habits and what their rooms were like and what they talked about when we were not around. All of this curiosity was at least partly prompted by the fact that our own primary school teachers were all members of religious communities too.

Some of these questions were partially answered when we drove to the sisters' camp in the summer. There we would catch glimpses of Sister Elizabeth and her peers swimming in the river in bathing suits, roller-skating in full habits at a local rink, or enjoying a picnic lunch and playing badminton or croquet or horseshoes. We always felt sworn to secrecy, especially in our younger years, as if we had been exposed to information hidden from ordinary Catholic kids. It was not so much like Dorothy in *The Wizard of Oz* discovering the sham power of the Wizard, but rather an encounter with the human dimension of women whom we held in high esteem.

Sister Elizabeth played a pivotal role in the history of our extended family. She had a cordial relationship with each of her siblings and with their spouses and children. At Christmas she sent all the children gifts, usually some religious object such as a rosary or a sacred medal or a book about a saint. As we grew older, we probably would have preferred something more secular, but because it came from Sister, the gift was prized on its own terms. As the only other member of my family who pursued a religious vocation, Sister Elizabeth was a great support to me in my journey to the priesthood. I was pleased to be able to celebrate her funeral at the I.H.M. convent at Marywood University in Scranton.

My Father

My father's full name was Edward Aloysius, so I am Edward Aloysius the Second, although I gained the nickname "Monk" in the fourth grade and was called after my father only in the earliest stages of my life and in certain formal settings. My mother called him Eddie and so did his family members and his colleagues at work. My father had one kidney removed when he was young and was not eligible to be drafted during World War II. In addition, during the whole time I was living at home he suffered from a duodenal ulcer and was on a bland diet and restricted in some of his activity. The recommended remedies of the day included drinking a lot of milk and taking regular doses of substances like Maalox, although subsequent research has proven that such therapies were counterproductive. One lesson that I learned from my father's mix of job-related stress and ulcerous symptoms was to seek for a balance in my own life so that I would not carry around a lot of emotional baggage.

My parents' move to D.C. was prompted by two job offers my father had received. One was to become a revenue agent in rural West Virginia, which entailed chasing down Appalachian moonshiners and trying to close illegal stills. The second was to become a claims adjustor for the D.C. Transit Company which ran the buses and streetcars in the metropolitan area prior to the building of the Metro subway system. On first hearing this story, I was immediately thankful that he had chosen the second path. How different my life might have been if he had not.

My father's job as a claims adjustor required him to investigate accidents and injury claims involving company vehicles and to make recommendations to his supervisors whether they should go to court or settle out of court (and how much the financial payment should be). This work involved interviewing the employees involved, the claimants, any witnesses to the event, and the police agencies if there had been a formal report. The problems the Transit Company had were, first, juries had a predisposition to punish the big, powerful, impersonal company if some poor citizen claimed to be injured, and second, the same doctors and lawyers appeared as part of the process in adjudicating the claim. Despite all of this, my father sought fairness in looking at the evidence and, as far I could tell, never grew cynical about the demands of justice or his responsibility to his employers.

Roots

I remember saying to my father when I was around twelve or thirteen that I wanted to follow his example and work for the Transit Company myself. I will never forget his demeanor as he told me he hoped I never had to face the dead-end realities that he did. Because he had only a high school education, he explained, he could never rise into the management ranks and would forever be a claims adjustor on the street. For the first time I realized what a sacrifice Dad was making for the family. His salary level was always relatively modest, and toward the end of his career the only significant benefit he enjoyed was four and eventually five weeks of paid vacation. Implicit in his concern for my early career aspirations was the notion that my education would be the key to rising above the limitations that he had experienced. It was a lesson I never forgot.

My father's religious convictions and his love for the Catholic Church were consistently manifest in our family life and in his attitudes about politics and current events. He was strongly anti-Communist, for example, and as a result he was an easy prey to the demagoguery of Senator Joseph McCarthy in the mid-1950s. He was a big fan of Bishop Fulton Sheen, and once we got a television set (about the last family in the neighborhood to purchase one), we were regular viewers of his weekly show. Like many Catholics of his generation, Dad felt special delight when a "Catholic" would win acclaim in some walk of life (Bing Crosby, Dennis Day, John Kennedy). Certain values were simply taken for granted: we ate fish on Fridays, kept the Lenten fast, and participated in the parish-wide retreats (which usually had separate sections for males and females). On Saturday afternoons we went to confession as a family, and under the influence of Father Pat Payton, C.S.C., we had periods of time when we would pray the rosary together ("a family that prays together stays together").

After my sisters and I were enrolled in Saint Anthony's Grade School, my parents both became involved in parish organizations. My father was on the parish council, or whatever it was called in those days, and he sometimes served as an usher at mass. He was a faithful attendant at the athletic and other extracurricular activities that were part of my grade school and summertime experiences.

My father joined the Knights of Columbus, the Catholic fraternal organization, in the 1960s and gradually worked his way up to the Fourth Degree, a kind of elite status. He was a faithful participant in the activities of the local K. of C. council. In retrospect I think that the male solidarity of the organization and the periodic wearing of fancy outfits—plumed hat, fur cape, sword—appealed to him since his work did not offer any special camaraderie or romantic ritual, and the religious orientation of the group was comfortably reinforcing.

In the 1960s and early 1970s, Dad became seriously involved in the civil rights movement and in ameliorating the discriminatory social conditions that prevailed in Washington and beyond. In Scranton he had known almost no black people, but in D.C., where in the 1940s and 1950s the city was around 50 percent black, he was exposed to a broad cross section of black society, from civic leaders and professional people to the poorest of the poor in the inner-city slums. For him, it was simply a matter of justice and Catholic values that one needed to work peacefully for social change.

So he joined the Knights of Saint John, a predominantly black Catholic fraternal organization created to preserve the status quo in a segregated society. He later invited some of the Knights of Saint John to join the Knights of Columbus, thus effectively integrating the K. of C. for the first time in the Capital City. This precipitated a round of behind-the-scenes attacks on my father's integrity and motivations, but despite opposition he prevailed and soon had a reputation in black Catholic circles of being a true friend and a courageous advocate for racial justice.

In 1963 when Martin Luther King, Jr., led his March on Washington, my father volunteered to be part of the hospitality committee and I assisted him. Despite predictions of blood in the streets, it turned out to be one of the most peaceful days in the city's history.

Roots

It was also one of the great moments of oratory in American history when King delivered his "I Have a Dream" speech.

After his retirement from the Transit Company, Dad volunteered on a regular basis at the Shrine of the Immaculate Conception on the Catholic University campus, about a mile from where we lived. His main responsibility was conducting tours of the large, elegant church structure. He also helped out with some of the masses, serving as lector and communion distributor. He loved this activity and always went to the Shrine with great enthusiasm. Sometimes he was called to lock up the main part of the church at the end of the day. This could involve encountering people trying to hide out or individuals who were mentally deranged (which was not uncommon in Washington tourist circles). On occasion, Dad would find some poor soul completely naked, claiming to have had a spiritual vision. He would call the police and gently urge the vagrant to put his clothes back on.

Because of his devotion to the Shrine and his personal piety directed to the Blessed Mother (the interior of the structure is characterized by altars and art celebrating the various national and cultural images of Mary), Dad wanted someday for our family to be in a position to make a donation to support its work and, thereby, to have the Malloy name emblazoned on the basement walls where donors were listed. When that day finally arrived, I came to Washington and celebrated a family Mass of Thanksgiving in one of the side chapels. The only ones present were my immediate family and an older woman who sat at the back. After I finished my brief homily, the woman began mumbling that I had never once mentioned the Blessed Mother. With that, my mother turned around and stared darts through the woman, who proceeded to leave. My father, ever cool in a crisis, simply encouraged me to continue as though nothing had happened. (A year or two later the same woman was arrested for stealing from the poor box with a string and some gum. When my mother saw the story in the *Washington Post*, she finally felt vindicated.)

My father lived to be seventy-seven—a remarkable age considering that he functioned most of his life with one kidney, survived persistent complications from ulcers, rebounded from a heart attack at seventy, and underwent surgery for colon cancer a few years later. He spent the last day of his life at the Shrine, conducting tours. He once told me that when there were lulls between visitors, he had a routine of going to different parts of the church where he would pray for different intentions—the needs of the family, social justice, world peace, the sick, and so on. I presume that is how he spent part of his final day. After the tour schedule was completed that day, Dad lectored at the late afternoon mass and helped distribute communion. Then he drove home, poured himself a drink, and sat down on the couch while Mom prepared dinner. The next thing my mother noticed was that he had keeled over with a heart attack. By the time the ambulance arrived, it was too late.

When I received the news, I was shocked and rushed back from Notre Dame to be with my mother and sisters. I had always wondered what it would be like to celebrate and preach at my own parent's funeral. As it turned out, once I adjusted to the reality of his death, I was comforted by an experience that I had had a little over a year before. I was on sabbatical from the faculty at Notre Dame and staying in our Holy Cross community house in Berkeley, California, where I lived with a group of about six other Holy Cross religious while engaging in research and writing. Almost on the spur of the moment, I invited Dad to come to Berkeley to spend a week with me and our community. With my mother's encouragement, he agreed. That week was just wonderful for both of us. He enjoyed the prayer life of the house and the social time around meals. We toured the sights, from Telegraph Avenue in Berkeley to Coit Tower and Fisherman's Wharf in San Francisco, to Sausalito and the beaches on the Pacific Coast. We talked a lot and enjoyed each other's company. Saying goodbye at the airport, he gave me a big hug and told me he loved me and was proud of what I was doing with my life. I told him that I loved him as well and

Roots

thanked him for being such a great parent. This experience was very much in the forefront of my mind when I participated in the wake service and the funeral liturgy.

Fittingly, on the altar at Saint Anthony's Parish for the funeral were black priests and married deacons as well as a good number of my Holy Cross colleagues. Dressed in their finery and serving as ushers and procession attendants were members of the Knights of Columbus and the Knights of Saint John. There was also a good contingent from our extended family, from the Serra Club (another one of his activities), from the Transit Company, and from the Shrine. For a man of modest achievements (by the world's standards), he had a great sendoff.

My Mother

My mother went to grade school and high school in Scranton. She and her sister, Geri, grew up in a household where their father worked and their mother was a housewife. When she was a young girl, Mom was afflicted with a congenital knee problem that required her to wear a knee brace and use crutches. That was a great burden for someone who later described herself as full of youthful energy and a desire to push the limits. When Mom was eleven or twelve and it appeared that medical solutions to her leg problem had been exhausted, her parents took her on pilgrimage to Lackawanna, New York, to the Shrine of Our Lady of Victory. A local priest who ran an orphanage there had established a special devotion to the Blessed Mother under the title of Our Lady of Victory. While she was there, Mom was inspired to attempt walking without her crutches. She was able to do it, and she and her parents saw it as a sign of a miraculous cure. From that day forward, Mom walked effectively, though with a slight limp. In thanksgiving, she pledged that each day she would pray the rosary and recite a novena to Our Lady of Victory, and she did. In addition, whenever there was a family crisis or someone felt the need for special prayers, she, my two sisters, and several other relatives would send a donation to the Shrine of Our Lady of Victory to help underwrite the costs of one of the children at the orphanage.

Throughout her adult life my mother could hear only out of one ear and the good ear required a hearing aid (I think this problem resulted from one of the diseases that she had when she was young). She never allowed this limitation to get in the way, especially when we were younger. As she grew older, however, even her good ear became more problematic and she had to resort to ever more sophisticated hearing aids. The family simply took the reality of my mother's relative deafness for granted. In closed settings or when individuals spoke distinctly and loudly, she had no problems, but in open spaces like shopping malls, churches, and office buildings, or in the great outdoors, she had difficulty. We sometimes accused her of taking advantage of her limitations, such as when she found a speaker or a homily boring or when she went to confession and did not want to be harangued. When I was older and could drive, Mom would have me take her to the hearing aid shop to buy new batteries or get her device fixed. At family gatherings it was not unusual for us to hear the high pitched whir of the hearing aid as she adjusted it to a new battery or a different environment.

Before my parents moved to Washington, my mother worked for a private detective in Scranton. She absolutely loved the work and the excitement that went with it. Years later she could recall in great detail specific cases, from domestic disputes to retail theft to kidnappings. I have sometimes been accused of being an ambulance chaser, and it is largely true. I have a prevailing interest in crime, police work, and adrenaline-inducing events like fires, accidents, high-speed chases, and public encounters between good and evil. Some of this interest I surely shared with my mother. But my father too enjoyed the human drama of urban life and often would be the first on the scene of accidents in our neighborhood. One year when the remnants of a hurricane di-

Roots

rectly hit the city of Washington, my father wanted all of us to get in the car so we could go to a high point and watch the storm. Out of fear for the safety of her children, Mom demurred. My father started out anyway with his three children but turned back after a tree blew down across the road right in front of us.

After she had stopped working and her children had moved away, Mom liked to be chosen for jury duty, the more prominent the crime the better. She especially wanted to be called to serve at murder trials where the stakes were high and where she felt she could draw upon her experience at the detective agency.

Mom was a great storyteller. When we were young, she regaled us with bedtime stories that never quite concluded (like the Perils of Pauline series at the movie theaters in the late 1940s). One of my favorites revolved around the man with the plastic thumb. Somehow or other he always managed to escape danger at the last minute. Mom had a secret ambition to become a writer of children's novels, but not until she was in her sixties did she give it a try. She finished one novel and sent it off to a publisher to no good result. Who knows how her writing career might have turned out if she had had better opportunities at a younger age? There is no doubt in my mind that my mother's storytelling when I was young and malleable prepared my imagination for my later love affair with books and reading.

When Joanne and Mary and I were young, Mom stayed at home to tend to our needs. In retrospect, this was a great benefit, since she was always home after school and she made sure we did our homework and otherwise used our time productively. One of the advantages of living in an apartment complex where most of the women were home in the daytime was that if something came up, there was always a next-door neighbor to pitch in.

As we grew older, Mom began to work again. For a number of years she served as secretary for the priest who was the public relations director for the U.S. Catholic Conference. This allowed her to be involved in important activities on behalf of the Church. She liked her boss and came to know some of the leaders in the hierarchy. Yet she was never impressed by titles or regalia, so her judgments about the people she met there had more to do with their qualities as individuals and their levels of friendliness and competence than with the fancy outfits they wore or their formal forms of address.

Later, when all of us had finished high school, Mom worked for the group that solicited and edited articles for what became the *New Catholic Encyclopedia*, a project centered at Catholic University. Much of her time was spent typing documents in final form. Later she often commented that if only she could have remembered half of what she transcribed, she would have been able to become a professor herself.

Her final job was as secretary to the editor of *The American Ecclesiastical Review*, a journal published at Catholic University that was once one of the preeminent Catholic scholarly vehicles, though by the time she began to work there it had become less central in the world of ecclesiastical publications. Nevertheless, Mom had good rapport with the editor and she liked being out of the house and engaged in interesting activity.

My mother preferred working for men rather than women. Although she was a feminist in the best sense of the term (especially when it came to equality of treatment and opportunity), she often found her female colleagues too catty or gossipy, and she felt that women administrators, at least in her generation, tried too hard to imitate their male counterparts. I never thought it would be worthwhile to debate these points with her (the old adage was right: "never argue with your mother"). She was also reluctant to see women assuming too many roles in the post–Vatican II liturgies. She would avoid lines where women were distributing communion if she could do so without making a fuss. That was just how she felt and I simply accepted it as her prerogative.

Mom normally did the cooking in our family, and in that regard we were a traditional family of the 1940s and 1950s. That did not mean that the rest of us had no roles to play. When I was old enough, I set out the plates and the silverware, but my most important function was to take the trash and garbage out to the receptacles in the backyard. I well remember coming home from college with a newly enlightened attitude: I considered it only fair that I should do the dishes and then dry them and place them in the cabinet. My mother and my sisters were tolerant of this enthusiasm until I dropped one too many dishes or, worse, placed china or silverware in the wrong places. Rather than precipitate a crisis, I gratefully returned to my previously assigned gender-specific role. One result was that I never learned to cook.

My mother worked marvels with the food that our financial constraints permitted us. We had some favorite meals—meatloaf (a great stretch-entree since more bread and less meat was always possible), Chef Boyardee spaghetti, tuna casserole, hot dogs and baked beans, Spam (a food I always hated but often the only meat available during the latter days of WWII), fried chicken, and occasionally fish, lamb, or beef. Mom had her own special recipes for potato salad, baked beans, and a tomato-bread concoction. She also baked cookies and made brownies from scratch.

My mother would periodically claim, "I may not be the best cook in the world, but I am the fastest." I often put her to the test by bringing home friends at dinnertime unannounced. This became even more pronounced when I was home from Notre Dame in the summer or studying at Holy Cross College seminary on the grounds of Catholic University. There is no quicker way to empty a refrigerator than to have a bunch of young, healthy males stop by for a meal. Later, some of these friends stayed with my parents during their transition to Washington for graduate study or work.

My mother was more liberal than my father when it came to matters of religion and politics. Early on, she quietly schooled me to make up my own mind about those doctrinal and moral claims she thought some Catholic authorities presented in an excessively rigid manner. For example, she had a number of Protestant friends when she was growing up in Scranton and she even (perish the thought!) had attended church services with them on occasion. In my mother's mind, the central Christian truths were relatively well established (creation, sin and grace, the incarnation, the life, death, and resurrection of Jesus, the presence of the Holy Spirit, the special role of Mary, the promise of salvation). With regard to the rest, she saw a clear difference between what might be called foundational truths and derivative truths. Especially in the moral realm, she had a realistic perspective on human nature. Things went wrong, people made mistakes, and sometimes relationships fell apart. That's simply the way the world is; she did not have to like it. She brought her children up to have a certain flexibility and resiliency.

My mother was basically what might be called a "low church" person. She liked quick masses, relatively brief homilies, hymns with only a few verses, and little folderol in general. My father preferred the opposite, and his involvements with the Knights of Columbus, the Serra Club, and the Shrine of the Immaculate Conception often forced my mother to bite her tongue at what she took to be liturgical extravaganzas. To be honest, I take after my mother in this regard, although for Christmas, Holy Week, and special occasions, I suddenly become "high-church."

My mother and father almost never voted for the same political candidate. By instinct my mother was a liberal Democrat and my father a conservative Republican. When they went to the polling booth, they both knew they would be canceling the other's vote. Somehow or other my father got involved with the Committee to Re-elect Richard Nixon. His responsibility was to go to a central location run by the Republican Party and call federal judges on the phone to solicit their financial support for the Nixon campaign. As a reward, Dad was invited to one of the several inaugural balls after Nixon was reelected, and he dragged my mother along. As she described it later, Dad went hobnobbing with the other enthusiasts while she found another disgruntled spouse and spent the evening expressing her displeasure at the state of American politics.

After my father died, my mother continued to live for a time in our house on 13th Street, but gradually my sisters and I realized she needed a more secure and supportive environment. We decided that a high-rise senior citizen facility in Takoma Park, Maryland, right over the D.C. line, was the best alternative. She became acclimated to her new life, made good friends, and still had relative independence: her own apartment, access to recreational and social areas, and the availability of an evening meal in the cafeteria if she did not want to cook. There was also a Sunday mass, which I sometimes celebrated when I was on vacation. (Mom advised me always to speak loudly and briefly, since most of the senior citizens in attendance could not hear very well.)

Her apartment was on the eleventh floor, and the two elevators took forever to get there since the residents' physical condition required long stops at each floor. Sometimes when I was visiting her, she would say to whoever was on the elevator, whether she knew them or not, "This is my son, Father Malloy. He is President of Notre Dame." I would look embarrassed and there would be a pause. Sometimes the response would be "Isn't that nice!" Other times, they would want to tell me about what their own children or grandchildren were up to. By the time we got to the eleventh floor I was delighted to have survived another mother-son moment.

Toward the end of her time at Takoma Tower, Mom began to experience periodic red rashes on her legs and other parts of her body. This was eventually diagnosed as the early stages of leukemia. Additionally she began to fear falling and was more and more reluctant to go shopping or to travel with the family outdoors. Eventually we three children sought a nursing home where she would have round-the-clock care and access to all three meals. Fortunately, she was able to move into the Manor Care Nursing Home in Chevy Chase, right at the northern end of Rock Creek Park. Having visited various nursing homes on pastoral visits, I knew how wide ranging the levels of care could be. Manor Care was clean and relatively well appointed and there seemed to be a dedicated staff. During her years there, Mom shared a room with three different roommates and outlived two of them.

I enjoyed lunch or dinner at Manor Care on a number of occasions and experienced firsthand the range of physical and mental disabilities the residents possessed. I would be chatting with one or two of her friends when someone in the dining area would cry out or shriek or complain about mistreatment. Everyone else would act as though nothing had happened. My mother's complaints were usually about the quality of the food, which tended to be bland and predictable, and the idiosyncrasies of her roommates. In fact, the conversation at the nursing home often reminded me of discussions among students in undergraduate dorms.

Before one of my visits, my sister Joanne expressed concern that some stories Mom was telling seemed to suggest that she was losing her mental poise. After we all went out to dinner together, Joanne asked me if I had noticed anything. I replied that Mom seemed fine. Then Joanne wanted to know what I thought of her reports about seven murders of people related to the home and about the woman whose Mafia relatives prevented Mom from using the bathroom. I said I thought the stories sounded plausible. In any case, after the doctor changed her medications Mom was back to normal and the crime wave disappeared.

By good fortune, I was in Washington at a higher education convention when Joanne called me to say Mom was in the hospital and near death. We were able to arrange for a private room at Bethesda Hospital in the oncology ward. For two days, her three children were able to accompany her in her dying process. She was mainly unconscious but we talked to her constantly and all of us had a sense that she recognized our presence. Finally, the nurse informed us that the end was near and we prayed for her as she died at the age of ninety-four. My mother was the first person that I saw die. It was a moving, peaceful, sad moment as she simply stopped breathing. After we shed our

Roots

tears and said goodbye, the three of us prepared to celebrate her life and death in the rituals of Christian burial.

Mother was waked at a funeral home in northwest Washington. We had a wonderful turnout of family, friends, colleagues from Notre Dame, and Holy Cross community members. In the room adjacent to the visitation area were endless floral displays sent in solidarity and comfort. We counted over a hundred bouquets, a much appreciated manner of supportive presence.

The next day we had the funeral at Saint Anthony's Parish in northeast Washington where Joanne, Mary, and I had gone to grade school. In my homily I tried to capture some of Mom's qualities and to convey our family confidence that she was at peace with the Lord. She was buried with my father at Lincoln Park Cemetery in northeast Washington. As someone told me at the funeral home, once you lose both parents to death, you are like an orphan, but I think that claim misses the essential role of memory. Dad and Mom both lived long and productive lives, and their influence on me continues in my religious faith, in my values, and in my sense of self. While they are missed, my utter confidence in the power of Christ's victory over sin and death gives me the assurance that I will be reunited with them someday in the eternal banquet promised to those who love Him.

Life at Home

My sister Joanne is one year younger than I am. After graduation from high school she went to Immaculata Junior College in northwest Washington, where she completed a degree that prepared her for a career in business. Eventually she married and had one son, John. In her professional life, she was employed by Marshall Coyne Enterprises, a real estate development firm in the D.C. area, where she managed a number of properties, including commercial real estate.

My sister Mary is two and a half years younger than I am. She attended the University of Maryland, where she received a bachelor's degree, and Catholic University, where she earned a master's degree. At Catholic U. she met her husband, John, and for a while they both taught in a D.C. public high school. Eventually they moved back to his home area in Manchester, Connecticut. Mary then began a professional career in human resources, working for a succession of banks and finally a large Catholic hospital. Mary and John have three daughters—Susan, Maureen, and Maggie—all of whom have graduated from Notre Dame.

Because my sisters and I are relatively close in age, we shared many experiences and had many friends in common. During the years when we lived in an apartment, the two of them shared a bedroom and I had my own sleeping space in a room in the back. The biggest challenge in the apartment was five of us sharing one bathroom. This was especially problematic as we grew older since teenage girls require a lot more beauty time than teenage boys. It was also a challenge when one of us was sick. But we made it work and never thought about the fact that other families we knew had more commodious living arrangements.

I learned a lot from growing up with two sisters. When their friends would come over to visit or for an overnight slumber party, or when I would overhear them talking about boys (many of whom I knew), I had ongoing lessons in female psychology. Women may be from Venus and men from Mars, but in our family despite any gender differences a fundamental equality was taken for granted. My parents spent equal time with each of their children when it came to helping with schoolwork and attending school events.

When I was ten or eleven and my sisters proportionally younger, I had one of those "the devil made me do it" moments and hid under their bed. I kept absolutely still until they fell asleep. When one of them hung her arm over the side of the bed I grabbed it, and the two of them let out a succession of bloody screams. My parents came run-

Roots

ning, fearing the worst, only to discover my prank. I was duly chided, order was restored, and we all went back to sleep. Over the years at family get-togethers the story grew with embellishments and the audacious claim that I set out to permanently traumatize my sisters.

The apartments we lived in during and after World War II were populated primarily by young families. Most of them dreamed someday of moving to more upscale areas, but in the meantime they made do and saved as much as they could. Mothers with small children generally stayed home while their husbands went off to work each day. If they were lucky, the families had a washing machine, but laundry normally was hung to dry in the backyards, a routine that afforded everyone a regular chance to chat. In a sense, a daily chore became a social occasion.

Like the other families we had our milk delivered. We also had regular visits in the back alley from trucks or vans that delivered ice or berries or watermelons or fresh vegetables. Once in a while the knifesharpener would proclaim his presence, and in the summer there were the Good Humor ice cream trucks with their distinctive recorded jingle on a loudspeaker.

As the children grew older and began to explore nearby yards, the mothers (and sometimes the fathers) came to know each other on a first-name basis. They shared recipes and remedies for toddlers' ailments and there was always someone available to serve as a temporary babysitter in an emergency. Since the daytime world was almost exclusively populated by women and children, no doubt the strange practices and propensities of husbands (and men in general) were subject to regular analysis. Who knows how many marriages were saved over the backyard fences?

There were some retired couples and a few unmarried groupings in the apartment buildings. On the ground floor of one building not far from us lived two older women who had a reputation for being gruff and unfriendly. Some of the older boys used to pull tricks on them and call them names before running away into the night. One

Halloween the shenanigans got a bit out of hand: the women's door had eggs broken on it and they had to endure continual disruptions of their peace and quiet. In anger and retaliation, when the next group of trick-or-treaters came along (this time a mix of sweet little boys and girls all decked out in costumes), the women opened the door and doused the children with a big bucket of hot water. Well, it took about ten seconds for the story to make the rounds, and the next thing we knew the apartment building was surrounded by a group of irate parents. Eventually, the police came, took a report, and ordered everyone to return home. Yet I am afraid those poor women knew no real peace until they decided, reluctantly, to move away.

One of the ways my parents built a social network among their friends was by playing cards. First of all, it was cheap; only a deck or two of cards and some light refreshments were needed, and the couples took turns hosting the gatherings. Second, they seldom played for money, so the final outcome of an evening together was hardly remembered a day or two later. My parents' favorite card game was bridge. The rules were not that complicated but the game was sufficiently complex to allow for strategizing, daring gambits, and effective team play. Some players were more adept than others, of course, but with a little luck even a rank amateur might have an evening of surprising success. My sisters eventually learned to enjoy bridge and sometimes filled in when there were uneven numbers or someone was sick. I, however, never got beyond learning the rudiments of the game. To be honest, I have always been bored by card games (except on vacation or in some rural retreat). When canasta was a big fad in the 1950s, I caught the fever for a while, but my enthusiasm soon dissipated. For much of my life I managed to avoid being trapped into evenings spent sitting around the house playing cards, Monopoly, Risk, or other domestic pursuits. I wanted to be outside with my friends instead, preferably on a playground.

My father did not believe in fans or air conditioners; he thought of them as an unnecessary superfluity. While my mother was more sen-

Roots

sitive to heat and humidity, she generally went along with him, so I grew accustomed early on to the long, hot summers of Washington. We had two main methods of beating the heat. The first was to sit outside in the late evening until the humidity subsided a bit and vestiges of an evening breeze began to appear. At the apartment this meant gathering on the lawn with neighbors and a cold drink and telling stories or speculating about the fortunes of local sports teams or passing on the latest neighborhood news. When we moved to a house with a front porch, we would sit on patio furniture and chat. If we entertained guests on summer evenings, it was to the porch that we invariably went for conversation.

Our second strategy for keeping cool required more effort. We would drive down to the Haynes Point recreation area across the Potomac River from National Airport, where we joined the thousands of other D.C. residents who gathered to toss a ball around, play Frisbee, walk along the riverfront, or just sit in a lawn chair and watch the planes land. As the sun descended, families would snack on junk food or juicy watermelon or some ice cream delight. In addition, there would always be coolers full of ice and soft drinks. The mix of people reflected the racial diversity of the city, but I never remember any trouble. Occasionally one of the groups would get a little raucous, but there was an unwritten code of acceptable behavior—and there were always the park police patrols to quiet things down in a pinch.

The family was always intent on taking full advantage of the relatively inexpensive recreational opportunities in D.C. We explored the Smithsonian buildings, the Capitol and White House, the Library of Congress, the Mall, the Zoo, Glen Echo Park, and Rock Creek Park. We attended free evening concerts in the summer on the steps of the Capitol Building, at the Jefferson Memorial, and at the original Watergate site where Memorial Bridge crosses the Potomac River. We traveled to Great Falls Park on the C&O Canal, and to Mount Vernon, Harpers Ferry, and Gettysburg. We even made it to Beverly Beach and other swimming spots on the Potomac River above where it empties into the Chesapeake Bay. We had a tradition of visiting the U.S. Naval Academy in nearby Annapolis during the June week when some of the senior midshipmen got married. On most of these occasions we would enjoy a picnic dinner in front of an elegant, historically significant setting.

Having eaten as an adult in some of the finest restaurants in the world, I can still claim that, given a choice for one special meal, I would choose a picnic. Perhaps that is because I have such cherished memories of when picnics meant outdoor fun, hamburgers and hot dogs, coleslaw, potato salad, baked beans, corn on the cob, sliced tomatoes—and the dessert *pièce de resistance*, brownies with ice cream or fresh watermelon. Depending on the location, we would toss around a ball or a Frisbee, listen to a Senators' game on the radio, or go for a long walk. Sometimes our patriotic juices would be activated by historical pageants or Sousa marches or fireworks beneath the Washington Monument. On the way home, we would feel like the luckiest people in the world.

One of the traditions we had as a family was to spend Sunday evenings working the crossword puzzles in the two local newspapers—especially after I was in high school and my vocabulary was sufficiently developed to be able to participate. Both my parents relished these moments and were proud of their skill. It was a rare moment when we retired for the night without filling in the whole grid, even though it might mean staying up quite late. I surely caught that bug. After a period when I was too busy to keep up with crossword puzzles, I have returned to this practice with enthusiasm in the last twenty years. I am what might be called a "semi-professional" crossword solver: I do four every day and five on Sunday. I have done all the back puzzles of the *New York Times*, the *Boston Globe*, the *Washington Post*, the *Los Angeles Times*, the San Francisco's *Examiner*, and the *Wall Street Journal*. This avocation does not include other forms of word or mathematical posers like Sudoku. One harmless vice of this sort is enough for me. After my parents retired and we children moved away from home, they often had to buy two copies of the same newspaper because one would get mad if the other one ruined the day's puzzle by filling it in partially.

In the late 1940s and early 1950s, radio was the most readily available form of entertainment. My mother used to listen to some of the soap operas while she did housework. In the evening there were popular shows like *Amos and Andy*, *Jack Benny*, and *Fibber McGee and Molly*. But what I looked forward to the most was to lie in bed with my little crackling portable radio on school nights and listen to *The Lone Ranger* ("Hi Ho Silver"); *The Shadow* ("Who knows what evil lurks in the hearts of men? The Shadow knows"); and *Sergeant Preston of the Yukon* ("On King! On you huskies!"). As I lay in my bed I could imagine myself heroically righting wrongs, protecting the innocent, defending women and children, and generally seeing that justice was done. Sometimes I would fall asleep before the adventure was resolved, but I rested contentedly knowing that the world was much safer.

We were one of the last families in our neighborhood to get a television set. At first none of us thought much about it, but eventually recess conversation at school revolved around the shows classmates saw the night before, and my sisters and I began to feel deprived. I can remember knocking on the door of a friend's apartment, being told he was watching television, and being invited in to join him. That, of course, was the reason for my visit in the first place. Eventually, like most children of my generation, I watched a fair amount of TV. I remember with special affection the *Howdy Doody Show*. Later, I was a loyal fan of *Dragnet*. As a family, we got into the fads of the moment with quiz shows like *21* and *The $64,000 Question*.

Television provided my first exposure to Notre Dame when I happened to watch an Irish football game in the 1950s on the Mutual Television Network (Washington being one of the few cities to have an outlet). Through the years I watched plenty of sports on TV, as well as regular doses of the news. Like most families of that era, my parents restricted our regular viewing time, especially during the school year. Only rarely was inappropriateness of the show's content the issue, however. More typically, it was getting our priorities right. School always came first, as did time together as a family: no TV during meals, no TV when guests were visiting.

One Christmas I decided to ask for a sled. I had seen just the type I wanted in a friend's basement. My parents accepted this as my first priority, and on Christmas Day I found a flashy, sleek sled under our tree. Unfortunately, D.C. went without any noticeable snowfall that winter and the sled sat in my closet unused. By the following winter I had grown interested in other things and so learned a good lesson about glitzy allure and neighbor envy.

My father always tried to do right by us kids at Christmas. We put emphasis on the religious dimension of the feast, but we also enjoyed the Santa Claus story and the tradition of gift-giving connected to it. Nevertheless, my father was a penny-pincher about one aspect of the season: he never believed in paying full price for a Christmas tree. Despite my mother's protests, he would wait until Christmas Eve to go looking for bargains, and we usually ended up with a scraggly tree that had already begun to dry out and was missing branches in key places. My mother would complain about the inferior fir, but my father would argue that the tree would be perfect once we wedged it into a corner and covered it with tinsel and decorations and topped it off with a star. My job was to dig up some wet mud from the ground out back and put it in a bucket to enclose the end of the trunk and keep the tree fresh through the Christmas season.

One year my dad saw a newspaper ad for cheap Christmas trees at a local tree farm in the suburbs. Once again on Christmas Eve we went bargain hunting as a family. We found the farm, paid our fee, and drove to a site where some strikingly beautiful specimens were available. It looked as though Dad had finally realized his hopes for a bargain. However, there was a problem. The owners of the farm closed shop soon after we made our purchase, and we had not brought along a saw or an axe. All we could find in the car was a butter knife. It took over an hour, with several of us taking turns, to saw through the trunk and secure the tree to the roof of the car for the ride home. I think I remember Mom saying under her breath "I told you so" with a certain suppressed glee. That was the last time Dad tried to beat the system.

It should not be surprising that intelligent, well-educated Christian believers sometimes carry over into their practical affairs what some might consider vestiges of superstition. In my family we said prayer before meals, a prayer for a safe journey before setting out on long automobile trips, and bedtime prayers, especially when we were young. But we also invoked the intercession of Saint Anthony if something was lost and Saint Jude if we faced a no-win situation. The thick crucifix on our wall contained a blessed candle inside, and threaded through the exterior were palm fronds from the celebration of Palm Sunday. In the summer when the city was hit by loud, impressive thunderstorms, my mother would first pull the plugs on all electrical appliances (lest lightning come through the circuit and burn the house down) and then take the candle out of the crucifix, put it in a holder, and light it, both for protection and for a source of light if the electricity failed. When our family was hosting a special meal or someone we knew was getting married or some group was having an event outdoors, it was always good form to place a rosary on the bushes outside to assure good weather. And when someone we knew was attempting to buy or sell a house, it made sense to bury a statue of Saint Joseph upside down in the dirt outside in order to invoke his blessing on the transaction.

Boyhood Days

My number one companion as a youngster was Denny Kane. He was a year older and somewhat stronger. We hung out together and engaged in the usual activities that young boys are prone to. We explored the nearby woods and hid out in the water main under the B&O railroad tracks so we could demonstrate our bravery by staying there while a train passed overhead. We threw rocks at make-believe targets, wrestled, tossed balls around, jumped fences, rode our bikes, and practiced curse words. As we grew older, I began to outstrip Denny in size and strength. Since he reached puberty earlier than I did, he was able to explain—rather feebly, as it turned out—what all that was about. But he sensed that he was losing his dominance in our relationship. His ploy when we disagreed was sometimes to sit on me until I would accept his point of view. My great moment of liberation came one day when I, Tarzan-like, told him that I had enough and chased him down the alley with a blunt instrument. God knows what I would have done if he had turned around.

Since my room was in the back of our apartment with windows facing into the backyard and the woods beyond, it was not unusual, when I was old enough to have a lively imagination, for me to hear sounds and perhaps voices in the night that I thought of as threatening or suspicious. We lived in a very safe neighborhood but I knew that hoboes rode the rails of the nearby Baltimore and Ohio railroad and sometimes lingered in the woods—I had seen them on occasion when I was prowling with my friends. We had one neighbor who sometimes drank too much and called the police to report suspicious noises and people. Little did I recognize at the time how vulnerable I was to her influence. Once my sleep had been interrupted, I would lie in bed plotting strategies of defense or escape until I made it through another night.

The woods behind our apartment were rather extensive, considering our urban location. They were bordered on the north by a series of residences for Catholic sisters who were attending the Catholic University of America, on the west by the B&O railroad tracks, and on the east by a development of two-story houses. The woods were a popular exploration spot with all the neighborhood kids. As we grew

Roots

older and wanted to get away from our mothers' watchful eyes, we began to wander farther and farther from home. In the woods we could imitate the Western movies we had seen the previous Saturday. We would choose sides as cowboys and Indians and hide behind trees, in secluded nooks, or under piles of leaves. Early on, our weapons were all imaginary, but later we had toy six-shooters like Hopalong Cassidy and Roy Rogers and the Cisco Kid. The chases and gunfights would go on until we grew tired, bored, or hungry. No one kept score. The enjoyment was in the game and the relentless pursuit.

A defining moment came when some of us were old enough to purchase B-B guns. Then the action acquired sound effects and we could see the movement of the bark when someone's B-B hit a maple tree head on. Our parents warned us about the dangers of such weaponry, but we were young and invulnerable and the risk was a big part of the excitement. Fortunately, no one ever lost an eye. And as far as I know, no one ever blabbed about our combat in the woods. It was a secret among friends.

As I look back, there was a kind of innocence about growing up in the 1940s and 1950s. We soon discovered that the hoboes who occasionally camped out in our woods were more scared of us than we were of them. (They clearly did not want the police to know they were around.) The closest thing I can recall to a shocking incident in my youth came when a mentally unbalanced adult male was accused of trying to impose his affections on a neighborhood girl in her early teens. There was no evidence that anything dire took place, yet I can remember all our parents suddenly feeling obliged to have that talk about the ways of the world and the dangers of inappropriate interest. Sex was never mentioned, nor was the word 'predator' spoken, but we kind of got the message. From that time on, the woods were more than a place to gallivant, they were a place where some unknown threat might be waiting.

Like all little boys, I went through versions of what I might want to do when I grew up. When I was very young I was attracted to the seemingly exciting work done by the men who picked up the garbage and trash from the bins behind our house. How much fun it would be to ride on a truck and wear a uniform and display your muscles for all to see. I never gave much thought to the negatives of the job, like the smell or the squishy stuff you had to handle or the pay scale. Later I wanted to become a police officer; it would allow me to wear a badge and carry a gun and save damsels in distress. Then there were the other fun things, like directing traffic and riding in a squad car with the siren on and the red lights flashing. Finally I settled on becoming a professional athlete—it did not matter which sport. I was attracted first to baseball because I was a big Washington Senators fan. But I also enjoyed football and basketball, so those were possibilities. My first step toward a professional baseball contract was playing catch with Dad in the backyard. At first I muffed too many tosses but eventually I got the hang of it. It was only in the last few years of grade school that I even thought about other options. No one in my family circle had ever gone to college, so I did not yet draw the connection between credentials and career. My horizons were wide open and my parents were constantly supportive as I continued to sift through possible adult roles.

The origin of my nickname, Monk, is probably the question I am asked most often. It has nothing to do with my religious vocation. When I was in third or fourth grade, two of my friends at Saint Anthony's School had an older brother nicknamed Bunky. He was a fine athlete and somewhat of a neighborhood hero. At some point I started calling him Bunk, probably because it suggested a more familiar relationship than we actually had. He decided to reciprocate and settled on Monk because it rhymed with Bunk and was alliterative with Malloy. After a while his brothers started calling me Monk too, and my classmates eventually accepted it as my operative name. My mother did not like it at first and refused to address me as Monk. To her, I was still Edward and my father was Eddie. But a couple of summers later I spent some weeks in Scranton hanging out with my cousin Tony Mc-

Roots

Nulty. When I returned home and Mom found out that Tony had renamed me Hockerhead, she quickly joined the Monk crowd. Like most juvenile nicknames, mine could easily have disappeared with the passing of time, but my career in athletics assured that Monk remained with me through the transition to Notre Dame and beyond.

From the very first, I liked having a distinctive, easy to remember name, and I cultivated its use. Even after ordination and joining the faculty at Notre Dame, I introduced myself as Monk. For better or worse, Monk is the name I go by. Some may think it undignified and some imagine it to be a religious title (like abbot), but I am undeterred. I always suggest to couples I have married that they might want to name their first child Monk or Monka. After they get over the shock and realize I am only semi-serious, they laugh it off as a joke. I am still waiting for the first courageous couple to step forth and take me at my word.

Play Ball!

I do not recall how old I was when I first started following the Senators. I used the radio to keep up with the long summer schedule of my beloved team. For home games there was always the background noise of the friendly confines of Griffith Stadium, but it was the way radio covered away games that particularly struck my fancy. In the days before they sent broadcasters along with the team, the game announcers would sit in a local radio studio and report the progress of the game from tickertape information. Because baseball is a slow game, this required the announcer to be quite inventive in filling in the details. Further, a sound technician had to make the appropriate noises of a bat hitting a ball or the ball settling into a mitt with a thwack. The crowd noise and cheers accompanying a big play were cued. I guess I never thought twice about how removed that coverage was from the real event on the field. Long before I had the chance to attend my first Senators' game with my father, I knew the thrill of victory and the agony of defeat. As it turned out, there was much more agony than thrill. The Senators were, by reputation, "First in war, first in peace, and last in the American League."

I have vivid memories of the routines that Dad and I would go through on days when he would treat me to a game. First, we would do some research in the local newspapers about the batting averages and pitching records of the players on our hometown team. Then we would find out who was scheduled to start on the mound for this game. We were less thorough in looking up the stats on the opposing team, but we always wanted to know their record at that point in the season and the win-loss record of their starting pitcher. Our second step was to decide what to wear to the game, which usually included a Senators cap for me and sunglasses for Dad. I would often bring a baseball mitt, since there was always the possibility that a foul ball would come our way. It was our custom to save money by finding a place to park on the street rather than pay in one of the official lots. However, since the neighborhood was pretty tough, we sometimes had to offer a "watching fee" to the local kids rather than risk car damage or, even worse, theft. Fortunately, this system always worked for us.

Finally we would arrive at the ballpark. The bleachers were our usual location and also the site of the greatest fan activity, particularly during weekend double-headers when the beer flowed freely. But sometimes Dad would be given a ticket in one of the boxes along the third base line. In either case, the prevailing rule was, if you could walk underneath the entry turnstile, you could get in for free. Since I sprouted up at a rather young age, it was somewhat comical to watch me scrunching down to beat the system as I was passed through.

By the time I got to high school I had a growing interest in the Washington Redskins football team. The Skins were the first franchise to have their own band and their own fight song: "Hail to the Redskins! Hail Victory! Braves on the Warpath! Fight for Old D.C."

In the first years, the team was quite successful. They had a great quarterback in Sammy Baugh and won the league championship in 1937. In 1942 they repeated as champions. But in the years after WWII they settled into the middle of the pack. Game strategy was changing and the Skins were one of the last teams to adopt the T-formation backfield. One advantage they did have was that in 1950 they became the first professional football team to have all their games televised.

At the beginning of my junior year of high school, I learned that jobs were available in the fall working in the concession stands at Griffith Stadium on Sunday afternoons for Redskins games and at Byrd Stadium on Saturday afternoons for University of Maryland football games. After an interview, I was chosen for both crews. I quickly found out that concession stand labor required little skill other than keeping a full stock of hot dogs, buns, popcorn, peanuts, ice cream, and soft drinks and balancing multiple orders in my head while being yelled at by customers. The job had a kind of feast-or-famine pace, with most of the business being done before kickoff and at halftime. In between, it was possible to sit down and rest or watch some of the play on the field. This was my first exposure to professional football with its gladiatorial quality and its expressive fans. (I would eventually become a lifelong follower of the sport, especially after the arrival of regular television coverage.)

Getting Around

The only vehicle my family had access to was Dad's company car. Before I was sixteen, he was the only family driver. My mother never learned how, partly because of her leg problems, so she was dependent on my dad or the streetcar or bus. After I got my license, I could help out with the driving load on long trips, but when it came to going on errands or helping my mother with shopping, one or both of my parents had to be in the car for me to validly use it. I always considered my father to be a safe and reliable driver, and as far as I know he was never involved in a significant accident. However, he shared with many men of his age a sense that he had an infallible sixth sense of direction, and he would never stop to ask if he was on the right road. Part of this confidence came from his regular wanderings around Washington to interview witnesses against the Transit Company. But his acknowledged success rate in finding obscure addresses within the city did not, in my experience, translate to equally happy results when he ventured afield.

I remember a trip into southern Maryland, which at that time was made up of tobacco and corn farms and an occasional small town. After he made a couple of U-turns and glanced once or twice at a map, my mother began urging him to stop at a gas station or farmhouse. But he would have nothing to do with such a foolish idea. He simply reasserted his prerogative as captain of the ship and drove on as if the cross street he sought was just around the corner. Maybe forty-five minutes later we finally found a recognizable landmark and, of course, it turned out that we had been going in the wrong direction for half an hour or so. On such occasions my mother never exactly said "I told you so" but she clearly felt vindicated.

On one family vacation to Scranton, we had just arrived in the downtown area and stopped for a snack. My father parked the car in a metered lot, and when we returned he got behind the wheel, turned on the motor, and started backing. To his surprise, the steering wheel spun around uncontrollably. It turned out that the pin connecting the wheel to the undercarriage had snapped. The problem was relatively easy to repair, but the mechanic informed us that if the pin had broken while we were on the highway, Dad would have had no control over the vehicle's trajectory. We said a prayer of thanksgiving that our family had been spared from potentially mortal harm.

In the wintertime it seldom snowed, but when it did the city's few plows tended to be reserved for the major thoroughfares. One or two inches was all it took to make every intersection a skating rink and every hill impassible. In the 1940s, 1950s, and even 1960s, radial tires were not available and most cars and trucks had rear drives. That meant that the wise car-owner possessed a set of chains for the rear tires. But owning a set of chains and connecting them to the rear tires were two separate realities. In the absence of a car-hoisting device, all you could do was get down your hands and knees after digging out the surrounding snow, and then hope against hope that the attachment clamps would hold up. I was the chain guy and my father was the steerer who had to back precisely over the chains despite the slip-slide effect of wintry conditions. Eventually we would get the chains rigged up and then go for a spin to make sure that everything was working. Usually, after all this effort, the sun would come out, the temperature would rise, and some of the snow on the streets would melt, but not all of it. So for a couple of days, Dad would drive around with chains on and we would hear the loud click-clack on clean pavement and the more restrained sound of the chains digging in on the remaining unplowed pavement.

The drive between Washington and Scranton took around eight hours. When we made our annual summer trips, Dad was the only qualified driver. We usually stopped halfway there for a bathroom break and a snack. Returning home from one such trip when I was seven or eight and my sisters proportionately younger, it had already turned dark by the time we reached Baltimore. In those days there was no inner-harbor tunnel, so we had to pass through the heart of the city. That night we were going through a relatively deserted inner-city neighborhood when out of nowhere a black woman ran past our car chased by a large black man with a long knife. The woman was screaming and her life appeared to be at risk. My father was clearly torn. Should he make some effort to help the woman? My mother, on the other hand, was petrified for the safety of her family. For her, the only move was to get out of there as fast as possible. The woman turned down a side street and disappeared from view with the man still in pursuit. There were no police around and, of course, no cell phones. In a kind of compromise move, my father proceeded forward slowly and peered intently down the street the woman had taken. By this time, neither of them was to be seen. The rest of the trip was uneventful, but even at my relatively young age I realized not only that we had encountered the dark side of urban life, but that my father and our family had been spared a set of decisions that could have quickly spiraled out of control.

On another journey back from Scranton when I was ten or eleven, darkness set in when we were midway between Philadelphia and Baltimore. We were listening to the Top 40 on the radio and chatting about one thing or another as we drove past a series of bars along the two-lane highway. I suddenly noticed a car weaving its way out of a parking lot ahead of us. I alerted Dad but he had already spotted the danger. The car made its way into our lane about twenty car lengths ahead of us, and its path became more and more erratic, veering over into the oncoming lane and back again. We suspected that it was just a matter of time until something tragic happened and we wanted to make sure that we were not the victims.

The next thing we knew a station wagon with a relatively large family inside passed us on the somewhat hilly road. Dad blinked his lights to try to alert the other car, but to no avail. A few minutes later we came over a rise in the road and saw, a couple of hundred yards ahead, that traffic in both directions had stopped and several cars had emergency blinkers on. We had no idea what we might find as we slowly slipped over to the side of the highway. We stopped and learned that, thank God, the station wagon had not been involved but the passengers had seen a car go airborne after wandering into the far lane and overcorrecting. We could see the drunk driver's smashed car lying twenty or thirty feet from the side of the road. There was no one inside and in the dim light there was no evidence of the driver.

By this time the police and emergency crews had arrived. Since we had been one of the first groups on the scene and had seen the events leading up to the accident, we gave our testimony to the state

Roots

troopers and waited around to see what would turn up. After the emergency crews rigged up their night lighting, they found the body of the driver about another twenty or thirty feet away. Contrary to our expectations, he was still alive and even able to talk. I still remember one of the police officers suggesting that it was always the drunks who survived such messes.

By the time we continued our journey home, we all knew we had been part of a real drama of threat, destruction, and potential death on the highway. We felt grateful that we had been protected from harm and that even the life of the foolish young driver had apparently been spared.

We went to Scranton to see my grandfather Malloy who lived there most of his life. Three of his sons, including my father, lived in the D.C. area with their families, so every once in a while Grandpa would make it to Washington. He had a lively personality and seemed to really enjoy hanging out with his grandchildren. He also was somewhat of a prankster. One of his games was to encourage us children to help our mother around the house by minimizing household labor. For example, he convinced us that after we had eaten our food we should take a piece of bread and wipe off the plate so that no visible particles remained. That way we would be members of the "Clean Plate Club" and we could simply put the crockery back in the cabinet to be reused.

My mother did not think this tomfoolery was at all funny, but she did not want to create in-law tensions. She would wait until Grandpa lost interest in the game and then she would tell us in no uncertain terms to put our dishes in the sink where they belonged. I think my mother's greatest fear was that we would go to school and spread the word among our peers about the exciting new "Clean Plate Club."

Although it seemed highly unusual at the time, after my grandmother Malloy died Grandpa Malloy married a former Methodist missionary who had served in Africa. He moved to her family home in the outskirts of Sunbury, Pennsylvania, and we went there to visit them twice. On the first occasion, I was around eleven or twelve. We had not met Grandpa's new wife before our visit, so everyone was curious to see what she was like. We were all on our best behavior as we sat on the porch before dinner, then we were treated to an excellent meal and retired into the parlor where we shared dessert. By this time, we were all more relaxed in each other's company. At a certain point, I began to ask Grandpa's new wife about her experiences in Africa (a continent I thought of as utterly exotic and mysterious). She told us how she had volunteered to serve there and how the local people dressed and how important music and dance were in their culture. Then, as she warmed up, she told us a story that absolutely grabbed all of our attention.

She was in bed on a pitch-black night in a hut that was open at the sides for ventilation. She was awakened from a sound sleep by the sensation that something was creeping across her body. Her first instinct was to swat it away with her hand, but when she lit the gas lamp next to her bed she discovered that her whole body was covered with ants. In fact, the entire room was filled with army ants that were moving in a procession toward some unknown destination. She had been told about such terrifying events by the villagers when she first arrived, and she remembered that one had to get out of their path. So after screaming for help, she ran off into the night, swatting away the ants on her body as she moved along. Eventually she made it to an ant-free zone where some of the locals helped her use motor oil to rid her body of the insects. We questioned her for more follow-up details, but by that time we three children had all decided that she was, in fact, an interesting lady.

It was our plan to stay overnight at their house. At the assigned hour, the three of us made our way up a set of creaky stairs to the second floor where I was to sleep in one room and my sisters in another. After my parents and the elder Malloys went to bed, the house was absolutely quiet. As I lay in bed my eleven-year-old mind began to replay the story of the ants. I began to hear noises, like the presence of some strange force. I began to itch, like my body was slowly but surely being beset. Then I would remind myself that it was all in my imagination. Nonetheless I slept fitfully all night, and the next morning my sisters revealed that they had had the same problem getting to sleep.

By the time we returned home the next day, I was convinced that someday I would have to make it to Africa where the depths of my religious convictions could be put to a real test by ants and other repulsive creatures.

CHAPTER 2

EARLY SCHOOLING

WASHINGTON IN THE LATE 1940S WAS FULL OF MEN and women who had served in the Second World War and now were home again, eager to marry or to be reunited with family. The demand on every type of social service on the home front was immense. The movement of many city dwellers to the suburbs spread out governmental responsibility for such services, but for trans-political entities like the Catholic Church it complicated the task of infrastructure development in areas such as parish life and the parochial school system.

My neighborhood in northeast Washington was called Brookland, and its alias was "Little Rome" because of all the Catholic Church–related institutions it encompassed. In an era when priests, brothers, and sisters were in abundance and most wore distinctive dress, it was commonplace in our neighborhood to see these religious figures shopping in stores, riding buses and streetcars, and walking along the streets. Although we never thought much about it, the area really was about as close to the part of Rome near the Vatican as one could find anywhere in the world. Throughout the years, the Catholic part of Brookland was just as important to one part of my life as Turkey Thicket playground was to another part.

Brookland at the time was family-rich and money-poor. Just about all our neighbors had multiple children and shared the almost universal sentiment that it was worth any sacrifice to provide quality education for them. The public school system was still predominantly white and our neighborhood was exclusively Caucasian, so decisions about public school (free) versus parochial school (tuition-dependent) were not decided on the basis of race or safety or even academic quality. Rather, a regular topic from the pulpit was that Catholic parents had a religious duty to send their children to parochial schools, and this principle was not subject to much debate.

In my neighborhood there were two Catholic primary schools—the Campus School (an experimental school run by the education department at Catholic University) and our parish school, Saint Anthony's. The Campus School was somewhat more expensive and a lot smaller. As far as I know, my parents never gave it much consideration.

Saint Anthony's School was right next door to Brookland School, the public alternative. We were allowed to use Brookland's outdoor recreation area for some of our recess activities when it was free. A stone fence with a wire barrier atop it ran between the two properties. When we played kickball, this fence constituted the equivalent of the left field wall. As we grew older, the challenge was to clear the ball over the whole barrier. Other than that shared use of outdoor space, we had absolutely no contact during the school day with the public school students. Our neighborhood was so overwhelmingly Catholic that I remember having discussions with my peers about why these other kids had not yet discovered the truth. We did not have any high theological theory about superiority/inferiority or any doubt whether they had souls, nor did we think them unworthy of being treated fairly.

It was not so much aggressive prejudice as ignorance and wonderment. Since we were not allowed to go to non-Catholic worship services, we thought of public schools in an "it's not our world" kind of way.

In the late 1940s and early 1950s it was taken for granted in my area of D.C. that children would walk to school. There was no particular fear of predators or hostile elements along the way. For the very youngest in the first and second grades, a concern about traffic safety and getting lost led mothers (it was almost always the women who were at home in the daytime) to either walk their son or daughter to school or send them off with a neighbor. Catholic schools had no access to public school buses nor a high priority to purchase buses of their own.

Older students served as safety patrols on the most heavily used streets and intersections. There were also adult monitors at the stoplights. It was a great thrill when I was finally old enough to join the safety patrol. We got to wear a badge pinned onto a piece of heavy white cloth about six inches wide that went over one shoulder and tied around the middle. After finishing patrol duty in the morning and afternoon, we rolled the cloth up into a ball and put it in our book bags. I was quite proud in eighth grade to be placed in charge of the safety patrol and given a different color badge to signify my rank. I also got to supervise the traffic at 10th and Michigan, one of the most heavily used routes.

I enjoyed school from the first moment I set foot in Saint Anthony's. I never went to kindergarten or pre-school, but both my parents spent time with me as my curiosity about the world developed. There was no *Sesame Street* and we did not even own a television at that time. I learned from my mother's stories, from the games we played around the house, and from the conversations on the front lawn of our apartment house on the hot, muggy nights of summer. Even though my parents did not pursue education beyond high school because of family financial responsibilities, they both prized education highly and, within their means, did everything they could to prepare us for the onset of formal education.

In my eight years at St. Anthony's School I had Benedictine sisters in every class. The principal was always a religious sister as well. The sisters wore a traditional habit that covered their hair and the sides of their faces, and their outer garment stretched almost to the floor. The Benedictine habit was not as exaggerated as some, but it established in our eyes a strong sense that these women were somehow consecrated to God and shared a common life and a common sense of mission. It was not, as we would soon discover, that they were all alike. Their personalities and temperaments quickly came through in their relentless effort to educate successive groups of six to fourteen year olds. We liked certain sisters more than others, and such preferences seemed to go the other way as well.

While behavioral expectations were clearly established, I have no memory of any excessive or offensive punishments, either by the standards of that time or of today. Most of our interactions with our teachers were positive, focused on the lessons of the day and our individual progress. When some child misbehaved, he or she was reproved, and usually that was enough to restore order. On those occasions, especially in the upper grades, when a student became disruptive, the offender was sent to the principal's office. The ultimate penalty, of course, was to call in the parents for a meeting with the principal. For most of us, the very thought was enough to ensure moral reform.

In that pre-litigious age, the presumption was with the teacher or the principal or (in the most severe cases) the pastor. In the postwar era, order was prized and hierarchy was taken for granted. Parents wanted good things for their children and the Catholic Church was prized by its members as a source of time-tested truth and solid value formation for the young. In a sense, you were expected to buy into the whole package. Catholic schools were the place where the three R's (reading, 'riting, and 'rithmetic) were supplemented by explicit religious instruction and practice, implemented by (in this case) women who had given themselves selflessly to Christ. Parents were not naive about the individual limitations of particular women religious, but they had confidence in the system as a whole and were willing to sacrifice to come up with tuition payments.

Homework was essential to the pedagogical theory of the day, both to assure seriousness of purpose in the student and to provide an opportunity for parental involvement in the learning process. It succeeded at both levels, at least with me. Mom and Dad were always willing to assist me with challenging assignments. In grammar we worked our way together from letters to words to sentences to the parts of speech, and over time I became adept as a speller and a reader. In math there were comparable steps, from addition and subtraction to multiplication and division and on to percentages and spatial configurations. We learned history and geography and literature and the rudiments of science. We memorized a lot, since rote was accepted as a valid way to master material. Along the way, I learned to recite the poem "Abou Ben Adhem" and the prologue of the Gospel according to John, as well as the Gettysburg Address and snatches from other culturally significant pieces.

I relished the grammar workbooks in which we had to complete a page or two each day for homework (circling verbs, checkmarking adjectives, crossing out misspelled words). As time went on, I looked forward to diagramming sentences, especially complex, compound ones which required the most work. Spelling bees were in their infancy as a cultural event, yet in Saint Anthony's School we competed in the spelling of obscure words until only one participant was left.

St. Anthony's did not have a cafeteria, so we had to brown-bag our lunch each day. My mother dutifully prepared the food the night before. Monday through Thursday fare was bologna sandwiches (sometimes with cheese) or peanut butter and jelly sandwiches, which were always welcome. To this would be added a bag of chips, a piece of fruit (usually an apple or a tangerine), and a Clark Bar. On Fridays in

Lent, a tuna salad sandwich or cheese sandwich was the standard replacement. For some reason, Mom's favorite special treat was a small box of raisins. She must have read somewhere that they were good for what ailed you.

Even though we were a parochial school, we were eligible for the free milk program, so our normal drink for lunch was milk in small, portable, waxed paper containers. The main problem was that the crates the milk came in were left outside the school by the delivery truck early in the morning. That meant that the milk, despite the ice it came with, got warm and sometimes soured in early fall and late spring, and often turned to ice in winter. No one would ever have thought about complaining, since the milk was free and purported to be healthy for young children. When things did not work out, we just adjusted our expectations.

Being chosen as an altar boy was a great distinction in the peer culture of Saint Anthony's. First of all, it was evidence of high regard by the teachers. Second, it was an overt public service role that made one's parents proud and seemed somehow connected with religious participation and good deeds. Finally, it required mastery of certain Latin phrases and some complicated liturgical logistics. In other words, being an altar boy allowed one to stand out from the crowd and assume a leadership role at an age when heroic models (like saints and missionaries) were quite attractive to young boys.

Fourth grade was the first year of eligibility. Because I was tall for my age and had done well academically, I passed muster that year and began formal training with the youngest of the parish priests, Father Decker. Other than the fact that he was afflicted with a rather severe stuttering problem, all of us found Father Decker to be a nice man, easy to work with, and sympathetic to the fears of new kids on the block, so to speak. He taught us how to put on our black cassocks and white surplices, how to hold our hands in a reverent palm-against-palm position, how to genuflect, how to light and extinguish the candles, and how to go through the various rubrical steps during the course of the Mass—including moving the mass book from one side of the altar to the other, bringing up the wine and water, washing the priests' hands, and holding the paten under the chins of the communicants.

The biggest challenge was learning the server's responses in Latin, a language none of us knew. "*Ad deum qui laetificat, juventutum meam.*" "*Suscipiat deum . . .*" The priest showed us in the training booklet what the words meant, but that memory lasted no more than a few seconds. We were preoccupied with the need to say the strange, almost unintelligible string of words in a way that sounded authentic, and that required practice and more practice. After a while, it became like memorizing a poem or the names of all the state capitals. When my duty day finally came, I was ready to respond like the bigger boys.

Being an altar boy was tantamount to joining a subculture within the school. We shared access to seemingly arcane knowledge, including speaking in a foreign language. We also got to know the priests more personally than did the other students—and as a result we were exposed to their idiosyncrasies. In the 1940s and 1950s, the pastor was assisted by three other priests, each of whom had a distinctive way of celebrating mass in terms of pace and manifest piety. Some days they were grumpy or critical of our performance; other days, they were full of compliments and encouragement. In addition to serving for Sunday and weekday masses, we took turns helping with weddings and funerals and special devotions like the novena to Mary under the title of the Immaculate Conception, which took place on Wednesday evenings. During Lent we assisted with Stations of the Cross on Friday nights and the high liturgies of Holy Week and Easter, which had a large cast of servers in multiple roles.

As I got older, I often was assigned to serve at funerals, which I liked since we were excused from school for the mass and the burial service at the cemetery. With my height, I usually carried the cross, flanked by candle bearers. At the beginning of the liturgy, when we made our way down the main aisle to the rear of the church to greet the casket and the funeral party, I would often tear up as I looked into the eyes of the grieving family members. I seldom knew the deceased personally, but the emotion of the occasion touched me. Some funerals involved a trip to Arlington National Cemetery across the Potomac in northern Virginia. For former military officers, they would play taps on a bugle at the end of the burial and fire cannons. For enlisted people, after taps an honor guard fired rifles. In that dramatic setting, with the endless rows of tombstones, I would almost always get choked up by the finality of it all.

Those of us who served regularly at funerals missed out on the stipend gift that servers usually received at weddings, but for novenas or other special paraliturgical celebrations, the priest would sometimes give the servers a quarter. Invariably, I would spend it at the Baldwin Bakery on six cherry-filled doughnuts which I would consume before I got home.

In a school play in the seventh grade, I was cast in two different roles with a costume change in between. In the first section, I played Steven Foster, the songwriter, and led the other students, who were dressed in period outfits, in a medley of Foster's major hits such as "Swanee" and "My Old Kentucky Home." Anyone who knows my level of talent as a singer will find that comical. I also had to dance a minuet with a female partner, which was even more of a challenge. After intermission, I returned on stage as George Washington, wearing a white wig and Revolutionary era clothing. This was a patriotic pageant that required little from me other than standing and looking presidential. Of course, my parents told me afterward how proud they were of my acting skills and even suggested I was destined for Broadway or Hollywood. I am sure that all the other parents made similar remarks to their children.

One person in my life who particularly instilled in me a love of learning and a sense of my responsibility to make the most of my talents was Sister Eleanor, my teacher in the fourth, fifth, and sixth grades. It was unusual to have the same teacher in consecutive years, but that was how it happened. She identified a few of us whom she believed to be the most promising in the class. Typically, the smartest were girls, but in our year it was three boys. That was a pivotal time in our lives; we were all approaching puberty and there were a lot of other distractions. Sister Eleanor would get together with us after class to do additional assignments and look at things the class as a whole was not studying. Most of all, she convinced us that we had a God-given intelligence, that we were capable of doing great things, and that opportunities would open to us if we would only use our capacities to learn.

She did this in a very unobtrusive, nondictatorial fashion, and she made it fun. The three of us were just delighted to have someone set us apart and encourage us. She gave us a tremendous amount of confidence, exposed us to some of the thrill of learning, and convinced us that we had a moral obligation to use the opportunities that were available to us. That confidence was important outside the classroom as well.

Prior to Sister Eleanor's extra help I had been doing well but I was not passionate about school. Education was important in my family and my parents sacrificed to send us to Catholic schools, but I did not have any models in the family for going on to college. I had many great teachers in my life, but Sister Eleanor was extraordinary. She had us cultivate a more developed vocabulary. She interested us in science projects. All the things we were studying in fourth, fifth, and sixth grades, whether history or geography or grammar, she supplemented. I always had been a strong reader, but with her guidance I became an enthusiastic one. Her theory, which is now mine, is that it does not matter what students are reading as long as they are reading—if they enjoy it they will keep moving on to more sophisticated material. They will have the passion and desire that makes a real learner.

In 1986, the year I was elected President of Notre Dame, there was a nice article about me in the *Washington Post.* Two or three weeks after the article appeared, I received a letter that read something like this: "Dear Father Malloy: You probably don't remember me, but I was your grade school teacher at Saint Anthony's, and I wanted to tell you how proud I and the other sisters are of your accomplishments." It went on to say a bunch of other laudatory things. I quickly wrote back: "How can you have ever imagined I wouldn't remember who you were? I was in your class for three grades in a row. More important than that, you were one of the decisive influences in my life. I didn't have the wisdom at the time to thank you properly, so I'm pleased that you wrote me, because now I can thank you as an adult for what in retrospect was a pivotal set of possibilities that you opened up for me." I have often talked about Sister Eleanor when I have given presentations to educators and I see a lot of heads nod.

Like most Catholic parishes of the day, St. Anthony's placed a heavy emphasis on Marian piety. We had regular novena devotions to the Immaculate Conception, and in October and May additional occasions were made to pray the rosary (with a special petition for world peace and the conversion of Russia). The highlight of May's events was the selection of the May Queen, who would have the honor of placing a crown of flowers on a statue of Mary. The crowning was preceded by a procession in front of the church and the singing of hymns that were perennial favorites on such occasions, like "Mother Dearest, Mother Fairest." The May Queen and her court were all decked out in white lacy dresses and wore white veils. Since I was a boy, I was not involved in the annual speculation among the girls and their mothers about who would be chosen. No doubt the Benedictine sisters played a heavy role in the selection; at a minimum a girl had to be an excellent student, religiously active, and a model of comportment. But it was also probably true that the sisters saw such recognition as a way of fostering religious vocations.

Saint Anthony's was a representative Catholic grade school of its time. There were two sections of each grade level with about thirty students in each. A modified kind of uniform was required, with the younger girls wearing a white blouse and blue jumper and the older girls sporting a white blouse, a blue skirt, and a blazer. By the seventh or eighth grade there were always one or two girls pushing the limits with a slightly higher hemline or something flashy attached to their blouses or blazers. The boys wore a white shirt with khaki pants and a sweater when the weather cooled. The boys' major problems with the rules were sloppiness and disheveledness. The sisters were always making them tuck in their shirts after recess.

Most classes used workbooks of one kind or another. We had regular homework and frequent tests. Memorization and rote learning were considered essential, especially in religion class where we were expected to know the standard answers from the Baltimore Catechism in the earlier grades ("Who made you?" "God made me to love, honor, and serve him in this world and to be happy with him forever in the next") and to master the essentials of the seven sacraments and the varieties of sin (original, mortal, and venial) and other such matters as we prepared for First Confession, First Communion, and Confirmation.

The whole school attended mass in the church once a week. From the sisters' point of view this was a dangerous time for discipline, since it was hard to keep track of all the students when they were packed into pews. The older boys had a propensity for trying to get away with something—like pinching one another to elicit screams or hitting someone surreptitiously in the back of the head. All it would take was a kneeler being knocked over or someone farting for peals of laughter to roll across the church. Not to say that there was no genuine piety manifest, but kids will always be kids.

As it turned out, I was sick with the flu when my class received First Communion. One of the girls had a similar misfortune, so two weeks later at one of the main Sunday masses the two of us, dressed in white from head to toe, had the privilege of walking together from the back of the church at communion time. Our hands were folded and all eyes were on us as we made our way to the rail. We felt like Princess

Early Schooling

Di and Prince Charles at their wedding ceremony, since we were the center of attention of the whole church.

After we had received First Confession and Communion, the upper grades would go over to the church once or twice a month for youth confessions. No one was forced into the confessional box but there was a strong expectation in that direction. From my perspective now, the priests must have been perpetually bored except for the occasional moment of humor that cropped up. (I was hearing a First Confession once when a little boy started off by stating he had committed adultery. I took a deep breath and began as gently as I could to figure out what he was talking about.) Since there was no one else in the church on youth confession days and the sisters had already read us the riot act about not making noise, it was possible when sitting near the confessional boxes to hear bits and snatches of conversation. In our class there was a boy with a very loud voice who confessed his sins to the whole church every week. All of us looked forward to the moment when he went into the box. It was like an early version of reality TV.

The religious values we were taught in school were consistently reinforced by my parents. We never missed Sunday mass, even when we were on vacation. We went to confession regularly. In my days as an altar boy, my parents and sisters often attended the novena devotions, especially when I was serving. In Lent we went to Stations of the Cross. On Good Friday, when we were old enough, we would stay for the three-hour service from noon to three o'clock. My father and mother both participated in societies that assumed special responsibilities in local parish life.

School dances were held in the school hall on Friday evenings. The grade school dances were quite popular with the girls but much less so with the boys. First of all, most of us did not know how to dance and it would have been a huge loss of face to admit that to our peers. Second, the girls were more mature than the boys, both physically and emotionally. Then there was the question of who would take

Early Schooling

the initiative in inviting someone onto the dance floor, and there was always the possibility of rejection. Finally, the physical setting did not lend itself to casual interaction: the girls would gather at one end of the hall and the boys at the other. If nothing developed after the music started, the girls did not hesitate to dance with each other. You could not have gotten the boys to do the same for a million dollars. While I went to some of the school dances under duress, I much preferred to be shooting hoops at Turkey Thicket.

By the seventh and eighth grades, the walk home from school tended to take a while. The block just north of the church was full of stores that became hangouts for students from Saint Anthony's and Brookland schools. Peoples Drug Store was a favorite since it had a soda fountain and a wide array of cheap items. Across the street were the local 5 & 10 cent store and the Baldwin Bakery (who could pass up the chance for a jelly-roll doughnut or some glazed pastry?).

Among the traditions of the 1950s were organized air raid drills that stemmed from a fear of nuclear attack and from the anti-Communist paranoia generated by Senator Joe McCarthy and the House Un-American Activities Committee. It probably made more sense to have such exercises in the capital than in the hinterlands of Vermont or Wyoming, but it is comical to think back at the utter inadequacy of what we did. At the ringing of the all-school alarm bell, we would duck under our desks and kneel down with our hands over our heads until the all-clear sounded. Sometimes we would watch films in class that described how to store food and water in the basements of our homes. Some blocks appointed Civil Defense wardens who, among other things, were expected to organize the post–nuclear bomb response.

Suffice it to say that all of us at Saint Anthony's were deeply committed to the American way of life and saw atheistic Communism as the great threat to our survival. The Fatima-induced prayer for the conversion of Russia at the end of each Sunday mass constantly reminded us of this perspective.

Saint Anthony's fielded football, basketball, and baseball teams that competed in the citywide Catholic league. Eventually, I played all three sports. In eighth grade, I was the tallest kid on the football team, and though never noted for speed, I was a fullback on offense and a linebacker on defense. Most surprising, I was the kick-off return specialist. I remember watching the football slowly sail through the air while everyone on the other team ran toward me with the single-minded intent of knocking my head off. On offense, the coach's strategy near the goal line was to give me the ball and hope that, with my height, I could fall into the end zone.

The most fun thing about football, other than wearing pads and a uniform and a helmet, was fumble practice. On days when it rained heavily, the coach would announce that it was time to practice recovering a fumbled football. Our job, in groups of four or five, was to slosh across the muddy field like a herd of pigs and dive for the ball. With a little head start, it was possible to slide on your belly for five or ten yards—sheer bliss for boys our age. When fumble practice was over, our uniforms were soaked in mud and grime and we felt like gladiators returning from the arena.

My basketball career started humbly enough when Mr. Gerard Kane, the father of one of my friends in the neighborhood, took me and his son Denny down to the basketball courts at nearby Turkey Thicket playground and taught us how to shoot a basketball. It was difficult to reach the ten-foot hoop since we were only in the fifth grade, but little by little I started to get a feel for it. My first attempts at scoring were restricted to a two-hand set shot. (Interestingly enough, my initial exposure to the game was restricted to a few dribbles and shooting at the hoop. Most of my friends would say I never did get around to learning the other skills, like passing, rebounding, and playing defense.) In the sixth grade, since I was tall, I tried out for the team and was the only one in my class selected. The next day on my way home from school, two disgruntled eighth-graders who had not been chosen jumped me and sat on me until they got bored and let me go.

From sixth to eighth grade, I continued to sprout and gain strength, and I felt a great sense of satisfaction as my skill level improved dramatically. I started practicing at Turkey Thicket playground during the summer and off-season. Over time, I moved from a two-hand set shot to a one-hand jump shot, which later in my career became my hallmark offensive move. Since Saint Anthony's had no gym, we had to practice and play our games in the gyms of other Catholic schools. The physical configuration of these facilities was not ideal for basketball; often, they had low ceilings near the baskets and walls or stages behind them. Even in the best of conditions, grade school basketball games were usually chaotic, with most of the time spent dashing helter-skelter up and down the court. Most games ended with the score in the 20s or 30s.

One year we practiced several evenings a week at the Saint Gabriel school gym. Our coach (who, like most coaches, was a volunteer with no particular credentials other than availability) decided that we needed to work on lay-up drills, so one evening he set up a small chair under the basket and told us to jump over it as we shot the basket. This was intended to improve our vertical lift and get us to focus on the basket. As might have been expected, several of us tripped over the chair and fell headlong to the floor. Eventually he abandoned this crazy experiment and we returned to our normal practice routines.

In basketball height and strength are crucial. There is a limit to what grade school kids can achieve until they hit their growth spurt after the onset of puberty. I had some advantage over my classmates because I was relatively taller, but the real change would come when I grew six inches between eighth grade and my sophomore year of high school. (Lying in bed at night I could even feel myself growing.) From that point on, basketball became my passion.

The third sport I competed in at Saint Anthony's was baseball. We had a lot of talent in that area, and the proximity of Turkey Thicket to the school and to where most of us lived meant we could play in the summer park league as well as during the school year. Most of us competed in both baseball and softball, and the Saint Anthony's team had almost the same membership as the Turkey Thicket fourteen-and-under recreation department team. Because we had so many talented young baseball players, I played catcher, which seemed out of position for someone tall. In softball, on the other hand, I was a pitcher, the coach probably thinking that my size would be somewhat intimidating. By the time we moved on to high school, we had won citywide championships in both baseball and softball in the summer leagues and had done well as members of the Saint Anthony's nine.

Our great thrill in the summer baseball league was playing for the championship in Griffith Stadium, the then home of the major league Senators. Because our starting pitchers had all come down with sore arms en route to the final game, I was named the starter and finished five innings, with us ahead, before moving back to catcher for the last two innings (games at that level were seven innings long). One of my claims to baseball fame was that I hit one out of the park, at least in the technical sense of the phrase. What happened was I hit a foul ball off to the first base side and it cleared the roof of the second deck and went out into the street. For a fourteen year old, that in and of itself was enough for post-game bragging rights. I have a picture in my office of the trophy ceremony at home plate: I have my chest protector and knee guards on, and in the distance, around second base, my father stands, beaming proudly.

At some point I was given the title "the Mayor of Turkey Thicket" by my friends because I spent so much time on the playground, especially in the summers. About half of the park was given over to baseball, softball, and football. There were three smaller diamonds used interchangeably for softball or children's baseball games. In the afternoons when most adults were at work, these fields were available for pick-up games, school practice sessions, and school or youth league games. In the evenings, usually around seven o'clock, they were reserved for men's and women's softball leagues. Many of the adult players were out of shape and just wanted to have a good time then

Early Schooling

retire to a local establishment for a few beers, but I was struck by the athleticism of the women, who played hard and seemed to relish showing their stuff. The worst thing I ever saw at one of the evening games was an umpire being attacked by a couple of irate fans. The police had to be called to restore order.

The other half of Turkey Thicket was given over to three full-length basketball courts (the center of my mayoral career), a clubhouse staffed by employees of the D.C. recreation department, eight tennis courts, a playground area for little kids, and oodles of open fields. This was a time when parents felt that their kids would be safe when left alone with their peers. The staff at the clubhouse had responsibility for the overall good order of the park, but other than scraped knees, sprained ankles, and occasional fisticuffs among the boys, their worst challenges were lost children and summer thunderstorms.

Turkey Thicket was a social and economic melting pot. Many of the kids came from apartment developments that were relatively inexpensive (that is where I lived until I went off to college) and attracted families with high fertility levels. However, other residents nearby owned their own homes, some of them quite pricey. There were no black families in the neighborhood at all. There may have been members of other racial groups, but their numbers were too small to draw much notice. For us growing up in the 1940s and 1950s, this was just reality as we knew it. But while the social revolution that the civil rights movement would set off had not yet begun, Turkey Thicket was a great leveler on economic grounds. You made your name and your reputation in the peer culture, not on which part of the neighborhood you came from but on how proficient you were in the playground activities, which usually, though not always, revolved around sports.

We were endlessly inventive in designing ways to have fun. A big favorite was three-player Nerf ball—one person would hit, one would pitch, and the other would field. The trick was to develop new types of curves, since the Nerf ball was light and hard to hit any distance. We also played touch football with a smaller ball and sidelines determined by where we placed our shirts. Depending on how many players were available, we would go at it with teams of from two to eleven. The offensive strategy was to send everyone long, throw a deep bomb, and hope someone would snag it. Sometimes we scored so many touchdowns that we had to tally the score by ones rather than sixes.

When we got tired in the heat and humidity of Washington summers, we would retire to an area near the basketball courts where there were a couple of picnic benches under a tree. If we had any money, we would get some soft drinks from McCarthy's store across Michigan Avenue and, if someone had brought cards, we would pick a game to play. Once in a while, when we were feeling frisky, we would play knuckles—a game designed to allow the winner to scrape the exposed knuckles of the loser's hand with the sharp side of the card deck. Most of the time the damage was minimal, but every now and then revenge would be taken for some slight and blood would begin to flow. We also played hearts and pinochle and rummy. But our favorite game was tunk, a version of poker that could be played either for fun or for small stakes. It was unusual for us to play more than penny ante, though as we got older the initial bet might rise to a nickel.

More often we competed at telling stories in order to seem more worldly or more aware. With the onset of puberty, regular attention was given to our female classmates or neighborhood girls who had caught our eyes. At the grade school stage, most of our observations about girls, about sex, and about the mysteries of life were part bravado and part shared ignorance. No one wanted to be left behind in the perpetual quest to be considered cool and worldly wise.

CHAPTER 3

"COME ON AND FIGHT FOR CARROLL HIGH!

COME ON AND FIGHT FOR VICTORY!"

IN 1945 THE ARCHDIOCESE OF BALTIMORE, WHICH included Washington, purchased land adjacent to the campus of the Catholic University of America for a new archdiocesan high school to be named after Archbishop John Carroll, the first American bishop and an important figure in U.S. history. Archbishop Carroll High School opened its doors in 1951 as an all-male school operated by the Augustinian Friars of the Province of Saint Thomas of Villanova. Right from the start, the school was intended to be a model of racially integrated education. Even before the *Brown v. Board of Education* decision by the United States Supreme Court in 1954, the Catholic Church in Washington took the initiative to serve a cross section of students from a variety of backgrounds and from every part of the archdiocese.

When I enrolled in the fall of 1955, Carroll had just had its first graduating class. In general, Carroll in its early years was between 10 and 15 percent African American, with a few members of other racial groups. The white students were mainly middle class, with a few from wealthy neighborhoods and a few from poor backgrounds. The other male Catholic schools in the area (Gonzaga, Saint John's, and Georgetown Prep) generally drew their students from a more affluent base, while DeMatha had a student profile closer to Carroll's.

From my home to Carroll was not a great distance but several hills along the route made it a bit of a challenge to walk to school each day. Of course, it was a lot easier on the way home. Carroll students from other parts of the city would either use the city buses or work out an arrangement to charter a small bus for the beginning and end of the school day. Upper-class students who were old enough to drive could use their cars or car pool, but this option was less common than it would be today. Although Washington did not get snow very often, an inch or two would make one of the hills along the route impassible since the city owned few sand or salt trucks. Like students everywhere, we would get excited when snow was in the forecast, hoping for a day off from school, and on rare occasions this actually happened. (A much quoted line from the later infamous Mayor Marion Barry after the city experienced utter chaos in the aftermath of a major snow storm was, "God gave us the snow. Now we will wait for God to melt it!")

I loved Carroll from the first moment I set foot in the school. I liked the change from Saint Anthony's and the opportunity to make new friends. The classes were challenging but I found early success in the classroom and sustained it all through my days there. Except for one Spanish teacher, all my teachers and athletic coaches were Augustinian priests and brothers. Class attendance was expected, and late arrival to school had penalties attached. Excuses about sickness or other impairment needed to be airtight since the principal's office regularly checked with parents over the telephone. Tuition was relatively low by today's standards but it was a real strain on my parents' budget. There was a dress code (white shirt, tie, and slacks in the warm weather, with a jacket or sweater added in the winter). The rules of conduct were intended to promote a healthy common life even if they sometimes went against the grain of male teenage desires. We could not chew gum or smoke inside the school, although there was a smoking lounge as a perk for seniors. Fighting, of course, was prohibited, but sometimes it was hard to tell the difference between horseplay and hostile confrontation.

Personal appearance was regularly corrected if we had our shirttails hanging out or our ties unknotted or our shoelaces untied. Discipline in the classroom was the prerogative of the teacher, with the presumed backup of the principal's office if necessary. Most of my teachers had a straightforward approach: if someone got out of line, a glance in his direction or a word of reproof was enough to regain control of the class. The most noteworthy variance from this style of control was displayed by our freshman math teacher, Father Cherbuck. He was a weight lifter by reputation and physically rather imposing. One day early in our first semester, he waited until some runty frosh was talking out of turn in the back of the classroom. Turning around, the priest summoned the malefactor to the front near the blackboard, picked him up by the armpits, and held him straight out a few inches off the floor. Time seemed to stand still, especially for the boy. Then he dropped him. Not saying another word, the teacher had the boy return to his seat. From that moment on, none of us would have dared to say boo in that class. And as boys are wont to do, we told the story of Father Cherbuck's impressive feat over and over again.

On the opposite end of the spectrum, our Spanish teacher during senior year was a retired Army colonel and the only lay teacher I ever had. He was a nice man but utterly naive and totally incapable of controlling his class. Once the students discovered this, the class embarked on a constant quest to see how far he could be pushed. It was not uncommon for individual students to ask permission to go to the bathroom and not return for the rest of the class. The worst incident I recall took place on the day of our fall semester final exam. One of the least-prepared students got the colonel's permission to go to the restroom early in the exam. He walked over to the Catholic University campus, found a Spanish-speaking student, had him fill in the answers, and returned before the end of the period to turn in the exam. As far as we could tell, the colonel never suspected what had happened.

I quickly became involved in extracurricular activities at Carroll. By graduation, in addition to playing basketball, I had served as student body president, head of one of the political parties, a member of the honor society, assistant editor of the yearbook, and assistant editor of the school newspaper. In my senior year I went out for baseball (as a kind of lark) and even became starting catcher, but I quickly found that my skills had not kept pace with the quality of the pitching and my heart was really not in it. After a conversation with the coach, we mutually agreed that I would be better served by honing my basketball talents.

One of my faculty mentors was Father Joe Duffey who, among other things, served as athletic director. He encouraged me to get involved in leadership roles among my peers, and it was he who suggested that I run for student body president. One time when he saw me not going to communion at a school mass he took me aside and pointed out that the other students were observing my behavior and could be influenced for better or ill by my example. On another occasion he invited me to come to his office where he asked whether I had ever thought about a religious vocation. I was a bit taken aback but I acknowledged that I had thought about it. We talked again about the topic and I told him that I just knew I needed to play college basketball and have a taste of independence by moving away from home. After college, who knew what might happen? Father Duffey was respectful of my answer, but in retrospect I am sure he helped prepare the way for my later decision to join Holy Cross.

As assistant editor of the school newspaper, I wrote a weekly column. It was a kind of Herb Caen or Irv Kupcinet type of commentary on school events, on people of note, or on whatever struck my fancy. Preparing it was not that onerous and I enjoyed the notoriety that came each Friday it appeared. It was the beginning of my public writing career. During my junior year, someone dared me to try out for the school glee club. I knew I lacked the necessary talent but I decided to go ahead with an audition. I was given a piece of music along with an accompanist at the piano. The director had already listened to many other candidates, so after I sang he merely looked at me and posed like he was shooting a basketball. I got the message. If only that moment could have been preserved for posterity.

The Augustinian priests and brothers lived in a separate but connected building behind the school. Normally, that space was *terra incognita*, but the altar servers were on a schedule to serve their individual masses before school in the morning in the many side altars of their chapel. As a result, we got to know them in a way many other students did not. Even observing their styles of celebrating mass revealed something about their different personalities. One of my favorites was Father Andy Boyle, the school librarian. He was a bit older than the rest and possessed a gentle demeanor. He had a great interest in things that boys our age thought were important. He encouraged us in our academic endeavors, always asked about our families, and attended all the major events at the school. Long after graduation, I corresponded with him periodically and I always received a Christmas letter.

Carroll was a well-run school with a committed faculty. It had strong school spirit, and as the fame of the basketball team increased, the school was frequently highlighted in the local newspapers. The school colors—green and gold—and the school song—"Come on and Fight for Carroll High"—were sources of pride for us. While most of the student body came from relatively humble backgrounds, we found in our athletic tradition a route to local (and later national) fame.

Carroll had its own gym, a multi-purpose traditional high school athletic space that was used for indoor physical education and for freshman and varsity basketball. It had rollback bleacher stands on two sides which, when jam packed, held maybe 1,500 people. On Sundays, varsity games were free for religious community members and diocesan seminarians from the many houses of study in the area. On a number of occasions over the ensuing years, bishops, priests, and brothers have told me that they saw me play at Carroll when they were in formation.

The school also had a locker room which served the physical education classes and all the varsity sports, indoor and outdoor. Outside the facility was a large grassy field for football, baseball, and track. At first sight it was impressive, but closer examination revealed that it was bedeviled by small rocks that kept creeping to the surface despite the efforts of the grounds crew. Every effort to re-sod the field led to the same sorry result. The main price for the rough condition of the field was paid by the students who practiced and played there, particularly the football players who often had nicks and bruises from the stones.

During my senior year when I served as student body president, one of my responsibilities was to represent the needs and interests of the student body to the principal, Father Edward Stanford, who previously had been president of Villanova University. I recognized early on that he was an experienced administrator. He was in his early sixties at that time, with white hair and a calm, unflappable way about him. He treated me with respect and listened to whatever issues I brought up, no matter how inconsequential.

The biggest crisis the two of us had to face revolved around a sexual overture one student made to another in the shower area. In the relatively prudish 1950s, this was potentially a really big deal. But Father Stanford discussed the matter with me calmly and in confidence. His priority was to protect the reputations of the two students and, insofar as possible, of the school. The offending student was asked to withdraw and encouraged to receive counseling (which he did), and eventually life got back to normal. This incident was my first exposure to the sometimes difficult, behind-the-scenes responsibilities of administrators. The fact that my principal handled the matter so well was an excellent model for my then unexpected future.

Punishment for minor offenses at Carroll was one or more days of "jug." This meant that after classes the offender reported to a classroom where a priest or brother supervised all the misbehavers of the day for an assigned period of time. There were unpleasant tasks to perform, such as completing an essay on such topics as "life inside a Ping-Pong ball" or "why virtue is better than vice," or writing a single sentence over and over, either in a notebook or on the blackboard. Occasionally students would be given some perfunctory manual labor task like helping the janitor clear the classrooms or the dining area. No one wanted to get jug too often, since it was basically a bummer, but there was a strange kind of pride in showing up once in a while. It gave one a chance to see who else was there and to establish a kind of solidarity of the bad (like an implicit teenage gang). I was too much of a do-gooder to appear in jug very often, yet I cherished the few times I was there as a sign that I had more sides to me than my public image suggested.

Carroll had a consistent academic curriculum for all its students. It was taken for granted that graduates would be well prepared for college. Each student or family had choices to make about what foreign language or science to take. I took Latin and Spanish for two years each, and chemistry and physics, each of which had a laboratory requirement. My physics teacher was Father Mullen, who offered us a first-rate introduction to the discipline. I remember one day going to the roof of the school to learn how to apply the principle of parallax for computing the height of the Washington Monument by measuring certain angles and using a telescope. It was not any big breakthrough in human knowledge but it gave me a sense of the relationship between theory and practice.

Father Mullen was the person responsible for my decision to study chemical engineering when I got to college—a big mistake. The

Soviet Union had successfully sent Sputnik into space, and the reaction in this country was a long lament about how far American scientific and technological education had fallen behind. There were many proposals to remedy the situation, some of which focused on motivating young people to enter these fields. One day in class Father Mullen gave an eloquent talk about how our generation had a moral responsibility, if we possessed the requisite ability, to pursue degrees in science and engineering (in effect, to stay ahead of the godless Communists). I had done well in math and science and I somehow figured that chemical engineering would be an interesting and fulfilling career path, even though I had no idea what a chemical engineer did.

It was quite common in the 1950s and 1960s for Catholic high schools to be single-sex institutions, even though Catholic grade schools were not. Part of this sprang from theorists who speculated that, with the onset of puberty, it was too distracting to the educational mission to mix the genders in the classroom. There was also a fundamental skittishness about sexuality as a moral area. But just as important was the availability of religious communities of female sisters and of male brothers and priests. These dedicated religious seemed to feel most comfortable in schools that resembled their own gender composition.

As an all-male school, Carroll was a lively, testosterone-imbued environment. Sports were big, both in levels of participation and in terms of conversation about favorite teams in the collegiate and professional ranks, with the Washington Senators and the Washington Redskins being perennial pro favorites. Sentiment was divided about the local colleges and universities, with Georgetown, Catholic U., and Maryland College Park all having supporters.

It was an era when males were not particularly adept at sharing their inner emotions or divulging every feeling. Teenage boys, Carroll students included, learned through the models provided by their own fathers and brothers and from the popular media. Roughhousing was acceptable (within limits), crying was not. Serious dating was discour-

"Fight for Carroll High and Victory"

aged but everyone was expected to go to the junior and senior proms. The pivotal male reality was access to a car, since on weekends juniors and seniors frequently congregated at drive-in movies and restaurants. Sometimes there were incidents of violence at such places, but most of the time it was mainly posturing among males to win the attention of the females present.

I never drank any alcohol until I was twenty years old and a junior at Notre Dame. In high school I abstained primarily because of my athletic commitments: I wanted to stay in shape and did not want to get into trouble. There were certain subcultures at Carroll where the use of alcohol was commonplace, usually among those from the more affluent neighborhoods. But drinking at school was simply taboo. To be caught with alcohol in one's possession or on one's breath was grounds for dismissal. The use of marijuana or other illicit drugs was identified in our eyes with jazz musicians or bohemian artists' colonies. I never knew anyone at Carroll who smoked pot or used heroin or cocaine. It was simply unthinkable.

Smoking tobacco was another matter. Although it was forbidden on school grounds, seniors had access to a smoking lounge at lunchtime and after school. Part of the lure of going there was that it gave one explicit permission to engage in an act otherwise prohibited. It was like a rite of passage. My one experiment with cigarettes came earlier, when I was twelve and spent a couple of weeks in Scranton with my cousin, Tony McNulty. He had a night watchman's job and I used to stay up with him, whiling the night away. He introduced me to cigarette smoking. But I soon found that it affected my breathing when I exercised, so when I returned home to Washington I quit cold turkey. I never felt the urge to smoke again.

Usually an all-male Catholic high school was paired with an all-female Catholic school in an effort to foster co-ed activities after school and on weekends. Carroll's sister school was Regina High in the Maryland suburbs—far enough away to make logistics complicated. Some Regina girls acted in the annual Carroll play and vice-versa, but when it came to the junior and senior proms, there was no way school officials could predetermine who might be invited. The girls I took to the two proms both lived in my Brookland neighborhood, and one of them was a good friend of my sister Joanne. I was never a social butterfly, so the prom experiences were important in their own right, as they are for many teenagers. For my senior prom I was double-dating with Michael Moore, who had permission to use his family car. I was dressed in my tux anxiously awaiting his arrival before we picked up my date. I looked out the window and saw a car pull up with a couple in the front seat decked out for a prom. I said goodbye to my parents, picked up my corsage box, and went out. When I got in the back seat, I realized that I did not know the couple in the front seat. They, in fact, were picking up someone to go to another school's prom. I apologized and returned, chagrined, to our apartment to await my real ride.

One memory that I have of senior prom was that the dance craze of the moment was the twist, and Chubby Checker reigned supreme. The dance was considered somewhat daring, especially with our faculty and parental chaperones looking on, but once the first couple started we all got into it. We twisted the night away, so to speak, and felt that we were part of a new, hip generation.

With Dwight Eisenhower in the White House, J. Edgar Hoover heading the FBI, and Senator Joseph McCarthy protecting the nation from Communists (real and imagined), the times during my high school years were fundamentally conservative. Ours was a generation respectful of authority (in society and in the Church), accustomed to relatively stable family life, instinctively patriotic, and full of high ambition. We had only a dim sense of what the breakup of entrenched patterns of racial segregation and societal discrimination would bring, or of how established notions of gender roles would prove precarious in the face of theoretical and practical challenges in the public forum, or of how quickly confidence in the leadership of the American social order would be lost in the face of scandals.

I kept my hair short all through my high school years, as did many of my peers. It was a matter of convenience for athletes, but it also displayed comfort with being part of the crowd and not needing to stand out. By my senior year, things had begun to change and some of my friends had begun to affect a modified version of the Elvis look, with ducktailed hair, flashier clothes, and a kind of strutting manner of walking. Within the school boundaries this was always curtailed by the prevailing administrative standard, but after school and on the weekends, and even more during the summer, these Catholic school conformists were transformed into hip teenagers with a mind and will of their own. Some of this was just the perennial move into greater independence by seventeen and eighteen year olds, but it was also the early stages of a cultural change that would eventually lead to the activism and cultural dissonance of the middle to late 1960s. It all seems clearer now than when I was living through it.

It is a curious experience to look back through the Carroll yearbook of my senior year (1959) through the eyes of someone in his sixties. Photographs of my classmates, of the faculty and staff, and of the school grounds all seem frozen in time. It was the tradition of the day to ask faculty and fellow seniors to sign their names next to their pictures. I was successful in gaining most of the signatures. It seems noteworthy that I am missing any message from Father John McDowell, the dean of discipline. Maybe I thought it was the better part of valor not to disturb him. My image appears frequently and in all my photographs except the basketball section I am wearing the same sports jacket, which probably reflected the extent of my dress-up capacity.

The book contains pictures of noteworthy events like pep rallies, the senior prom, students relaxing in the smoking lounge, horseplay on the outside grounds, phys. ed. in the gym, the all-school masses and retreat groups. There were 184 students in my graduating class, and by the end of our senior year I knew them all to one degree or another. Those were good and exciting years, and our class not only enjoyed a positive rapport but we were attending a school at the pinnacle of its reputation because of the success of our basketball team. At Carroll, one had much to cheer about and be proud of. Most of my classmates married and went on to raise families. A few pursued the priesthood. The vast majority received a bachelor's degree. Several went on to do doctorates and became faculty and/or administrators in higher education. Others went into education at the secondary level, including at Carroll itself.

From Good to Great

My arrival at Archbishop John Carroll High School turned out to be providential not only scholastically but in other ways as well. A number of elements were coming into place just then for what would turn out to be the most successful high school basketball team in American history. At the start, Carroll had a good but not outstanding team. By the time I graduated we had established ourselves as the best team in the country by the newspaper polls of the day. The following year, when the last of the superstars graduated, the team finished an amazing run of fifty-five straight victories.

The first component in this tradition was the head coach, Bob Dwyer. An effective strategist, a strong motivator, and a talented recruiter, he recognized early on that Carroll had a unique advantage as a top-flight academic institution that had deliberately become racially integrated before the rest of the region's public and private high schools came to grips with the social changes underway. While Carroll's modest tuition might seem prohibitive for some African Americans, Coach Dwyer was able to negotiate scholarship funds for a limited number of worthy and needy individuals. In the course of two years, he recruited Tom Hoover, John Thompson, and George Leftwich. Hoover transferred from a public school for his junior year, and Thompson and Leftwich came in their sophomore years. The other members of the team, including myself, came by more traditional methods of recruiting. Without Bob Dwyer's vision, Carroll would never have been able to attract the core of outstanding talent that was key to the team's success.

Coach Dwyer was a realist when it came to the racial realities of the day. He knew that our integrated team would be subject to a fair amount of attention, especially if we performed as well as he expected us to. He also sensed that we would be prey to unpleasantries in the all-white and all-black environments where we would be playing, and he was alert to the potential negative influence of some types of hangers-on who might claim a role in the recruitment process of the colleges interested in our star players. When I saw the hit movie *Remember the Titans* about the integrated football team in our area of northern Virginia who had a black coach and won the state championship in the same period of social transition as the Carroll team, I felt they had told our story under the guise of a different sport.

By the time the Carroll basketball team finished its record winning streak, we had been adopted by the *Washington Post* and the *Washington Star*, and also by the average citizens of D.C., as a hallmark of positive racial integration. In my junior year I was the single white starter with four black teammates. In my senior year we were two whites (Walt Skinner and myself) and three blacks (Tom Hoover, John Thompson, and George Leftwich), while our top subs included a mix of black and white players (Kenny Price, Doug and Billy Barnes, Mike O'Brien, and Tom Moore). Since access to our games was limited by the relatively small gyms in which we played, many more people knew about us than saw us play. Some people thought that I was black (because of the nickname) and that George Leftwich was Jewish.

In some of our venues, the spectator response to our team was downright hostile. But we usually went out to an early lead and took the crowd out of the game. One of our worst experiences was one night after a decisive victory at a suburban Maryland all-white public high school. It turned out that we shared a common shower area in the locker room with the home team. They told us to go first and then informed us that they were going to fumigate the area before they showered themselves. I was embarrassed for my race, but my black teammates just took it in stride as one more thing they had to deal with.

In the summer I would sometimes go with some of my black teammates to playgrounds in all-white areas of northwest Washington (like Chevy Chase or Georgetown) because they had lights at night and good cotton nets on the baskets. By this time our reputation preceded us in the playground subculture where reputation was everything and no story was too wild not to be believed by a few. Once I was at Chevy Chase with Tom Hoover and George Leftwich, among others. It was not hostility that we met there but naiveté. I told a small group of playground aficionados that Tom Hoover could take a quarter off of the top of the backboard. Furthermore, I claimed that he could dunk from behind over the top of the backboard. I saw them gulp and then go off to share the amazing news with their friends. I am sure that for the rest of the night they were waiting for Tom to display one of those feats.

One weekend during the spring of my senior year and after the basketball season was completed, my father agreed to drive Tom Hoover, George Leftwich, and me up to Villanova University, where Tom and I were being recruited and where Tom and George Leftwich would eventually play. This was long before the big budgets for athletic recruiting, and we figured we would go to Philadelphia together and look things over. About halfway there we stopped for a meal along the interstate in Delaware. In the restaurant, we sat, and sat, and sat some more. Finally, the manager motioned my father over. He told him he would serve him and me, but that the two black boys would have to take their food outside and eat in the car. My father looked the man in the eye, told us to get up, and we left together in an act of protest and solidarity that would be remembered long after the fact by all four of us. Many years later at a reunion of our team at a downtown

"Fight for Carroll High and Victory"

hotel in Washington, Tom Hoover made reference to this incident as a defining moment and offered words of praise for my father as a man of integrity.

The summer between my senior year and going off to Notre Dame, some wheeler-dealer organized a four-city (D.C., Baltimore, Philadelphia, and New York) all-star tournament at Spingarn playground in northeast Washington near RFK Stadium. This was a poor, inner-city neighborhood that was almost all black. Games were organized at three levels—high school, college, and professional. When I received my invitation, I quickly accepted and looked forward to the opportunity. I knew that I would be starting in the back court with my teammate, George Leftwich. The main thing that I remember about the event was that I was the only white player on any of the teams at any level of play. I was thrilled with the implicit validation that this represented.

In the summers of my high school years, Turkey Thicket playground became one of the few places where black and white athletes regularly congregated to play basketball together. Part of this had to do with its adjacent full-length courts and part with its relatively convenient location. But the draw of Turkey Thicket was largely a result of the influence of Elgin Baylor, who during thirteen years in the NBA was a perennial All-Star and generally regarded as one of the great basketball players of all time. During my sophomore and junior years of high school, Elgin was starring at Seattle University. He was the first black player from the D.C. area to gain a national reputation and, in a sense, he was at least partially responsible for D.C. becoming known as a great recruiting area once colleges and universities started to integrate their rosters.

Elgin was also a great showman. In the summers he would sometimes show up at Turkey Thicket with a caravan of ten or twelve cars full of players and wannabes. It did not take long for the word to get out, and soon my home court was besieged by players from all over the area. When Elgin was there, the action on the other two courts would stop and all eyes would be on the king. Among his other gifts, at 6'6" he had a God-given ability to hang in the air until his defenders came down to earth. Then he would kiss a sweet shot off the backboard or, when he felt like it, conclude with a rim-rattling dunk. No one could guard him, so his team tended to win as many games as they wanted to. Then off they would go in triumph.

In the playground world that I inhabited for most of my pre-college years, all that mattered were talent, confidence, and a positive reputation. You had to arrive early, when the teams were being selected, and hope you would be lucky enough to assemble a group capable of running the string, i.e., going undefeated. Full-court games were usually to 21 baskets, changing ends at 11. Half-court games, sometimes made necessary by the large number of players, were to 15. On most occasions, offense reigned supreme. Ideally, a team would have a speedy point guard who liked to hit the open man, and a shot-blocking, rebounding specialist who only got to shoot on offensive rebounds or tip-ins. That would leave three others to carry the offensive load. Playing defense with any intensity (something usually forced by coaches during the regular season) normally only followed mano-a-mano encounters between talented players when pride was at stake.

Most of the top flight basketball action at Turkey Thicket occurred on weekday evenings and during the afternoons on weekends. The rest of the time, the courts were available for neighborhood kids or for practicing one's skills hour after hour. There were days in the summer during high school and college when I might spend two or three hours shooting jump shots from every angle of the court and from every distance, after which I would try to make fifty or sixty foul shots without missing. I knew instinctively that I had a real gift as a shooter with almost unlimited range. I also knew that I was not very fast, could not leap particularly well, and had only average-size hands so my ball skills were limited. My route to success was going to be on the offensive side of the game, for better or for worse.

"Fight for Carroll High and Victory"

It was during one summer late in my high school career that I became connected to Red Auerbach, the legendary coach and later general manger of the Boston Celtics. Red was at the peak of his career and kept a home in Washington, where he had his roots. It began one day when I received a telephone call from a man claiming to be Red Auerbach and asking if I would be interested in joining him and a group of players he would invite for some informal games on Chevy Chase playground on a Sunday afternoon. At first I was suspicious, but I thought what the heck and decided to go over there and see what would happen. When I arrived, there was Auerbach and a mix of about fifteen high school, college, and professional players. I was flabbergasted but pleased to be included.

Red picked the teams and the action began. We played for ninety minutes or so, then Red treated us to drinks from the local dairy store and regaled us with one story after another about the Celtics, about professional basketball, and about some of the star players in the league. I could have sat there all day. Several other times that summer I received calls from Red and we reenacted our special, by invitation only, event. One time I was playing on a team with "Jungle Jim" Luscatoff, who had a reputation in the NBA as an enforcer not to be messed with. After I received a hard foul he came to my defense. I thought how handy it would be to have Jungle Jim on my side all the time.

Some years later at a Notre Dame game in New York City, Red Auerbach came down to our bench after warm-ups, but before the game started, to say hello and to offer kind words about me to our coach, Johnny Jordan. Everyone on the team, of course, knew who he was and they were duly impressed by this personal relationship that had suddenly been revealed. Since my basketball career at Notre Dame was less than sparkling, it became a cherished moment when the coach of perennial NBA championship teams implicitly suggested to Coach Jordan that I should be playing more.

One of my regrets is that during my high school and college career we did not have the 3-point shot. At my best, I think I could have held my own with any of the contemporary players when it came to 3-point efficiency, and that applies to present high school, college, and professional 3-point distances. The long-distance shot was my forte, my claim to fame. It was just that I came along too soon.

When my old teammate John Thompson was covering an NBA game on television, there was a half-time contest in which someone from the audience could win a big prize if they could make a shot from half court. The person chosen turned out to be a Catholic priest dressed in clerical garb. He did not come close. John then said to a national audience, "The only priest I know who could have made that shot is my former teammate, Monk Malloy, who is now the President of Notre Dame."

Over the summer between my junior and senior years of high school, I was eager for competition in order to refine my skills. Along with several of my Turkey Thicket–oriented friends, I decided to compete in three different summer leagues. This was the era before everything was hyper-organized by shoe companies and profit-seeking entrepreneurs. There were no national camps, no media rankings of college prospects, and no Internet websites. In a sense, the student athletes had the initiative and we could play for fun and enjoy high levels of competition. We did not have a coach, so all the details had to be worked out by whoever took the initiative to form the team. This meant paying the entry fee (we all dug deep into our small nest eggs of expendable cash), registering the team members, distributing the game schedules, and, most difficult of all, figuring out the transportation. We could play in three different leagues because most of the time the games were scheduled on different nights of the week. But sometimes there were conflicts, and then we would arrange to switch starting times to give ourselves a reasonable chance of making it from one location to the other. The worst challenge arrived one night when

"Fight for Carroll High and Victory"

we had three separate games in three rather far-flung places. Somehow or other we made it to the last game with seconds to spare.

Sometimes our team had access to a car, and then everything worked like a charm. But sometimes we could not come up with any transportation and had to hitch rides. Often the shortest distance from home to the league courts was unwalkable, so we had to plot the odds on alternate routes. We could take public transportation in a pinch, but that cost money and was not as exciting as hitchhiking. Our team had six or seven players, depending on the evening, so we had to split up into smaller units. My preferred partner was Doug Barnes, not only because we were good friends but also because he had a baby face and looked younger and more innocent than he was. At our favorite corners for hitching a ride, Doug would approach a prospective driver while I (and maybe one other guy) sort of hid behind a tree. Doug would turn on the charm and when the Good Samaritan said yes, he would throw in the tag line, "Can my friend(s) come too?" Before the driver had a chance to say no, we would all be in the car.

The three leagues we competed in that summer were the Jelleff's Boys' Club in the Georgetown area of D.C., Chevy Chase playground near the D.C.–Maryland border off Connecticut Avenue, and Takoma Park playground in the nearby Maryland suburbs. They were quite far apart and represented three entirely different approaches to promoting summer activity for young people. What they had in common was no black teams and no black players, a combination of location and long-established tradition. Georgetown and Chevy Chase were affluent, nearly all-white neighborhoods. Takoma Park was then a largely white, middle-class suburb. There was no one agitating for change since there were comparable all-black leagues around the city where the level of competition was, in fact, much better.

At Jelleffs there were some teams with coaches and players who had been together since grade school. None of my teammates ever hung out there, so we just played our games and left. Chevy Chase was more interesting for me because I often went there to play informally and because I helped to integrate it by bringing some of my teammates. At the end of the summer I led the league in scoring at over 30 points per game and was awarded the MVP trophy. My teammates were generous in feeding me the ball and, like most summer leagues with no coaches around, the name of the game was offense and more offense. The Takoma Park league had the fewest good teams and we dominated the competition there, but it was not as enjoyable overall.

Our main form of relaxation after a game was to buy a quart of grape or orange drink and some chips or cookies from the local High's Dairy Store and sit and rehash the game until we stopped sweating enough to return to our neighborhood. On our hitchhiking nights, the collective stink that we could throw off was more than enough to assure that all the windows would be open in our vehicle of transport.

If someone asked me then or today what experiences of basketball were the most enjoyable for me, nothing would surpass the hours upon hours of pickup games at Turkey Thicket and around the network of playgrounds in the metropolitan area, which meant D.C. and Maryland. A close second would be the summer leagues, where there was never a moment when I did not feel open for a shot and where I had no hesitation about acting on my instincts. I think most of the basketball players of my generation would say the same.

In my freshman year at Carroll, my basketball efforts were restricted to the freshman team. It played a limited schedule and primarily worked on fundamentals. I also went through a growth spurt, and by the beginning of my sophomore year I topped out at 6′3½″. This made me taller than the average American and taller than most of my peers, but not particularly impressive in the world of scholastic basketball. A few generations earlier I would automatically have been thought of as a prospective center or, at worst, a forward, but by the time I arrived on the scene I was able to use my height to advantage as a shooting guard. My commitment to the sport, especially my endless

"Fight for Carroll High and Victory"

hours on the playground perfecting my shot, enabled me to gain the coaches' attention rather quickly.

In 1955–56, my first year, the Carroll varsity had a good but not a great team. But when I moved on to my sophomore year, there was a much higher level of expectation in the air. The two stars were Jimmy Howell and Willie Wells, both African Americans who had complementary skill sets. Howell was a guard with a good outside shot and a wonderful head fake that often got defenders into the air, at which point he would jump into them to merit two free throws, if nothing else. (Howell went on to become the principal of a local public junior high school and a top-notch collegiate referee who was assigned to the NCAA championship game on more than one occasion.) Wells was an inside player with tenacious rebounding instincts and nice soft shot from within four or five feet of the basket.

I had the good fortune to be chosen as a starter in my sophomore year, even though I was very thin and was counted upon primarily to hit the open jumper from anywhere outside the foul line. In the second semester that year, Tom Hoover transferred into Carroll and all of a sudden the quality of the team improved dramatically. Like me, he was still more raw potential than finished product, yet the word on the street was that Carroll was becoming a team to be reckoned with. That year we finished the season with a 22–4 record—really 22–3, since one of our losses was to the Georgetown freshman team, which did not count as an official game. This selective scheduling of games against local college frosh teams would increase during Bob Dwyer's term as head coach. He saw it as a way of pushing us beyond the level of most of our interscholastic competition.

By my junior year, those who followed high school basketball figured Carroll had a chance to be a powerhouse. In addition to me and Tom Hoover, we had an exceptional rebounder and leaper in Maurice Walker. Beginning their sophomore years were John Thompson and George Leftwich. Thompson would grow to 6'11" and although he was thin and relatively inexperienced, he frequently had to play in practice against Tom Hoover, who was 6'9", about 240 pounds, and very strong. These practice combats prepared both of them in a way that would have been impossible otherwise. Leftwich was a smooth-as-silk point guard who could both penetrate effectively and hit the outside shot. He was also capable of bringing the ball up against both zone and man-to-man presses, an important consideration since teams could be expected to press our much taller than usual high school team.

Our 1957–58 team set the stage for what would be the extra-ordinary achievements of the next two seasons. Carroll played an enhanced schedule that included contests against four college fresh-men teams: Maryland, American U. (twice), and Georgetown. We beat American both times and lost to Maryland by 7 points and to George-town by 10. During the regular season we played twenty-five games against high school teams, winning twenty-four and losing one. Then, in the city championship playoff with teams from the public and parochial leagues, we lost in the final game, 67–62.

Despite our disappointment in losing that game, we still had two more opportunities to finish the season on a positive note. We were invited to play for the first time in both the Knights of Columbus tour-nament in D.C. and the ESCIT (Eastern States Catholic Invitational Tournament) in Newport, Rhode Island. The K. of C. tournament had begun three years before the 1958 match-up; it was created to bring together the best Catholic high school teams from the East Coast and beyond. No D.C. team had yet won the championship but hopes were high. In the first round game we beat Norfolk Catholic 51–22, and in the second round we defeated Central Catholic of Troy, NY, 45–27. (The star of Central Catholic, Armand Reo, would later be my team-mate at Notre Dame.) In the championship game we lost to Arch-bishop Molloy, 61–47. In this game, the older and more experienced team won.

It rankled that we lost the city championship and K. of C. champi-onship games but we had one last chance to establish some positive momentum for the 1958–59 season: the ESCIT tournament in Newport. We were excited about the trip and about one more opportunity to taste the thrill of victory. ESCIT prided itself on providing extracurricular activities for the players, including luncheons and dinners with invited speakers, tours of local sites, and entertainment. In our first round game we survived a strong performance from Saint Aloysius (Jersey City) by a 63–61 score. In the semi-final we defeated the pre-tourney favorite, Trenton Catholic, 53–42. Later that night, Tom Hoover was admitted to Newport City Hospital with an upset stomach and a sore throat, but by the next day he had recovered sufficiently to be in the starting lineup for the championship game.

It was a great way to end our long season when we defeated All Hallows (NYC) 66–45 for the ESCIT championship. We drove back from Newport in a multi-car caravan and when we arrived at Carroll, 600 students and parents were there to greet us in the gymnasium. Not all of us made it back at the same time but the exuberant crowd waited from seven o'clock to nine thirty so that we all might have their cheers. When the local newspapers selected All-Star teams at the end of that basketball season, George Leftwich was First Team All-Met, Tom Hoover was Second Team All-Met, both Leftwich and Hoover were First Team All-Catholic, and I was Second Team All-Catholic.

Leftwich, Hoover, Thompson, and I returned for the 1958–59 season and we went 28–0 against high school competition, including seven post-season games, 21–0 during the regular season against high school opponents. The best competition came from other D.C. Catholic schools, particularly Gonzaga and DeMatha, but we had better personnel and a coach who was a good strategist. As we had done the year before, we played four games against college frosh teams (at that time, first-year college players were ineligible to play on the varsity, so their teams were the equivalent of a recruiting class plus walk-ons). In these games we were 2 and 2, but the games were considered exhibition contests and did not count against our record. Nonetheless they had the desired effect of pushing us to play against higher levels of competition.

The biggest disappointment we had in 1957–58 was losing to Cardozo in the city championship game. So, when the city championship of 1959 came around, we were excited to play before what would turn out to be a record 8,000 fans at Cole Fieldhouse on the University of Maryland campus. I remember the Cardozo team coming out and every member performing spectacular dunks in the warmups. While we had our share of dunkers, it was not our style to try to intimidate before the game began. We simply concentrated on getting loosened up and mentally prepared. As quickly as the game began, it became no contest. Every member of our starting five played his special role: Tom Hoover blocked shots, rebounded, and scored. John Thompson rebounded and scored in close. Walt Skinner shut off the passing routes, made some quick steals, and scored when needed. George Leftwich handled the ball in the open court, fed the open man, and scored on jumpers and layups. And I waited for my chances and hit long jumpers. The final score was 79–52, but the outcome was never in doubt. We had gotten the monkey off our back and could bask in our status as the best team in the D.C. area.

Our next opportunity to push the legend to the next level was the Knights of Columbus tournament held at Georgetown University's McDonagh gymnasium. In the opening round we decisively defeated Queen of Peace, 73–42. In our second game we beat Pacelli, 59–36. For the championship game we were really psyched. We had lost to the same opponent, Archbishop Molloy, the year before and we were still embarrassed from disappointing our hometown audience. Four thousand fans crowded into the McDonough gymnasium at Georgetown for the contest, which most figured would be close all the way. Instead, we trounced Molloy 75–44. Coach Dwyer described it as the high point of the season.

The last opportunity that we had as a team was a return to Newport, Rhode Island, to play in the ESCIT tournament. It had been a long season, and our bodies were growing a bit weary, but there was something about the magic of a season that none of us wanted to come to an end. In the opening game we beat Power Memorial 61–43. In the semifinal we defeated All Hallows 84–62. As we prepared to play Trenton Catholic for the championship, we knew it was our final game together. We were pushed hard by underdog Trenton Catholic. Somehow or other I was the only one who seemed able to hit an open shot. It was like we were playing in quicksand; we had no legs. One shot after another bounced off the rim and we made more than our share of errant passes. But in the end we prevailed, 67–65, and as it turned out, it was my best offensive game of the tournament; I led Carroll with 19 points.

What it came down to for us was will power more than skill or finesse—we simply did not want to end the year with a loss. Trenton Catholic had a good team and was well prepared, but we hung on for one last victory to finish the season 28–0 against high school competition.

Although I was at Notre Dame by then, the following year's Carroll team (with George Leftwich, John Thompson, Walt Skinner, John Austin, Kenny Price, and Billy Barnes playing key roles) went on to continue the school's unbeaten streak against high school competition to 55–0, a record that stood for a couple of decades.

Where non-believers see fate or destiny, believers see God's providence. The sacrifices my parents made to send me to Archbishop John Carroll High School provided the opportunity for me to receive a first-rate secondary education. This in turn prepared me well to go on to a major university. Furthermore, the decision by Archbishop (later Cardinal) Patrick O'Boyle that Carroll would be in the forefront of efforts at racial integration meant that I would enjoy a more diverse group of peers than would be true almost anywhere else in the D.C. metropolitan area. The presence of Coach Bob Dwyer, who convinced the Carroll administration to give him some leeway in recruiting basketball prospects, meant that as a varsity player I was surrounded by an extraordinary group of teammates, and together we would be able to achieve an amazing level of success. The influence of the Augustinian priests and brothers who were my prime mentors reinforced by their example what would later emerge as a clear call to me to pursue the priesthood. The desire of the *Washington Post* and *Washington Star* to celebrate examples of integrated cooperation and friendship provided a unique chance for the Carroll team to represent the hopes and dreams of a city at a time of major social transformation.

These and many other factors seem to me in retrospect to have blessed my life from those teenage years on. What is hard to capture is how many others, with no direct ties to Carroll, became taken up in the saga as it unfolded. Through most of my adult years I have run into people who either recognize me or have heard who I was and would begin recounting how and why they embraced the Carroll teams. I have been stopped by bellboys, cab drivers, corporate executives, Church leaders, former referees, and playground legends. Members of Congress and cabinet secretaries who spent time in D.C. in their youth will inevitably bring up those days of glory as they remember them. Most of these interlocutors have been male, but not all of them. When the conversation begins, it is as though time has stood still.

About ten years ago, our team had a reunion at a downtown D.C. hotel. Just about everyone was there, including Coach Dwyer. The assembly included a mix of former Carroll peers and mentors as well as old friends and competitors. I was accompanied by my sister Joanne and her son, Johnny. The atmosphere was festive and nostalgic, with stories being swapped and everyone grazing on the hotel buffet. Toward the end several of us made speeches full of gratitude for the happy days we had spent together. However, my most lasting impression was that no one there felt that their time at Carroll or their membership on the team was the end of their life story. All of us had moved on to new challenges and new opportunities. For that I was grateful.

In my senior year at Carroll, as a result of the success of our basketball team, I was in the position of having many options as I contemplated college. I wanted to attend a Catholic school with an engineering program somewhere outside the D.C. area. I sensed that I was ready to take on the challenge of living away from home in a totally new environment, but I wanted to choose a Catholic school with a supportive religious environment. My engineering interest was entirely the result of my success in high school math and science and the influence of Father Mullen. As our team continued its unbeaten streak I started to receive overtures and then concrete offers from more and more programs, and by the end of my senior season I had more than fifty offers. Some schools may have wanted to use me as a lure to recruit John Thompson and George Leftwich the following years, yet I was not concerned with the motives of the recruiters but with how exciting it was to be able to pick among so many institutions.

I had offers from the major military academies, but they were easy to eliminate because I was not attracted to a military vocation. I remember saying to someone that if I had to put up with the rigid discipline of the academies, I might as well go into the seminary. Pretty much all of the D.C. schools (Georgetown, George Washington, Catholic, American, and Maryland) were interested in me, but I was inclined to go outside the local area. Because of my grades, the Ivy League schools (Harvard, Princeton, Yale) promised that they would meet whatever need I had, which was their way of claiming that they did not give athletic scholarships as such. I was gratified to receive attention from these fine universities, yet I somehow had the impression that being a Catholic at Harvard or Princeton would not be an easy route, so I never had any serious interest.

I gave some consideration to schools on the East Coast like Saint Joseph's, Fordham, Saint Bonaventure, LaSalle, Mount Saint Mary's, Saint John's, and Boston College. I was also pursued by Loyola of Chicago, DePaul, Marquette, and Seattle. In the end, my top three schools were Villanova, Notre Dame, and Santa Clara. Each was Catholic, had an engineering program, and had well-established basketball traditions. I had visited Villanova a couple of times and knew that Tom

Hoover had decided to go there; it had an attractive campus and was run by the Augustinian community who had been my teachers at Carroll. It was not that far away from D.C. and they were in the process of recruiting a strong class. But something held me back. Perhaps it was that I thought Villanova would be too close to my high school experience.

In any case, I arranged to visit Notre Dame in the spring of my senior year. Jim Gibbons, then the assistant basketball coach under head coach Johnny Jordan, visited me at home and set up the logistics for my official visit to the campus. He arranged for me to be hosted by co-captains Armand Reo and John Dearie. Armand and John were both about 6'6", fun to be with, fine students, and great representatives of the institution. All my intuitions during my visit told me that this was the school for me.

Prior to visiting the campus, I only had isolated impressions about Notre Dame. I remembered seeing the football team play on the DuPont network, and I knew in a general way about its legendary football figures like Knute Rockne and Frank Leahy. But I had no family connections to the school and I had never seen any brochures. Like most Catholics of the 1950s, I was a Notre Dame fan in general, primarily because it was an icon of Catholic success. Beyond that, if I had not been recruited I would never have thought about applying. When I returned home from my campus visit, I discussed my impressions with my parents and rather quickly wrote back accepting the University's offer.

In the process of being recruited I learned a number of life lessons. One was how easy it is for a seventeen or eighteen year old to lose perspective when a host of coaches and recruiters tell you how crucial you would be to their program. You already have enjoyed a high level of peer recognition and received media attention unusual for a teenager. Then through letters and visits you feel like you are the center of attention. Second, some of the recruiters will test you by bending the rules. For example, I received sideline overtures connected to illegal benefits from more than one school's supporters. While this sort of recruiting had no impact on me, I wondered how students from really poor backgrounds might have reacted. Finally, I discovered that once you decide on a school, all the other interest dries up. You have gone from being a pen pal to a potential opponent.

As part of the recruitment process, when I was still undecided I agreed to have a full physical, since the military academies required it and my parents thought it would be a good idea in general. I had the physical at a downtown facility adjacent to a group of doctors' offices which included our family physician. Because I was overall in good physical condition, I did not have any anxieties about the tests. However, when the report came back I was told that my EKG indicated I might have a heart murmur. My first reaction was, "How could that be?" I had just spent a season of strenuous physical activity without any problems. Yet, once the question was raised about a possible organic defect, I started to have some real concern. It was agreed that I would visit the office of a respected heart specialist who had more sophisticated equipment and more experience in dealing with abnormalities of the heart.

Once again, I went through a variety of tests and went home to wait for the results. Another week went by and I was called in for a consultation with the specialist. At his office he quickly informed me that he had good news. It turns out that I was born with a slightly concave chest and, when the testing device sent signals from the heart to the machine, that deflected the echo just enough to suggest that my heart was not functioning properly. I went away thanking God that it had been a false alarm. If the early indications had been true, I would never have been able to play competitive basketball again and I would have lost all the scholarships I had been offered.

CHAPTER 4

"LOVE THEE NOTRE DAME"

EXCEPT FOR MY RECRUITMENT VISIT, I HAD NEVER been on the Notre Dame campus until I arrived to begin my freshman year in 1959 All I knew ahead of time was that I was assigned to live on the first floor of Farley Hall and that my roommate was George Lamb from Glen Cove, Long Island. In those days before the Internet, when Notre Dame was all male, there was no sense of urgency about getting in touch with your roommate.

We drove to Notre Dame, a trip that I would make countless more times by a variety of modes of transport. My father and I took turns driving and I was glad to have a chance to spend concentrated time with my parents. We all knew that this was a major transition in our lives. I could not move into my dorm room until the morning after we arrived in South Bend, so we had a reservation at a downtown hotel. The three of us were tired from the long trip and went to bed relatively early. This was a good idea in theory but there was one practical problem: our rooms were right above a bowling alley on the first floor of the hotel and we spent several sleepless hours listening to bowling balls knocking down pins. What was intended to be a restful night before starting my college career was instead hours of tossing and turning accompanied by imagined scenarios of my first days of college.

Farley Hall opened in 1942 with Father Hesburgh as rector. It was designed to hold 330 young men and was situated in the so-called north quad, a concentration of dorms primarily housing freshmen and focused around the North Dining Hall. At the time on-campus undergraduate housing options depended on class status—there were freshman, sophomore, junior, and senior halls, and each year the members of a returning class would move *en masse* to one of the dorms designated for that class. Because everyone in Farley was new to college, it was a great challenge to the hall staffs to handle so many testosterone-driven seventeen and eighteen year olds from all over the country. Our rector was Father Joe Haley, C.S.C. (affectionately known as Mumbles because of a minor speech defect). He was a good priest who cared about the students and had a reputation for fairness in dealing with rule violations. An additional Holy Cross priest was assigned to each of the floors in Farley, and in most of the other halls as well.

Living conditions in Farley were rather crowded, at least by today's standards. On the other hand, most of us brought to college much less electrical gear and equipment. We had bunk beds, two desks with chairs, and a sink with a mirror on the wall. We had to supply our own desk lamp and bedding, although the University provided sheets and towels which were replaced once a week. The bathroom and shower areas took care of the needs of the floor. Common areas included a fairly large, traditional-style chapel on the first floor and a study lounge and storage area in the basement. Maybe because I came from a modest background, I felt right at home in Farley from the day I arrived. I liked the male environment with its casual mode of interaction, its informal style of dress, and its light-hearted banter. Our first week together was how I imagined military boot camp to be.

Since Notre Dame residential life was created on a French boarding school model, the presence of significant adult others in the dorm, primarily Holy Cross religious, was taken for granted. So was the accountability structure, which had academic, developmental, religious, and moral reasons for its existence. Compared to the early days of the University, when the Main Building and later Saint Edward's and Sorin Halls were the only residence options, the rules were rather moderate, yet to many of my contemporaries some of the regulations seemed excessive. The irony would be the dramatic changes in the Notre Dame rulebook by the time I graduated.

In 1959–60, the first noteworthy prohibition was a restriction on where students were permitted to go in the South Bend–Mishawaka community. Certain neighborhoods were off-limits. I never really understood why, but since I did not have a car (no on-campus students could), I did not feel oppressed by this stricture. While off-campus no-go zones were a minimum concern, we soon became aware of three other rules that set the tone for life in the dorms. The first was lights out after eleven o'clock on weeknights and after midnight on weekends. There was a master switch in the rector's office that turned off the electrical sources in our individual rooms. This policy was clearly intended to foster regular hours, especially for study, and to inhibit the rambunctiousness of young men away from home for the first time. It meant we had to plan our days and evenings in order to get enough study time in before the lights were dimmed. Most of us thought that this rule was absurd, so it did not take long for strategies to be devised to offset its impact. One was to use flashlights. We learned that some upperclassmen had rewired their rooms and installed blackout screens on their transoms, their interior windows, and at the bottom of their doors; most of these students turned out to be engineers or sons of electricians. A final option was to spend prolonged periods on the toilets in the restrooms, where a 60-watt bulb on the ceiling made it barely possible to discern words on paper.

The second rule was morning check, which required us to appear fully clothed at a desk immediately outside the hall chapel three mornings a week. Although the rationale was to foster the habit of regular mass attendance, there was no requirement to actually go inside the chapel. I should add that from the days when Father (later Bishop and Cardinal) John O'Hara, C.S.C., was prefect of religion, Notre Dame was a campus with a strong eucharistic orientation. In the *Religious Bulletin* he published for many years, Father O'Hara would keep tabs on the rates of mass attendance campus-wide—with an occasional correlation between this statistic and the success or failure of the football team. I never resented morning checks except insofar as they forced me to get up somewhat earlier than I would have otherwise. In any case, I went to mass rather frequently during the week, something I probably would have done anyway.

The third rule of note was night check, which meant one of two things—either be in the dorm at ten o'clock when the hall staff went room to room to see who was there, or be back in the dorm by lights-out. After the ten o'clock room rounds, all entry to the residence hall was through the main entrance where a security guard oversaw the sign-in process and ensured that returning students were sober and well behaved. This gave the security guards a special place in the student body psyche—it was important to have a good relationship with these individuals who could seriously affect one's status with the rector. Some students even resorted to sharing packages of goodies from home with the guards. Unlike morning checks, where the main reason for violations was oversleeping, night check problems usually involved staying out later than expected on the weekends or missing the last bus back to campus from town. An often tried solution was to sneak into the dorm through an open window with the complicity of a dormmate, or through an unguarded door, then claim that there had been some mistake at the ten o'clock check in.

The most distinctive aspect of the Notre Dame *in loco parentis* environment was the restriction on female presence in the dorms.

Saint Mary's College next door was an all-female school but with a student body much smaller than Notre Dame's, which meant that most coeducational events took place on the weekends, sometimes supplemented by busloads of female students from Saint Mary of the Woods College or Barat College. After parietal hours began, no women were allowed in our dorms. In the 1950s when I arrived, parietals were standard at many other schools, even in the public system, so this constraint did not seem so unusual to us.

In the late 1950s and early 1960s, the drug of choice on campus was alcohol, as it is today. But the rules prohibited the possession and use of alcohol on campus for all students. Those who were over twenty-one could drink off campus but they were expected to be sober when they returned. As far as I knew, the use of marijuana, cocaine, heroin, or any of the other harder drugs was non-existent in the student body. If anyone was a user, he never talked about it, nor did I ever see any evidence of drugs at social events.

I did not touch alcohol until I was twenty, so in my freshman year I was relatively immune from any controversy in that regard, but some of my peers had come to college accustomed to drinking beer in high school. They constantly railed against this prohibition and tried to devise ways around it. Only the bravest attempted to stash alcohol in their rooms. It was much more common to find someone who was of age who would buy a couple of six packs and then hunt up a place where the beer could be consumed clandestinely. The other option was either to use fake IDs to get into off-campus bars, or to find establishments that regularly bent the rules.

Other forms of behavior that were *verboten* included fighting, subscribing to adult magazines, espousing positions contrary to Catholic teaching, damaging common property, being disrespectful to those in positions of authority, cheating on tests, harassing other students, and theft. You could smoke, however, and nothing was ever explicitly said about ill treatment of women or members of racial and ethnic minorities.

We were required to wear a sports coat and tie to the evening meal in the dining halls, and most of us kept the same sports coat through our four undergraduate years. By the time we graduated the garment was a mere shadow of the original; the right arm would be encrusted with bits of food and sometimes there was a long rip up the back. Acceptable ties could be anything from a regular business-style cravat to a bow tie to a clip-on. The formal requirement to dress for dinner had become a kind of joke by the time I arrived. As long as one adhered to the letter of the law, enforcement by the dining hall staff was minimal.

In my first week in Farley Hall I had an interesting experience with the dining hall system. I have never been a big breakfast eater, so my first few mornings at Notre Dame I skipped breakfast at the North Dining Hall and did not think twice about it. About the fourth or fifth day, as I was waiting in the dinner line for the student checker to validate my ID, he looked at me with a somewhat stern expression and asked why I had been missing breakfast. He said Notre Dame freshmen were required to eat the morning meal and I would need a note from Father Matt Miceli, C.S.C., the rector of Lyons Hall, granting me permission to eat dinner the next night. I thought that he could not be serious, but then I figured this was Notre Dame and maybe I just had not gotten the word.

That evening I wandered over to Father Miceli's office and told him I needed a note excusing me for missing breakfast. He looked at me with that strange gaze rectors learn to adopt when dealing with student quirkiness and proceeded to scrawl something on a piece of paper, which he put in an envelope, sealed, and handed to me. Then he sent me on my way. The next evening I made my way down the same line with the same checker. Just as I came close to pulling the envelope out of my pocket, he abruptly turned toward me and said, "I hope you didn't take me seriously last evening." I laughed with a strange mix of embarrassment and anger and answered, "Of course not." When I got back to my room, I made sure no one was watching

"Love Thee Notre Dame"

as I pulled the envelope from my pocket, ripped it open, and read it. The message neither chastised the upperclassman for taking advantage of my naiveté nor made me look like an utter sap. If nothing else, this story reveals my state of mind as I began my career at Notre Dame. I was intent on getting off to a smooth start, even if it meant giving the benefit of doubt to what seemed an irrational system.

My orientation to Notre Dame is generally a blur to me now. I know that we moved into the dorm rather smoothly and got registered in the Navy Drill Hall, where we wandered from station to station to get the required cards for each class. My most vivid memory is of the Freshmen Retreat talk given by Father Ned Joyce, C.S.C., in Sacred Heart Church. He welcomed us to Notre Dame, urged us to work diligently, comforted those who were already homesick, and informed us that if we looked to our left and our right, one of those young men probably would not make it to graduation. Little did I guess how close I would come to being one of them.

George Lamb, my freshman roommate, was a thin, blond-haired, young man around six feet tall who had dreamed all through high school of going to the Air Force Academy and becoming an astronaut. He had worked hard to gain support from his local congressman but ended up as the first alternate, so in a sense he was at Notre Dame by default. He was a nice guy and a fellow engineer and we got along fine. Like most first-year students, of course, we sometimes had our disputes. Most nights after lights-out we would lie in our bunk beds and discuss the day's events or world events or our classes or whatever. Every once in a while when I felt particularly obstreperous, I would declare that it was immoral to put lives at risk as astronauts and that the whole space program should be shut down. He would get mad and then we would joust, first orally and then physically. Because I was bigger and stronger, I would pin him to the floor and sit on him until he relented. His mode of getting even was to trash intercollegiate athletics, and especially basketball, as a waste of time and unworthy of being offered by a Catholic university.

When semester break came around, George decided to reapply to the next class at the Air Force Academy. At the end of our freshman year, convinced he would be admitted, he withdrew from Notre Dame. As it turned out, he never made it beyond the alternate list at the Academy. When he reapplied to Notre Dame, he was denied re-admittance. I never saw him or heard from him again.

Almost all my classes were in either O'Shaughnessy Hall or the Engineering Building. While the weather was nice, I traveled the campus walkways, but when fall rains arrived, followed by the frigid winds and slippery snows of winter, I decided to explore indoor options. I would exit Farley on the south side, walk through Breen-Phillips, cross a short distance to the side door of the basketball arena, then take a slight detour to the west and exit near the north side entrance to Nieuwland Science Hall. From Nieuwland I would continue on through the Chemical Engineering Building (now the Art Department), turn left outside and cover the few yards to the northwest entrance to O'Shaughnessy. For an engineering class I would exit O'Shaughnessy under the clock tower and hurry to the Engineering entrance. The total time outside during this five- to seven-minute jaunt was less than a minute.

I was always a fast walker with long strides. During my junior and senior years when I lived in Badin Hall, my friends used to tease that I held the campus speed record for walkers from Badin to O'Shaughnessy. But it was just one of my methods of coping with the lack of an indoor route during the frequent days of bad weather.

As every student knows, it is a challenge to get into the right routine for study amid such distractions as talkative roommates, campus events, and sheer procrastination. I remember being advised by academic counselors to study for fifty minutes, take a ten-minute break, and then repeat the process until I completed my assignments. The problem was always that the ten-minute break so easily became extended until all momentum was lost. One of my ways of coping was to

"Love Thee Notre Dame"

leave my room and move all my stuff to the basement study lounge in Farley, where calm prevailed and it was unlikely that anyone would interrupt with an invitation to walk over to the Huddle or play touch football on the quad. Plus, the study lounge was set up with long wooden tables and relatively uncomfortable hard wooden chairs. While it was not impossible to fall asleep in those chairs, it was less apt to happen than in one's room right next to the bed.

Later in my freshman year, I began gravitating to Nieuwland Science to study. Some of the lecture halls there had tiered rows with wooden seats and movable desk tops, and sometimes I could have a whole room to myself. I always cherished privacy when I was studying, and the very act of walking over to the Nieuwland was an implicit commitment to spend the evening in serious academic work.

NCAA regulations required student athletes on full scholarship to have a campus job. In my time, each scholarship athlete rotated among four jobs through the month. The first was the easiest—to keep the bulletin boards clean. The second required the most energy—to pick up the mail from the post office and place it in the student mail boxes in the dorms. I actually enjoyed this option because it was physical labor and it provided a sense of who among my peers was the most successful pen pal or received the most packages from home. It was also a way of inferring who had a romantic relationship left over from high school (the perfumed letters were a giveaway).

The other two job choices put one closer to being an agent of the hall staff, with both the peer power this included and, in some cases, the potential for corruption. One job was to take a turn overseeing morning check at the hall chapel. At the end of the morning the checklist had to be turned into the rector for his perusal. Most of the time things worked out fine, but on occasion a fellow student would be in trouble for having missed too many mornings and would try to convince the student athlete at the desk to sign him in when the rector was not around. It would not have been difficult to pull this off, but it exposed the student athlete to a huge risk. And like most such violations, the tendency was to expect the collusion regularly, which ratcheted up the odds of getting caught.

The fourth job was night check, which meant going from room to room at ten o'clock to determine who was present in the hall. Usually I was responsible for only one floor, so I could carry out this task in a leisurely fashion. It was a wonderful way to get to know the students in the dorm and for them to get to know me. At its best, Notre Dame is a place where student athletes have a chance to be regularized, to spend time with their peers away from the demands of athletic preparation and game participation. In my era, it was taken for granted that we would be held to the same academic and behavioral standards as everyone else, and night check was one way that this was reinforced. Here, too, some students tried to suborn the athlete into checking them in when they were spending a night on the town. In most cases, the persuasion was not physical coercion but an appeal to friendship or a promise of mutual benefit. The hardest ones to turn down were teammates, who could broker tit-for-tat arrangements if we lived in the same hall.

There were three ways to go downtown from the campus—walk, hitchhike at the campus Circle, or take the bus. On weekends, the real problem with all three forms of travel was getting back to campus in time for the midnight dorm check-in. The last bus from downtown was always full and included students who had imbibed. The mood could get raucous. If a student missed that bus, panic would set in. He could get lucky if an upper classman with a clandestine car could be found. Otherwise, he either had to run, call a cab, or take his chances with the night guard in the dorm—or else ascend the fire escape to gain entry through a student window and concoct a story about how he had unfortunately been missed at night check.

A popular off-campus restaurant in my freshman year was the Philadelphia in the center of downtown South Bend. It was right at the end of the bus line and a convenient place to visit before or after a movie. On weekends when I decided to walk somewhere with my friends for a night out, we might go to Sunny Italy restaurant on Niles Avenue (which is still going strong) or Giuseppe's, where we had to sit in the non-drinking area. We would not have thought in a million years of going to the Morris Inn or an upscale restaurant east of the campus called Eddie's, since they were out of our price range. When visitors were in town, there was always the café in the middle of the South Dining Hall.

By the end of the first semester I knew everyone on my floor and a good percentage of the rest of the Farley dwellers. It helped that I enjoyed meeting people and that I worked hard at learning names. Dormmates tended to congregate at meals and play touch football and Frisbee on the lawns. On weekends we often went to the movies in Washington Hall—they were free, and we could let off steam until Brother Movie (as we called him) would threaten to cut off the showing unless we behaved. Before or after the movie we would visit the Huddle and spend some of our discretionary funds. On home football weekends, of course, there was plenty to do, from the Friday night pep rally in the Fieldhouse (after we tramped around the campus following the band), to the festivities at the outdoor venues before and after the game, to the occasional concert or lecture.

While weekday masses were celebrated in the dorm chapels, Sunday masses for the undergraduate student body were held in Sacred Heart Church, which was regularly filled to capacity. Confessions were held in the church on Saturdays and on Sunday before mass, and it was commonplace to see long lines of penitents waiting their turn, as was typical in Catholic parishes around the country at that time. Some confessors had reputations as kind and tolerant and were known to impose light penances. One of these was Father Joe Barry, C.S.C., who had been a chaplain in World War II. We all suspected that there was no sin Father Barry had not heard. One afternoon I was waiting in his line at the back of the church when all of us heard the priest in another confessional box say, "You did what?" in a rather loud voice. Instantaneously, everyone waiting in that priest's line switched to Father Barry's.

The Grotto was a popular place of devotion in my undergrad years, as it is today. I lit many a candle seeking the special help of the Blessed Mother as I faced one crisis or another, real or imagined. May Day devotions at the Grotto were always heavily attended.

Father Ted Hesburgh was in the eighth year of his presidency that year. In the 1960 yearbook he agreed to submit to a relatively long interview with a group of student leaders. The heading in that section of the book reads "What is this excellence? The President discusses a problematic present, an optimistic future." It is interesting to look back today at what Father Ted and the students who were my peers thought the major issues were. Ted placed a great emphasis on nourishing the graduate school, on the quality of the faculty, on building financial resources, and on putting the role of football into better perspective. The students were preoccupied with easing the rules, emphasizing undergraduate education, and becoming a more female-friendly school.

Two of Ted's quotes particularly strike me in re-reading this section. The first is: "We want as good a football team as we can have consistent with that ideal of a fine university. I don't think the ideas are contradictory. . . . My own impression is that people outside of the University are a lot more concerned about football than those in the University." (Ironically, the new coach, Joe Kuharich, would go on to have the worst four-year record of any football coach in Notre Dame history.) The second quote is: "My impression is that the rules are much more relaxed today than they were ten years ago. What the picture will be ten years from now I have no way of knowing. . . . Personally, I think it is a good idea not to have cars." (Major rule changes would come in 1961 before I graduated, and in 1966 after I was a seminarian.) These are reminders that even the most perceptive of leaders do not always recognize what the future might bring.

One Notre Dame reality that all of us took for granted was that the University administration was largely made up of Holy Cross

"Love Thee Notre Dame"

priests. In 1959–60, in addition to Father Ted, Father Ned Joyce was executive vice president, Father Chet Soleta, C.S.C., was vice president of academic affairs, Father Jerry Wilson, C.S.C., was vice president of business affairs, Father Jim Moran was director of admissions, Father A. Leonard Collins was dean of students, Father George Bernard was vice president of student affairs, Father Glenn Boarman was student chaplain, and Father John Wilson was acting director of the Notre Dame Foundation. The only lay person on the list was Jim Armstrong, secretary of the Alumni Association. This overwhelming predominance of Holy Cross administrators could not be sustained, especially after a largely lay Board of Trustees was created in 1967.

The size of the undergraduate student body in 1959–60 was approximately 5,000 compared to around 9,000 today. While the University prided itself on its academic standards, not that many serious applicants were turned down, a sign that the overall applicant pool had not grown to the dimensions it would achieve in later years.

Sporting Matters

The athletic world of Notre Dame in 1959–60 was overseen by Moose Krause, a former All-American in both football and basketball. As Moose would later admit, his forté was not administrative detail but representing the University to its multiple constituencies. At that time, all-male ND offered programs in football, basketball, wrestling, swimming, track/cross country, fencing, tennis, golf, and baseball. There were also non-varsity programs in skiing, bowling, and sailing in addition to the Bengal Bouts.

My main interest other than basketball was in Notre Dame football. I went to all the home games and sat in the student section of the stands. While there was great initial enthusiasm with a new coach, Joe Kuharich, the Irish ended that season at 5–5. I noticed the notoriety around campus that the star football players received. The campus gossip mill followed with great attention the lives and behaviors of George Izo and Monty Stickles, Angelo Dabiero, Bob Scarpitto, George Sefcik, and Joe Perkowski. The first two were noted as men about town and received their fair share of reported sightings and rumors.

As a basketball recruit, I arrived full of confidence and enthusiasm. Having just finished an undefeated season in high school, I was eager to establish myself at Notre Dame. Since practice could not officially start until mid-October, the Rockne Memorial gym was the natural gathering place for the varsity players to compete against each other and against the best of the non-varsity athletes. I never particularly liked the Rock gym because it had hard rims (a disincentive for shooters) but it was the best we had available in an indoor setting. I also played outdoors at the bookstore courts.

Jim Gibbons, the assistant men's basketball coach who recruited me, had a good rapport with me and my three scholarship classmates—Bill Kurz, John Andreoli, and John Matthews. Long before practice got started, Coach Gibbons would get together with the four of us to see how we were doing and to offer encouragement and advice. He was a stickler for class attendance, church participation, and good citizenship. We never had a doubt that we were expected to live by a high standard of personal conduct. (We soon discovered that Coach Gibbons was a master at remembering names. Many years later, after I became president, Jim served as the highly regarded director of special events and assistant vice president of university relations—a role in which his comfortable way with people and his astuteness in name retention were great assets.)

As the season approached, the Notre Dame varsity knew it had to compensate for the graduation of star player Tom Hawkins. I had met Tom on my recruiting trip and was impressed with him as a person. He was the only black player on the team, and after he graduated Notre Dame became an all-white team once again. After my experience on the integrated Carroll team, this seemed odd, but there was not much I could do about it. Although an effort was made the following year to recruit my ex-teammates John Thompson and George Leftwich, I do not think Coach Jordan's heart was in it, and the absence of any black players was surely noticed by John and George, especially in comparison with Providence and Villanova where they eventually matriculated. Not until my senior year, when Larry Sheffield became a sophomore, was this racial void filled at Notre Dame.

The most sobering reality for me was that freshmen were not able to compete at the varsity level, nor did we have a schedule of games against other freshmen teams. Once practice began in earnest in October, we ran the drills and competed every day against the varsity players but we could not play in the games. So it was not in the coach's best interests to give us much playing time in scrimmages, except to simulate the style of opposing teams. Coach Gibbons would sometimes work with us separately, but that did not satisfy our competitive juices. After that experience, I have never as an administrator favored eliminating freshmen eligibility in any intercollegiate sport.

We practiced and played our home games in the Fieldhouse. It was old and relatively dilapidated even in my day, long before it was replaced by the Joyce Center. An oval indoor track circled the raised basketball floor at one end and there was a dirt-floor open area at the other. During basketball practices the court stood like a desert mesa above the surrounding track, with netting at either end to prevent stray balls from escaping and, more importantly, to protect players on mad dashes down the court from stumbling and falling over the side. In the coldest part of the fall, there could be football, basketball, track and field, and fencing teams all practicing simultaneously, and the noise level could make it difficult for the coaches to communicate with their respective teams.

One of the great characters of that era was the head equipment manager, Mac McAllister, a little pipsqueak with a grating voice and an acerbic style of interaction. He seemed to think the goal of the student athletes was to find some way to beat the rules and steal some of his equipment, and he was going to make sure that never happened. He also did not believe in any frills, so the uniforms were collegiate-unspectacular, the towels thin, the soap in small bars, and the basketball shoes replaced only when they were falling apart. Mac used to call everyone "piss ant," a swear word mild enough that he could get away with it in front of the priests. One day in my senior year, sophomore Walt Sahm gave Mac some lip and Mac threw a heavy paperweight at him that shattered the wooden board behind Walt's head. It took only minutes for that story to get around and for Mac's general don't-mess-with-me reputation to be reinforced.

In high school I never lifted one weight or otherwise engaged in the intense physical training that is commonplace today. The prevailing wisdom was that weights and the accompanying muscle enhancement would ruin one's shooting ability. Instead, we ran sprints and did jumping jacks and other such stamina-improving exercises. Surprisingly, when I arrived at Notre Dame I found nothing changed. There might have been a barbell or two in the innards of the Fieldhouse, but participation in such activity was entirely voluntary and even discouraged for most of us. As a result, while most of us put on some weight simply as a function of growing older, almost no one could claim that they improved their vertical jump or their capacity to take a pounding under the backboard.

Coach Johnny Jordan was a Notre Dame graduate from Chicago who had played on the team during his undergraduate years. He coached for a number of years in the Chicago Catholic secondary system before returning to Notre Dame as head coach. (His undergraduate peers at Notre Dame, Ray Meyer and George Ireland, went on to successful careers at DePaul and Loyola of Chicago respectively.) Coach Jordan was deeply Irish and manifestly Catholic, and he seemed a perfect fit for Notre Dame. Early on he had productive teams characterized by strong interior play and scrappy defense. Dick Rosenthal and John Smyth (later Father Smyth) personified this style of play. By

"Love Thee Notre Dame"

the time Tom Hawkins arrived, college basketball was becoming more wide open and dependent on athleticism. The jump shot and high-powered offenses were becoming more typical in the teams that made it into the NCAA. And more schools were welcoming black players.

By my time at Notre Dame Coach Jordan had become wedded to a 1–3–1 offense, with a point guard, a high post player, two wing players, and a low post player. The system had some of the elements of what later was known as the Princeton Offense, and the goal was to lull the defense by constant cuts and picks and an occasional backdoor play. The point guard and the high post player were critical to the effectiveness of the formation. Overall, it was kind of a grind-it-out approach that stressed subordination to the system rather than individual free-lancing. The 1–3–1 could be effective against a superior team if the players were patient, but it was difficult to catch up if the team fell behind. Moreover, Notre Dame had run the same offense for so many years that opposing teams did not really have to scout us; they already knew what to expect.

Coach Jordan, for some strange reason, insisted that all of his players shoot underhand free throws, no matter what their conversion rate had been in high school. Since I had shot around 85 percent, this made no sense to me, but none of us had any discretionary authority in the matter and I too learned the underhand stroke. At the beginning of my sophomore or junior year Coach informed us that we would not run any fast breaks. He insisted that we play a slow-down style. I could not believe my ears.

Since we did not travel with the team, my contact with Coach Jordan was somewhat limited during freshmen year. When invited, we scrimmaged with the varsity, but after drills we spent a fair amount of time just standing around while the first two teams went at it full court. Then the rest of us would stay around to run more drills, play two on two, four on four, or five on five, either half court or full court. At the end of practice we would shoot foul shots in our by now distinctive fashion.

The 1959–60 Fighting Irish basketball team finished the regular season at 12–11. They were invited to the NCAA tournament but lost in the first round. Although it was Notre Dame's fifth NCAA appearance in the last eight seasons, they lost in the early rounds in all five. The most over-achieving player that year was Emmett McCarthy, a hard-nosed competitor with no identifiable basketball skills who was perfectly suited for the 1–3–1. My most noteworthy basketball moment came when Emmett was playing defense against me by pushing and pulling and grabbing my shirt. After a few minutes of this, I grew so frustrated that I reared back and punched him in the face. There was utter silence for a second and no one said a word, since I was generally known as a mild-mannered player. Emmett went off to the side to have the trainer examine what turned out to be a black eye. Then Coach Jordan blew his whistle and we went on with practice. Not a word was said officially about what happened, but I am sure that behind the scenes it was the talk of the team for a few days.

Perhaps the hardest thing about being a freshman with no opportunity to play was having to stay behind for road trips. It was not so much missing the chance to visit new places or the camaraderie of the team as it was the seeming disgrace of being left behind. Never before had I been a part of a program where my role was so ill defined. I was with them but not of them. When the season ended, I still figured that my best days were ahead. I clearly was one of the best shooters on the team and I was convinced that I and my three freshmen teammates would become major cogs in the year ahead.

Academics Matter More

The most problematic part of my first semester of college, to my surprise, turned out to be my academic performance. Once classes started, I began to have misgivings about my choice of major. In those days, before the First Year of Studies concept was in place with its

"Love Thee Notre Dame"

flexibility and strong counseling component, I was considered a member of the College of Engineering, and so I would remain at least until the end of freshman year. The two most disconcerting classes for me were math and engineering drawing. The main trouble in math was that I thoroughly disliked the teacher, and as the semester went on I started skipping classes. In engineering drawing I had conceptual problems—I could never quite learn how to plot images as seen from new angles (like simulating a piece of machinery from the top or bottom or various slices from the side). In frustration, I began to read more and more novels. Not that I sat around idle, I was focusing on things other than my primary coursework.

First semester did not end until after Christmas break in those days, which meant that final exams took place in January. As I prepared for my first set of college finals, I studied hard to try to make up for my deficiencies. I knew it would be a close call in math but I figured I had finally mastered engineering drawing. In fact, I thought I got 100 on that final. And then I received my report card: I had flunked both math and engineering drawing (I received a zero on my final). I was now on academic probation, less than a percentage point away from flunking out. I was absolutely shocked. I took the bus downtown to the State movie theater and sat through two showings of the hit film *A Summer Place*. Being in a darkened theater gave me the freedom to cry my eyes out as I tried to come to grips emotionally with the greatest setback I had yet undergone.

By the time I returned to campus I had made up my mind to seek help, and I made an appointment to meet with Professor Bill Burke, who at that time headed the equivalent of the first-year advising office. He was quite helpful, and his encouraging words were critical to reestablishing my self-confidence. He recommended that I take a battery of tests, and when the results came back, English and history emerged as likely choices. I chose English, but in order to transfer to the College of Arts and Letters I had to raise my grades enough to be off academic probation.

The pivotal course in that endeavor was a five-credit math section taught by Jake Kline, who served as Notre Dame's baseball coach and adjunct professor of math. His nickname was "99" Kline, since he reportedly had sworn never to keep anyone from the playing field or the altar (referring to student athletes and seminarians). His friendly rival at that time in academic beneficence was Father Tom Brennan, C.S.C., who was known as "88" and had a similarly kind reputation. I applied myself completely in Professor Kline's class, never missed a day, and ended up with a 5 on the 6–point system; I was a bit peeved that I did not receive a 6 since I knew I was close. I performed equally well in my other courses, especially enjoying my first class in philosophy with Professor Ken Sayre. In my newfound academic enthusiasm I even wrote Professor Sayre an anonymous thank you note at the end of the semester.

None of my talks to undergraduates as Notre Dame president, especially first-year students, was as well received as my retelling of my own first semester woes. I used to end by bragging that I was now president of a school I had almost flunked out of.

Then and Now

One of the most dramatic differences between undergraduate life then and now was in the available forms of communication. I wrote home about once a week in the first semester and progressively less often thereafter. My mother wrote back providing encouragement to me in my studies and brief updates about family news and other local matters. About once a month she would send me $25 for spending money; all other major costs were covered by my scholarship. My parents also paid for my trips back and forth to home.

Our dorm rooms were not equipped with a telephone, so we were forced to use the one telephone available at the end of each hallway. Some of these phones had the semi-privacy of an enclosure, but most

"Love Thee Notre Dame"

were not so sheltered. Unless one whispered, all conversations were public (which put them on a par with many cell phone conversations of today). That meant that one's love life, tame as it might be, was part of the general rumor mill. It also provided a kind of sympathy reaction toward students whose parents were excessive doters. Sometimes, roommates and hallmates could thwart parental over-involvement by routinely saying, when they answered the phone, that their son was not available.

In a case of what today one calls helicopter parents (always hovering around their children and trying to run their lives), there was a student in Farley whose mother moved to South Bend to be closer to him. Needless to say, this was a source of some consternation on his part and some speculation on ours. When I told my parents about it, my mother periodically teased me that she was thinking of moving to South Bend. When she finally met the woman in question at Junior Parent Weekend, she never said a word.

During my four undergraduate years, I came to realize that 630 miles is a long distance. All my round trips were by whatever seemed the cheapest available mode of transportation. The majority were on the B&O Railroad, which required getting a ride to LaPaz, Indiana, about twenty miles south of the campus—a trip usually arranged by the campus Baltimore-Washington Club, the sole purpose of which was to facilitate transportation for students from the area. One year the club was energetic and arranged for a charter flight to Washington National Airport. The flight home was fine, but when we arrived for the return journey there was a ten-hour delay. My peers and I sat it out at the airport where we entertained ourselves quite comfortably.

My most interesting trip home was over spring break during senior year when I decided to hitchhike with one of my friends—purportedly to save money but really for the adventure of it all. We started out well enough and our first ride took us east on the Indiana Toll Road to one of the rest stops at the western end of the Ohio Turnpike. From there we were able to make it to a rest stop near

Youngstown where, unfortunately, we were confronted by an Ohio state trooper who threatened to arrest us if we were not out of there in ten minutes. We were saved by a kind truck driver who saw our plight and offered to drive us into Youngstown where we could catch a Greyhound bus. That sounded like the best option, so we jumped into the cab of his semi and off we went. I experienced firsthand how much interstate truck drivers get bounced around in their work.

The driver let us off on one of the main roads in downtown Youngstown, next to a city bus stop. But it was Sunday morning and no local buses were operating to take us to the interstate bus terminal. When a friendly churchgoer pulled over, we explained our dilemma and he drove us to the station. It was then just a matter of waiting for a bus going east. We eventually made it home, but I never again saw hitchhiking long distances as a viable option.

Freshman year of college is a great time for larks and antics. All someone has to do is suggest some prank and the plot is underway. I remember two such moments in my year in Farley. The first involved moving every piece of furniture out of a room, so that when the occupants returned it was completely empty. The other demanded much more time: a large group of us wadded up enough paper balls to fill a room completely. When the unsuspecting roommates opened their door, all they saw was a wall of paper. (This, of course, I completely oppose as an administrator since it makes the room an absolute fire trap.)

We had daily maid service to clean the rooms, make the beds, and otherwise assume responsibility for the good order of the dorm. Many of the women were from ethnic backgrounds (primarily Polish and Hungarian) and were Catholic. They often befriended (or should I say bemothered?) the boys and were always available for advice or an adult perspective. Some worked in the same dorm for twenty or thirty years and became more of an institution than the rectors, who were more frequently changed. Each dorm also had a janitor who saw to ongoing maintenance as well as trash patrol and minor plumbing and

"Love Thee Notre Dame"

electrical tasks. Both the maids and janitors were sometimes exposed to the worst sides of student life (like vomit-filled bathrooms and isolated physical damage of the property) but they seemed to take it all in stride.

The primary forms of in-hall discipline revolved around one or another form of confinement. To be "campused" was to lose the privilege of going into town or traveling off Notre Dame property. This punishment was usually imposed for some limited period of time, but it could also be indefinite. Some rectors favored, as a form of punishment, a system of hourly visits out to the police guard post at the Circle where the miscreant had to sign in. Because this involved sleep deprivation, it was normally a short-term punishment. A third form of control was to require a student to be in the dorm each evening by night check time. This was worse than being campused because it also curtailed one's mobility around the campus itself.

Despite the range of offenses that could get one in trouble, I never felt that I was living in a police state or that somehow my fundamental human freedoms were curtailed. Occasionally we would learn about someone getting suspended or kicked out of school entirely, but these were unusual events. For most of us, it was the lesser forms of disciplinary sanction that we had to deal with, and like young people everywhere we learned the tricks of the trade from the upperclass students and considered our peers who got into serious trouble either stupid or unlucky.

Summer School, Then Zahm

Because of my poor start academically, it was determined that I would attend summer school between my freshman and sophomore years. I lived that summer on the fourth floor of Howard Hall, which got extremely hot and humid in the dog days. Most of the time we wore a minimum of clothing and slept in our underpants at most. It was not unusual to take four or five showers a day. Academically, I took two classes which met daily for the eight weeks of summer school.

Summer students from Notre Dame could be divided into three groups—student athletes trying to reduce their course load; students in precarious academic straits who had failed a required course; and aspiring pre-meds who wanted to get organic chemistry or some other backbreaking requirement out of the way. Classes were small and personal in the summer, but the pace was relentless. If you did not study every day, you would be in trouble quickly.

Despite the pace and the living conditions, I very much enjoyed summer school. The weather was great for playing on the outdoor basketball courts, the sun shone brightly in the early evening, and the campus felt twice as big as it did during the gloom of winter. There was a weekly free movie in the engineering auditorium, and students tended to linger longer at the South Dining Hall and in outdoor gathering places. A trip to the Lake Michigan dunes could be arranged on weekends if someone had a car. Late night entertainment included a fair amount of card playing, sometimes for small amounts of money. Bill Kurz, my soon-to-be sophomore roommate, developed a reputation as an accomplished bridge and poker player. This would be his downfall the following summer when, despite the fact that I was assigned to motivate him to study, he flunked out.

One of the hangouts in the summer was the South Dining Hall cafeteria. There we could buy a soft drink and a snack in the evening and just hang around. The same was true of the Huddle in the Student Center, which was well known for its hamburgers, snacks, and desserts. I liked to walk or run around the lakes, both to keep in shape and to be touched by the beauty of the setting sun refracted through the polluted air generated by the steel mills of Gary to our west. I also enjoyed stopping at the Grotto to light a candle and say a prayer. For me, the Grotto has always been most impressive after sunset when the candle power radiates to its full effect.

When I went home to D.C. after summer school, I played basketball and hung out with my friends. Already I could sense that my experiences at Notre Dame were much different than those of my former Carroll classmates, many of whom were either living at home and attending local schools or working. I did not consider myself better than they were but I knew we no longer had as much in common.

In my sophomore year I moved to Zahm Hall and lived with Bill Kurz, a fellow basketball player. Bill was 6'9" and weighed about 250 pounds. He was from Cairo, Illinois, and had been a dominating player in high school, if only because of sheer size. But at Notre Dame, he had two problems. First, he had a tendency to put on weight (a quart of Cherry Coke and a bag of donuts were his favorite late night snack). Second, he had a hard time disciplining himself to study. He had the ability but often lacked the grade point average to prove it. Bill and I got along pretty well. He was basically a down-home country boy with simple tastes and a nice way with people. We had arranged for extra-long bunk beds for our room. Bill chose the upper bunk and I would sometimes look up at night at his sagging mattress and worry that I might be suffocated overnight.

Bill and I had different tastes when it came to room temperature in the winter. He liked to keep the windows open and I liked to crank up the heat. When we would reach an impasse (usually jokingly), I would grab his little fingers and pull them back until he relented. He could, of course, have crushed me like an insect if he wanted to. After Bill flunked out at the end of summer school before his junior year, he enrolled at Saint Louis University, which had also recruited him. He eventually played basketball there and married the coach's daughter. Many years later, Bill and his wife and family would visit the campus each summer after I was ordained. He seemed to enjoy sharing his experiences from his Notre Dame years. Unfortunately, a few years later he died suddenly of a massive heart attack. I only found out about it when his wife sent me an official notice and a nice card.

Zahm Hall was a pleasant place to live. It was just across the north quad from Farley Hall so I knew the territory, and I still ate my meals in the North Dining Hall. Like most sophomores, I knew that I had survived the rigors of the first year of college, and I was enthusiastic to be taking courses that were inherently interesting to me. One of my teachers that year was Professor Bob Turley, who taught philosophy in such a way that we were introduced to the perspectives of some of the great thinkers of the modern world—Darwin, Marx, and Freud, among others. The class was overwhelmingly Catholic in its makeup and in the cultural presuppositions of its members. What Professor Turley achieved with great skill was to encourage us to be open to the insights of such seminal intellectual figures without feeling our Catholic faith was being undermined. He opened up for me a way of engaging in reflection about fundamental questions that made learning fun and rewarding. I am extremely grateful that I had a chance to have him as a teacher.

That year I began to take courses in my designated major, English. By the time I graduated, I had taken two courses apiece from Professors Joseph F. X. Brennan (one of the most articulate people I have ever met) and Donald Costello (who introduced me to the study of film and theater in addition to fiction). Most of my English courses were focused on fiction and poetry, English and American. While there was still a kind of latent snobbishness in some of the faculty that underprized American literature compared to British, the new faculty who were coming into the department had been trained in different and more sympathetic methodologies. We did read established female authors but few minority writers. The revolution that would strike English departments, and the rest of the academy, when the whole curricular issue was opened for discussion was still about a decade away.

For chemistry lab I had Professor Emil Hofman, who would later become dean of the Freshmen Year program and one of the most famous teachers at the University. He possessed an amazing capacity to

"Love Thee Notre Dame"

lecture while simultaneously writing on the blackboard with one hand and erasing with the other. He was an effective conveyor of compli-cated information but also a somewhat intimidating presence, and we pitied anyone who came to his classes unprepared. One day to our complete shock he appeared in class with new hair (i.e., a wig) where previously he had been bald. In some classes this might have elicited a giggle or daring comment, but not in Professor Hofman's chem lab. We simply stared straight ahead and acted as though nothing had changed (at least until we were far out of earshot).

In my junior year I had Professor Ed Cronin from the Great Books Program (later the Program of Liberal Studies) for a two-semester seminar. An expert on James Joyce, he was best known for his lively seminar leadership and his extensive comments in red on our papers. In class he looked the way we imagined a scholar should—tweed coat, wispy uncombed hair, and a pipe that he spent most of the discussion trying to fill and light. He would wave his pipe demonstratively as he made his points about ancient culture, the notion of virtue, the pica-resque novel, or who deserved to be in the inner rings of hell.

Professor Cronin delighted in taking on classes that, in their composition, his colleagues might have thought unchallenging. In one thirty-person class I took, about twenty were jocks or varsity athletes, several of them from the football and basketball teams. Professor Cronin (who came from simple roots and who was active in the local Democratic Party) took great pride in making connections between the issues in great literature and the concrete experience of the stu-dents entrusted to him. The bigger or more impervious the student, the more Professor Cronin felt compelled to ignite the spark of gen-uine learning.

By the end of my second seminar we had worked our way through the Greeks and Romans, Augustine, the medieval period, Shakespeare, Dante, Milton, Cervantes, and more modern writers like Melville, Twain, Dostoevsky, Cather, and Joyce. For me the course was a turning point, opening me up to literature from other periods of history and other cultural settings. During my presidency, when I began teaching seminars with a heavy emphasis on world literature and film and a correlative interest in issues of diversity, I would look back on my two semesters with Professor Cronin as a formative model of how to proceed.

During my first two years at Notre Dame I ate most of my meals in the North Dining Hall. At the time it was aesthetically comparable to Motel 6—purely functional in design and organization. We went through one of the multiple entrance doors, showed our ID to the checker, picked up a tray, chose an entrée, and filled up with bread, salad, dessert, and something to drink. The food options were limited and there were frequent student complaints about mystery meat, recycled stews, and indigestible globs of noodles. We were limited in how much milk we could take and it was *verboten* to take food back to our rooms (although everyone did). The culinary *pièce de résistance* was roast beef for Sunday night dinner. True this entrée was a step up, but it was sliced so thin you could almost see the plate through it.

The South Dining Hall, where I ate during my junior and senior years, served pretty much the same food but it had a certain elegance, with its two large dining wings and its wood paneling and high ceilings. Then as now, students from the same dorm tended to congregate in the same part of the dining hall. Very few of us ate breakfast, especially after lights-out and morning check ended in 1961 and we began to live more typical student hours, which meant staying up until the wee hours and sleeping in. My own experience of dining hall eating was tempered by my participation in the training table during my three seasons on the varsity. Because practice ended late for most athletic teams, we had special dining privileges, including large portions of food and unlimited milk. This was probably first introduced to beef up the members of the football team but we all benefited. It also made us the envy of the student body.

Beyond the dining halls there were a limited number of venues for food and drink. The two most popular were the Huddle in the Student

"Love Thee Notre Dame"

Center and the Visitors Café in the South Dining Hall. Around this same time, however, the first on-campus pizzeria appeared (at the rear of the Navy Drill Hall). Many of the dormitories also introduced in-hall evening food sales run by student entrepreneurs. These tended to feature high caloric items like pizzas, bread sticks, and various types of junk food and soft drinks. Years later a constant stream of delivery cars from area pizza and sandwich shops would become a regular feature of campus life.

For the basketball team, there was always a team meal the day of a home game, and the fare was almost always T-bone steak or a slab of roast beef, plus a baked potato, a vegetable, and toast with a small jar of honey. This cuisine conformed to the prevailing theories about energy sources that were both healthy and effective. On road trips we would eat in a variety of restaurants, sometimes to great fanfare. One of my favorites was Sam's Deli in Indianapolis. I also enjoyed Terry Brennan's beef place in Chicago and Win Shuler's restaurant on the way to Michigan State. The varsity team was usually bused to the away games that were within reasonable distance, but we flew charter on Purdue Airlines to games farther away, or via commercial flights when we played on the east or west coast. Purdue Airlines was a for-profit part of Purdue University's academic program in aviation science. Among ourselves, the general opinion was that they had the least attractive flight attendants we had ever seen. This was probably only male bravado but it did reinforce the notion that playing away from the friendly confines of Notre Dame's Fieldhouse needed to be all business.

One of the traditions on away games was that Chicago lawyer Ed O'Rourke, a friend of Coach Jordan, would accompany the team on the road. He arranged his personal schedule in a way that allowed him to make all the trips. Ed was always a friendly presence, a win-or-lose supporter of the team and coach. The amazing thing is that he has preserved this form of support to this very day despite all the changes in the head coaching position. It has also been a long tradition that a

Holy Cross priest accompany the team on road trips and celebrate mass before the game, as they still do for home games. While the degree of religiosity varied considerably among my teammates, no one would ever have dared question this tradition.

On the road we were expected to dress in coat and tie and to acquit ourselves fittingly as representatives of the University. I knew of no major breaches of this code while I was on the team. However, by my junior and senior years when relations between Coach Jordan and some members of the team had broken down, the bus trips could get pretty unpleasant, especially after a loss.

The announcer for the ND student radio station was Don Criqui, who went on to a highly successful career in sports broadcasting and telecasting. He could mimic the patter of Howard Cosell long before I knew who Howard Cosell was.

The Badin Years

In my junior and senior years of college I lived in Badin Hall. It was an almost ideal setting for undergraduate life with its mix of singles, doubles, triples, and quads, its second-floor outdoor porch facing the Hammes Bookstore and Gilbert's clothing store, and its location next to the bookstore basketball courts. In the basement was the University barber shop (where crew cuts prevailed and business was constant for the eight or nine barbers who worked there) and some social and study space for the dorm. Father Joe Garvin, C.S.C., was the rector. He was a gentle, soft-spoken man and a scholar in medieval studies who assisted Canon Astrik Gabriel in the Medieval Institute, one of Notre Dame's areas of great academic strength. Father Garvin genuinely liked students, and someone had to do something really stupid to get into trouble. When stay hall became a possibility after junior year, most of us stayed in Badin for a second year.

"Love Thee Notre Dame"

I was elected hall vice-president in junior year and hall president as a senior. As hall president, I would periodically meet with Father Garvin to talk over hall business and try to convince him on behalf of my hallmates about some priority or some event we wanted run. One of the presidential initiatives I took was to purchase a range of newspapers and magazines for the use of the men in the hall. It might be said that I read them first and that the hall subsidized my own intellectual interests, but that would be only partially true. The bull sessions in Badin were vigorous and challenging, and I always had the sense that we were coming into our own as learners. One of the residents on the second floor of Badin where I resided was Buddy Hill, a black Jamaican who had a wonderful voice and was a member of the Notre Dame Glee Club. Sometimes on Sunday afternoon he would play Ravel's *Bolero* or other classical music on his hi-fi. This gave us the sense that we were a hotbed of the arts as well.

Badin had the tradition of sponsoring a pep rally from our porch before one of the home football games. In format, it was not much different from the pep rallies that Dillon Hall has put on in more recent years, but the star of the show was always Father Garvin, just about the last man one would expect to generate enthusiasm for an athletic event. When his turn to speak came, the dorm residents generated thunderous applause, no matter what he had to say. This was partly a spoof on the whole notion of pep rallies, and I am sure Father Garvin always wondered why we insisted that he be part of our rally.

My most noteworthy administrative involvement with Father Garvin was the result of a project gone awry. I asked some Badin students to find a Christmas tree for our porch. To save money, they decided to cut down one of the trees on campus and they chose a beautiful fir from the sweeping driveway in front of what is now Carroll Hall but was then called Dujarie Hall (it served as a formation house of Holy Cross Brothers). They performed the clandestine deed late one night when snow was falling and dragged the tree back to Badin and set it up on the porch. When the brothers found out, they called Notre Dame security, whose crime-solving skills led them through the tell-tale snow right to the porch where the illuminated tree was shining in all its glory.

Father Garvin apologized to the brothers and assured them that we would replace the tree in the spring. On Arbor Day we marched from Badin to Dujarie in double file with a young sapling in a wheel-barrow, with me as hall president and Father Garvin as hall rector leading the group. When we arrived, some of the Dujarie residents awaited us. One of the Badinites recited Joyce Kilmer's poem "Trees," then Father Garvin, decked out in his cape and carrying a holy water dispenser, blessed the tree and sprinkled it. We then placed the tree in a spot near where the original tree had been and covered the base with dirt. Thus ended Badin Hall's number one public offense during my regime.

In my senior year we decided to run a hall-wide party at the Young Republican Club in downtown South Bend. Because beer would be served, I wanted to be sure nothing happened that would at-tract the attention of the South Bend police. I decided to use hall funds to hire a member of the football team who was also heavyweight champion of the Bengal Bouts. It turned out to be an excellent expen-diture of funds, since no one wanted to mess with him. We made it through the night unscathed.

That year I was initiated into the Monogram Club and experi-enced the hazing that then went along with the event. We showed up at the old Fieldhouse at the assigned time, and the class of in-ductees was brought to the locker area where we were blindfolded and stripped down to our jockstraps. Then we had hot ointment ap-plied to our arms and genitals and we were led into the open part of the Fieldhouse, which had been filled with dirt, manure, water, and various foul-smelling substances. We were ordered to get down on our hands and knees, moo like cows, and move speedily across the mire. Eventually, we were told to stand, take off our blindfolds, and be cleaned off with hoses. We then returned to the locker area and put our clothes back on. From there we were led to a ritual at which long-standing members of the Monogram Club welcomed us into their ranks.

At the time I did not know what to expect and it seemed like relatively harmless fun. But when star quarterback Daryl Lamonica refused to participate and filed a complaint, the athletic administration ended the days of hazing for the Monogram Club and any other student group. In retrospect that was exactly the right thing to do. That sort of behavior too easily gets out of hand, and the bullying instincts of a few can take advantage of the naive and the vulnerable.

Going into my sophomore year, my hopes were high for my chances to make a contribution to the Notre Dame basketball team. But the chosen starters were John Tully, John Dearie, Armand Reo, Eddie Schnurr, and Bill Crosby. The only consistent scorer was Armand, and the team had a habit of defeating top teams and losing to mediocre ones. It tended to play with inspiration at home and with less enthusiasm on the road. At the end of the season, the record was 12–14, the second poorest in John Jordan's ten years as head coach. Perhaps the most memorable game that year was a 64–63 victory over highly rated Saint John's in the ND Fieldhouse, it featured a long fist-fight on the court with some supportive participation by fans who sat close to courtside. The Fieldhouse by that time had developed a reputation as a bad environment for visiting teams, and more and more of the competitive programs refused to play us there.

My sophomore teammates and I saw little playing time, and by the end of the season the team was rent by considerable carping, most of it directed at the head coach. Conditioning drills consisted of wind sprints and calisthenics but no weight lifting or isometric exercises. Practice sessions usually consisted of dribbling and passing drills and two-on-two, three-on-three, and five-on-five contests. For those like me who were far down the pecking order, there was a lot of standing around during full-court competition. That made it difficult for

"Love Thee Notre Dame"

those of us who sat on the bench to show any improvement during the regular season.

In the spring of 1961 I was chosen as a new member of the Blue Circle Honor Society. This self-selecting campus undergraduate group had fifty-five members, half of whom were replaced each year. It was a very formative moment for me since the Blue Circle was a cross section of the movers and shakers on campus, deliberately chosen to represent various constituencies (I was clearly a jock-electee). It was also the leading voluntary service group on campus. Among its activities were running freshmen orientation, organizing campus-wide pep rallies, overseeing the logistics for the student trip to an away football game, sponsoring Christmas parties, ushering at Washington Hall, staffing campus tours, and providing leadership training. Some of my best friendships at Notre Dame came through my participation in the Circle in my junior and senior years.

The summer between my sophomore and junior years, the University implemented the most drastic rule changes of its history to that point. (In 1966 another series of changes would take place that became, in a sense, the great dividing line between the old and new Notre Dame, at least as far as the structure of residential life was concerned.) The 1961 rule changes were precipitated by a series of organized protests run by student leaders, including my ordination-classmate-to-be, Ollie Williams, and culminating in a noisy rally in front of Corby Hall. In earlier times, all the participants would have been subject to dismissal just for challenging the status quo, but in 1961 Father Ted Hesburgh welcomed the student voice.

The changes were relatively modest. Lights were no longer turned off in the dorms at eleven o'clock. Morning checks were eliminated. Students were no longer restricted to two midnights a week. The main impact was to allow students to study all night if they wished, or to visit each others' rooms, or just engage in bull sessions until the wee hours. They no longer had to rig up clandestine lighting systems, risk punishment for moving around the hall after hours, or feel pressure to

"Love Thee Notre Dame"

show up outside the chapel fully dressed in the early hours of the morning.

By the time I began my junior year in 1961–62, I was deeply embedded in the distinctive Notre Dame subculture. I had eaten at Frankie's and Eddie's and the Philly and Sunny Italy. Along with my fellow Blue Circle members I had become a regular at Giuseppe's. I had learned all the walking paths to the various establishments as well as the bus route and hitchhiking stations serving downtown. After I hit twenty, I had moved from being a non-drinker to an occasional imbiber at those local way stations whose proprietors looked kindly on customers of whatever age; I guess I was close enough to the twenty-one cut-off point and looked old enough to pass. My most dramatic encounter with the law in this regard took place during my junior year when we were having a dinner get-together with pizza and beer in one of the back rooms in Giuseppe's Restaurant and the alcohol agents showed up. We were warned before they discovered us and we ran out the back door and kept going all the way back to campus. I never found out whether anyone paid our bill but that was the least of our concerns at the time.

It was exciting to be temporarily on the lam like a wanted criminal, but later I came to see such raids, at least in the early 1960s, as a kind of game in which the alcohol agents just wanted to scare students so underage violations did not become too pronounced. In my senior year, I was in a downtown Irish bar on Saint Patrick's Day when I saw a group of underage students run out the backdoor in great haste. One of them had looked out the window of the men's room and noticed several police cars. He did not know that the bar's back door faced the parking lot of the city police station.

By junior year the administration was under increasing pressure to do something about the social life on campus. That fall the University sponsored an open house to which hundreds of students from other colleges and universities were bused for an afternoon of coed sports and folk singing. Also that fall there was a Limeliters concert in the Student Center, a homecoming dance, a sophomore cotillion, a roaring twenties party, and a Brothers Four concert. For most undergraduates of my era, the absence of women on campus meant that most formal social events were of greatest interest to those who had a steady relationship either at Saint Mary's or at some nearby school. For the rest of us, social encounters with women were almost nonexistent. Like it or not, the basic campus social dynamic was male and revolved around the dorm.

In Joe Kuharich's third season as head football coach, the Fighting Irish finished 5–5. I earned a little extra money selling programs at home football games. I developed a system of working the parking lot on Saturday mornings but finishing up in time for the kickoff. There was a fair amount of grumbling in the student section as the season moved on. The early support for Joe Kuharich was waning.

My junior year on the basketball team was a great disappointment for me and for the team as a whole. We finished with a 7–16 record. My role was minimal, and like most bench warmers I could imagine how much better the team would be if I had more playing time. In many ways, the team was a prisoner of Johnny Jordan's 1–3–1 offense. The team makeup was such that we conformed to the stereotype that all-white teams were not very athletic and could not run a high-powered offense. Sam Skarich, another seldom used sub, and I were the best shooters, but the 3-point shot had not yet been authorized and the coach preferred playing those he thought had a better chance of making a short-range jump shot, a low pivot hook-shot, or a lay-up, particularly off a backdoor cut. Opposing teams tended to play a zone defense that forced us to shoot from the outside.

By the end of the season team morale was horrible. Coach Jordan had health problems which were exaggerated when we were on the road. Moose Krause, the athletic director, had challenges of his own at the same time. Even expressions of concern from the team captains turned out to be ineffective. By the end of my junior season, I recognized that chances were slim that I would ever have a major role on the

"Love Thee Notre Dame"

team. Practices were a burden to suffer through in order to keep my scholarship.

Although my basketball career was undistinguished and full of frustration, I was pleased to see some action during my senior year, enough to merit a Monogram letter. On occasion during my years under the Dome I would imagine how things might have been if I had pursued one of my other scholarship offers. Yet even if I had played a starring role elsewhere, I would have missed out on the non-athletic part of the Notre Dame experience and all it has meant to me ever since. My college education was paid for, I made lifelong friends, I received an excellent education, and I discerned my life's vocation. How lucky can a person be?

One result of all this was that I turned my time and emotional energy to other pursuits. I decided to make a run for senior class president with Scottie Maxwell, a football player and my next-door neighbor in Badin, running for vice president. Larry Shubnell, another Badinite, agreed to be our campaign manager. Although our decision to run came on a whim, both Scottie and I took the challenge seriously. We adopted the campaign slogan "Vote for M & M" and, within a limited campaign budget, gave out small packets of M&M candies. Scottie and I divided up the junior halls and set ourselves the goal of making our case in person to every member of the class. We came close. It was an interesting exercise, since I found out that I already knew a good percentage of the class by name and face. Our biggest disadvantage was that we were both residents of Badin, one of the smallest dorms. By the end of the campaign period, we figured that our odds were pretty good but we were naive about many things, especially how to survey our constituency.

When the results were in, I ran second to Eddie Eck, and Scottie won election as vice president. Eddie had given out small ink pens with his name on them as part of his campaign effort. I took some consolation from the fact that his pens ran out of ink a few days after the election. Despite losing, I enjoyed the electioneering and learned a lot along the way. Once it became clear that I would not be class president, I ran for hall president in Badin and was elected. The job required a relatively small investment of time. I knew the men in the hall quite well already, and with the coming of stay hall, most of my classmates remained in Badin for a second year. This provided for great continuity but allowed for the influx of new blood as well.

I entered my senior year at Notre Dame with a clear sense of a call to become a priest (see the next chapter) and with a real commitment to the intellectual life and to exploring everything Notre Dame had to offer. Before the year was over, I had gone to my first debate tournament, my first Collegiate Jazz Festival, my first fencing match, the Bengal Bouts, all the student plays, the film festival, and various lectures on campus. I had seen Ray Charles in concert and Peter, Paul, and Mary. I had heard Father Hans Kung speak on "Church Authority and Freedom of Conscience," a topic that seemed to reflect the spirit of reform of Vatican II. That year construction began on the gigantic Hesburgh Library, which would transform the campus forever.

By reputation, the two strongest departments in the College of Arts and Letters in my undergraduate years were English and history. In addition to doing assigned course reading, I took it upon myself to explore Dostoevsky, Turgenev, and Gogol, Moliere, Joyce, Beckett, Camus, and Sartre, the Beats and the various contemporary authors who were pushing the limits of respectability. I even started a list of all the books I was exploring, some of which would not be safe to use in a Notre Dame classroom setting for many years to come. I also began in a formal way to expand my vocabulary by buying books full of etymologies, prefixes and suffixes, obscure usages, and convenient mnemonic devices. I noted unfamiliar words in my readings, subsequently looked them up, then worked hard to make them part of my vocabulary.

I wrote a few short stories and even a poem or two, but I never had a gift for creative composition. Most of my poetry was written in free form in moments of intense reflection or difficulty. When I reread

"Love Thee Notre Dame"

one I felt it did not reflect my normal view on reality, since I am an optimist by nature. I was embarrassed to find that my verse was full of self-preoccupation, obscure references to troubling moments, and a kind of adolescent angst. That, plus its lack of quality, are the main reasons why none of it has seen the light of day.

I did not fancy myself as an intellectual. I was always put off by my peers who liked to debate obscure philosophical or theological topics for the sheer delight of winning the argument, or claiming to. I was fully aware of my own lacunae academically and was disinclined to pretend to a sweeping competence in anything. But I was learning a lot in the classroom, in my extracurricular activities, and in late night bull sessions. I was more like Marco Polo or Christopher Columbus discovering new worlds than like Thomas Aquinas or Darwin offering new syntheses of available knowledge. That year the yearbook honored thirty-five of my graduating class as Who's Who. I was not one of them, but I do not remember feeling concerned about the non-recognition one way or another.

The football team in what turned out to be Joe Kuharich's last year finished 5–5. The consensus was that ND had some outstanding talent, but many players under Kuharich's pro-style system were playing out of position. Several went on to successful professional careers in the NFL. When the administration bought out Kuharich's contract (with an eleven-year settlement), Hugh Devore became the interim coach, a position he would hold for one year until Ara Parseghian was wooed away from Northwestern. The 1962 team had two black players, but the achievement of an integrated team comparable to other top programs would be years in the making.

The basketball team that year was 17–18 in regular season and 0–1 in the NCAA tournament. An influx of young talent, not the Jordan style of play, was primarily responsible for the improvement over the previous year. The team would have been even stronger if two of its best sophomore players—Larry Sheffield and Ron Reed—had not been declared ineligible after the fall semester. After their departure,

Coach Jordan was sufficiently committed to the rule of seniority that he felt obliged to use me, at least selectively. I had my best game in a win at Detroit. I also started at point guard against Saint John's, I think because my father was present, even though I was not a good ball handler. Ironically, the coach of Saint John's was Lou Carneseca, who had been coaching at Bishop Molloy High School when we beat them at the K. of C. Tournament in my senior year of high school.

As graduation approached, I began to worry, at least mildly, about a missing link in my academic record. Back when I was a freshman, physical education was a requirement, and one component was passing a swim test, come hell or high water. Students were not allowed to graduate without satisfying the requirement. The problem was, I could not swim (and still can't). Several attempts to learn earlier in my life only proved conclusively that I am hopeless in the water. My first attempt came in the eighth grade when my mother saw a newspaper ad for free swimming lessons for children under eighteen. The course began with simple exercises, like blowing bubbles in the water and doing the dead man's float. When test day arrived, I climbed to the top of the diving board, said an Act of Contrition, and dived. To my amazement I found myself standing on the bottom of the pool. I held my breath and walked sideways to a ladder before my lungs gave out. One of my instructors informed me that I was a sinker, not a floater.

As a varsity athlete at Notre Dame, I did not have to enroll in phys. ed. when I was in season, and because I was studying chemical engineering, which required labs, there were no available phys. ed. time slots. During the next few years I simply put the issue out of my mind. The night before the commencement ceremony I had a nightmare in which I saw myself walking up to receive my diploma and finding it blank. Gratefully, that did not happen and I finished my undergraduate career at Notre Dame as a non-swimming bachelor of arts.

Graduation goodbyes were difficult, even for a group of men schooled in the cultural expectations of the 1960s. Many of us spent the days before graduation pledging lifelong friendships. Late one

"Love Thee Notre Dame"

night I sneaked out of Badin with one of my friends. We bought a six pack of beer and were lying on a small pier in front of Moreau Seminary, talking about life and God and the future, when we saw a police car coming in our direction. We were not sure if we had been spotted, so we hid in the water under the pier. When the security guard reached the pier, he shone a flashlight and asked if anyone was there. He clearly knew that we were and only wanted to scare us. After a few minutes he left and we sneaked back into Badin. How my life might have changed if this otherwise minor incident had prevented me from graduating. In any case, it is a story never before told.

Because the 1963 commencement exercises took place in June, the weather that day was about ninety-five degrees. Commencement was held in the area around the flagpole on the South Quad. Lester Pierson, the Prime Minister of Canada, was the speaker, and at least from a student perspective he was long and boring. Nevertheless it was an exciting moment for me and my parents and sisters. I was the first one in my family to attend college and the first to graduate. While I had several degrees yet to pursue, there was something especially satisfying for all of us that I had gained a B.A. in English from Notre Dame.

CHAPTER 5

THE CALL

IN THE SPRING SEMESTER OF JUNIOR YEAR, I
overheard a corridor conversation about plans for a summer service
project in Latin America. My interest was piqued, and I learned that a
Notre Dame student group called CILA (the Council for the Interna
tional Lay Apostolate) was planning a two-month trip to work with
the Maryknoll missionaries in Peru. Father Larry Murphy, M.M., who
at the time was working on his doctorate in philosophy at Notre
Dame, had proposed the trip to the CILA members. I was too late to
be selected for the Peru venture, but it turned out that Father Ernie
Bartell, C.S.C., who was serving on campus before going off to Princeton to begin work on a doctorate in economics, was willing to accompany a second group to Mexico, and there were enough volunteers to
constitute at least one, if not two more CILA contingents.

With that news, I started to get really excited. As a scholarship
athlete, I did not have to worry about working in the summer to
help pay my tuition, room, and board. Unlike the summers after my

freshman and sophomore years, I was in good shape academically. I had never been out of the country (except to cross to the Canadian side at Niagara Falls), and the prospect of experiencing a new culture was intriguing. I also liked several of the other students who were on the list of volunteers.

That first summer CILA sent three separate student entourages to Latin America, one to Peru under the guidance of Father Larry Murphy and two to Mexico led by Father Ernie Bartell. The volunteers got together about once a week for orientation sessions led by the two priests and other campus personnel with special expertise. Fluency in Spanish was not required (although a couple in each group were fluent) but we were expected to work on the rudiments of the language in our spare time. Although I had studied Spanish in high school and at Notre Dame, I was better at reading than at oral comprehension or speaking. To help pay for our trips, each of us was expected to look for sponsors—family members, hometown organizations, businesses, or individual donors. We promised potential benefactors that if they supported us, we would provide a full report after the summer. I ended up being the report writer for our group in Aguascalientes, Mexico, an experience that led me to become a regular practitioner of the art of the travel journal.

A total of thirty-one students participated in the three projects. Although the two groups which went to Mexico were both supervised by Father Bartell, those of us in Aguascalientes saw him only periodically since he lived at the other site at Tacambaro in Michoacán Province, a hundred miles away.

Aguascalientes (Summer 1962)

Seven of us drove from campus to Mexico in three donated station wagons that contained our basic gear, food, and utensils. When we finally set out after all the weeks of preparation, great excitement

Mother and me at two months,
August 1941

A proud father and his young son

Shooting my first
jump shot

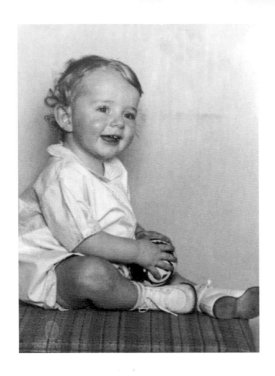

At one year old with
my curly
blond locks

Me with my Uncle John
and Aunt Clare

Boyhood pals,
Denny Kane and me

Denny Kane and me—
two kids on patrol

(*above left*)
First Communion,
June 5, 1950

(*above right*)
Father, myself, Joanne,
and Mary at the time
of First Communion,
June 5, 1950

The slick look,
June 1950

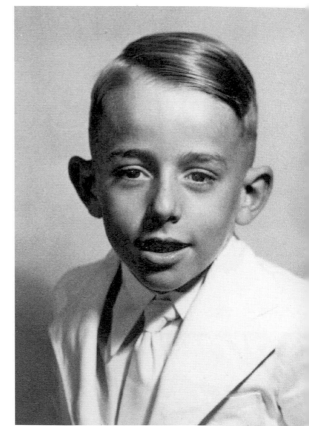

Mary, myself, and Joanne with our father, about 1955

Grade school days

Eighth grade graduation and our first television

(below)
The Optimist Club team from Turkey Thicket playground after winning the twelve-and-under citywide baseball championship at major league park Griffith Stadium. I am wearing my chest protector, with my father proudly standing behind me.

The 1956–59 Archbishop John Carroll High School championship team. This was a team of complementary skills, high morale, and uncommon success. *Front row (l. to r.):* Kenny Price, Tracy McCarthy, Jim Bradley, mgr., Tom Berry, mgr., George Leftwich, Bill Romig; *Second row:* Coach Bob Dwyer, Walt Skinner, Monk Malloy, Bill Barnes, Doug Barnes, Mike O'Brien, Tom Moore; *Back row:* John Thompson, Tom Hoover. Dan Hogan, mgr., was absent when picture was taken.

The three seniors— Doug Barnes, Tom Hoover, and myself—joyfully accept the winner's trophy from the 1959 Knights of Columbus tournament, with *(r.)* Coach Bob Dwyer and Father Andy Boyle and *(l.)* Father Joe Duffey.

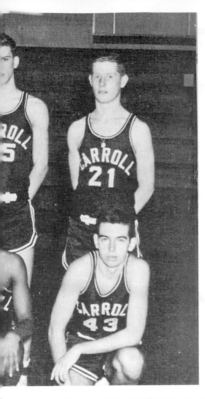

With three classmates at Carroll High, 1959

(left) Scoring on a lay-up, Carroll vs Gonzaga High

(below) Father, myself, and the Kane brothers—the jaunty look

Champions
of the
Chevy Chase
summer league

All-Metropolitan First Team, 1959

The Knight of Columbus championship, 1959

The candidates go before the people at Carroll High student elections

Senior picture,
Archbishop Carroll
High School,
June 1959

Senior prom 1959,
Maureen O'Brien
and myself

Mother and father in their go-to-meeting best

Home on vacation
from Notre Dame

Notre Dame basketball team, 1960–61

CILA in
Aguascalientes,
Mexico,
summer 1962

CILA group with local bishop in Aguascalientes, Mexico, summer 1962

The Shrine of Cristo Rey (Christ the King) near the geographical center of Mexico, a place of pilgrimage and devotion where I experienced my mountaintop call to become a priest.

CILA group in Mexico, summer 1962

"Pancho" Malloy
in Mexico,
summer 1962

Nick Vitalich and myself,
Notre Dame graduation,
June 1963

CILA in Peru
on Lake Titicaca,
summer 1963

CILA in Peru,
Pat Whelan
and myself

Tom Jones, Charlie Corso, and myself as Holy Cross novices
in Jordan, Minnesota, summer 1965

Receiving my master's
degree in English Literature
at the Grotto,
summer 1967

Ordination picture,
April 9, 1970

Mary, Joanne, mother,
father, and myself
at Ordination,
April 4, 1970

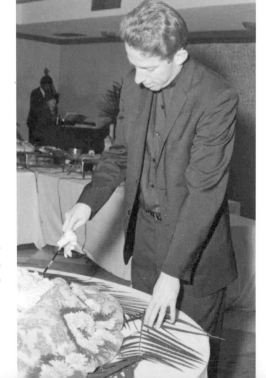

Cutting the cake,
First Mass celebration,
April 1970

First Mass, St. Anthony's Parish, Washington, D.C., April 1970

Baptism of
Dave Sheil
in the Log Chapel
at Notre Dame,
May 8, 1976

Mother, father, and myself, April 1970

was in the air, but the reality of what we were undertaking struck home only when we passed into Mexico at the border check point between Laredo and Nuevo Laredo. The first week of June was hot and dry as we drove through Monterrey, Saltillo, and San Luis Potosi on our way to Aguascalientes, which is north and west of Mexico City. It took us four days to reach our destination.

In addition to me, the others in Aguascalientes were Tom Kapacinskas, Larry Shubnell, John McGroarty, Jack Hildebrand, Tom O'Dea, and Jack Mattox. Tom O'Dea was fluent in Spanish and looked somewhat older than the rest of us, so he was appointed our on-site director. Each member of our group was to live with a different family of local residents. We ate breakfast and dinner in our respective houses and lunch in the local seminary. None of the host families spoke English well, so we were required to communicate as best we could in Spanish. Our sponsor was the bishop of Aguascalientes. Our main job was aiding Mexican laborers in the parish of Divine Providence. We worked on a drainage ditch for two weeks and later helped make cement and carry it to the site of a new convent they were building. We also did other manual tasks like bending steel wire and moving pipe. Besides the construction work, we took trips through the area to observe living conditions and the contrast between wealth and poverty that existed in the region. We played basketball with the seminarians and others, baseball with the workers, and used athletics as a way of relating to the people. We also helped distribute surplus food, visited the country club, and participated in discussions with other Americans who lived and/or worked in the area.

Our sense of mission was strong. Our goal was to have an interchange of ideas and experiences with Mexicans of all financial and cultural levels in order to impress them with our interest in their problems and those of the Church in Mexico. And we hoped to examine the characteristics of Mexican culture that we might bring back to our own society. Although we cited our physical work as the immediate reason for being there, at no time did we consider it our primary rationale. In religious terms, we hoped by means of example to impress the people with the fact that we were serious Catholic Christians as manifested in our daily participation in the Mass and communion.

In retrospect, I think that the mix of physical labor and extra-curricular involvements worked reasonably well. The main limitation was our language deficiency. Although our good will usually carried the day, we missed out on some of the in-depth analysis of Mexican society. What we carried home with us in our hearts was the impact the place made on our senses, the raw reality of a new culture and new physical circumstances, and the wonderful people we met.

I lived with the Guerrero family. He was an eye doctor and a member of one of the more prominent families in the city. She participated widely in charitable work. They had six children, ranging from four to eighteen years old. At all times I was treated as a member of the family, and I will be forever grateful for this exposure to the best of the Mexican spirit of hospitality.

The biggest problem we had as a group was health related. Every one of us, at one time or another, suffered from dysentery or some form of intestinal disorder. As we discovered, this simply goes with the territory. For centuries, Mexicans have been using human manure to fertilize their crops, so almost all the drinking water (and some of the food products) are contaminated. It is imperative to drink only boiled or bottled water, but it is easy to slip up (is the ice in a drink safe or not, and what about the lettuce?) and then pay the price. Fortunately, none of us got amoebic dysentery or hepatitis or any other long-term medical plague.

The local newspapers covered our activities, so our presence was known to more people than those we encountered directly. One newspaper photo showed our group wielding pick axes; the text in Spanish read: "Under a hot sun, the university students from Notre Dame were working yesterday, far from Indiana, from their homes, from all that is theirs, at the side of humble Mexican laborers. They contribute a grain of sand in order that hope will be reestablished in a forgotten slum." An accompanying article, titled "The Best Ambassador," went on to say, "In one of the poorest slums of Aguascalientes are found working a group of North American university students who came to know Mexico and to know the Mexicans. . . .Yesterday they worked in the hot sun. With pick and shovel they opened the drainage for what will be the Chapel of Divine Providence." Another article summarized our involvement by saying, "Great work of social benefit is being undertaken in this diocese by a group of students from the University of Notre Dame, who are making a visit in our city in order to promote activities of a social and religious character. . . . For now the most important work that has been begun is the construction of a church."

During our time in Aguascalientes we were able to take a trip to Tacambaro to visit with the members of the group there and to observe the differences between that locale and our own. The lifestyle of the people, we discovered, was strongly affected by environmental differences. Tacambaro was more tropical in vegetation and in the ways that the poor lived off the land. The Aguascalientes families were more dependent on organized efforts to provide the basic necessities.

Someone in Aguascalientes had the great idea of organizing a fiesta with a local mariachi band. In an album of the trip we collected photographs of our group members dancing with some of the local teenage girls decked out in their finest clothes. One of our favorite getaway spots was a restaurant owned and operated by an American-born black man named Bill Wright, who originally went to Mexico to play baseball and stayed on after marrying a Mexican woman. His restaurant was the only place in the city that served authentic American-style hamburgers. A favorite place to visit was a local orphanage run by Catholic sisters. These children were so cute and hungry for attention and affection that we were always warmly received. Being so far from our own families, these moments were a precious reminder of our common need to belong.

Every afternoon, almost precisely at four o'clock, it rained for twenty or thirty minutes. It just poured, then the sun came out, and that was it for precipitation for the day. In the slum area where we toiled, the sewage and drainage systems were minimal, so we had to wait for the water to be absorbed into the dry earth or else get used to the mud.

On the trip to visit our colleagues in Tacambaro we chose to visit Mexico City on the way. Mexico City is situated in the middle of a huge volcanic crater at an altitude over 7,000 feet, so the climate is cool and dry. The present city is on the site of the old Aztec capital of Tenochtitlán. Our time in the city was limited so we focused on visiting the pyramids, the central square including the Cathedral, Chapultepec Park, the Archeological Museum, and the Basilica of Guadalupe. Moving between these traditional tourist areas gave us a sense of the scale of the city, one of the largest in the world, and the great contrast between the richest and the poorest neighborhoods. We also attended the Ballet Folklórico México, a Broadway-style show of traditional Mexican music and dance.

Another trip took us somewhat north and west of Aguascalientes to the town of Guanajuato, one of the most beautiful places in the country. On the way back, we decided—I am not sure why—to visit the Basilica of Cristo Rey (Christ the King), which sits on a mountaintop near the geographical center of Mexico.

Cristo Rey: An Unmistakable Call

The Basilica is reached by ascending a winding mountain road. Along the way we passed little shrines bedecked with hand-written letters, prayer cards, photographs, and a collection of left-behind crutches and other medical devices. The letters described in emotional detail some favor granted (sometimes the gift of healing for some bodily infirmity) through the intervention of Christ the King. Although we had never heard of the Basilica or the devotion that is centered there, we were immediately struck by the special status this holy place had in the hearts of those who had preceded us there.

At the summit, which afforded a sweeping view of the countryside, we toured the Basilica, stopping to say a prayer near the main altar. Back outside, we stared up at the dominating image of Christ the King which can be seen from miles away. Then the rest of the group went off to continue exploring and I was left alone. For some reason, I welcomed this sudden isolation, and I walked over to one of the viewing areas that look down to the valley below and across to the distant mountains.

All was quiet and I soon found myself in a state of reverie. It was as though time stood still and all the cares of the moment had dissipated. I was at peace. How long I remained so disposed I cannot say. All I know is that I had a sudden and compelling sense that I was being called to become a priest. I did not hear voices or have a vision. I simply had a feeling of certitude about my vocational call.

Looking back on that moment from the vantage point of four more decades, I can recognize that such experiences do not come out of the blue. What I knew then (and still do) is this grace-filled encounter with the living God had been paved by the influence of my parents and family, by the worship and faith formation I had known from a young age, by the years I had attended Catholic schools, by my service as an altar server and the priests I had come to know in the process, by the environment of Notre Dame, especially its residence life tradition, and now by my choice to come to Mexico on a summer service project that brought many of the previous elements into sharper focus.

Like many boys of my generation I had thought positively about the priesthood during my formative years. Most of the priests I encountered in our parish, at Carroll High, and at Notre Dame had seemed like good and holy men. I liked some more than others but I just considered that to be a fact of life. In high school, when Father Joe

Duffey had extended a formal invitation to consider becoming an Augustinian, the time was not right. I knew instinctively that if I went into the seminary directly from high school I would not have been happy and probably would not have persevered.

Maybe the best way to put it is to say that by the completion of my junior year of college I had begun to get serious about what I wanted to do with the rest of my life. I had begun to attend daily mass. I knew by then that I had no realistic chances of playing basketball after college; I simply was not good enough. I also sensed that I would enjoy working in a university setting, especially at a place like Notre Dame.

After my nearly disastrous academic start, I felt that I had come into my own as a learner and as someone genuinely interested in the world of ideas. Yet it was an open question whether I possessed the requisite passion and discipline to pursue the doctorate to qualify myself to become a college professor. I had been a peer leader both in high school and college and I was confident in my abilities to speak in public, to run a meeting, and to properly execute an agreed upon set of priorities. What was uncertain was how to decide what area of endeavor would allow these leadership skills to bear good fruit.

On that mountaintop in Mexico, all of these tugs and pulls in my inner life came together. For the first time I could proceed with full confidence that Christ was definitely calling me to become a priest in the Roman Catholic Church. All of this took place in a relatively brief moment of time. It stood out not for its length but for its emotional intensity. When I was back among the Aguascalientes group I did not say a word. I simply kept this dramatic gift of vocational enlightenment to myself for the time being.

When I returned to campus for my senior year, I knew that eventually I had some important choices to make. As was my wont, I decided to reveal my Cristo Rey experience first to Father Bartell, who by then was off at Princeton. He was "safe" because we knew each other from our time together in Mexico and yet he was preoccupied with his graduate work and would not be inclined to put any pressure on me.

In an exchange of letters, I revealed my state of mind and my sense of calling, and then asked all kinds of questions about the difference between diocesan clergy and members of religious communities, about what seminary life was like, about the possibility, if I joined Holy Cross, of becoming a priest-teacher, and about the nature of the vows religious priests take. Slowly but surely, Ernie answered my questions and kept encouraging me to continue pursuing my inchoate inclinations.

Meanwhile I had begun a correlative conversation with my parents. They were not surprised I was considering the priesthood (it is hard to fool those who brought you into the world), yet they took a low-key approach. They let me know they would be proud of me whatever I decided to do, and if I did enter the seminary it would be my choice alone whether to stay. By the end of the first semester of my senior year, I was satisfied I had asked all the right questions and knew enough to proceed to the next step. Father Bartell encouraged me to make contact with Father Ralph Fisher, C.S.C., the Holy Cross vocational director. I filled out the requisite papers and went through some interviews. By midway in the spring semester I had been accepted to join the candidacy program at Saint Joseph Hall on campus in the fall of 1963.

The next challenge was to decide when and how to tell my family members and friends. My sisters were easy, since they clearly knew something was up and, I suspect, were prepared for the news ahead of time by my parents. I waited until after the season was over to tell my basketball teammates and hallmates and other friends. What was amazing was how supportive everyone was. Some told me that they suspected it all along. Others simply affirmed our friendship and were pleased that I had a clarity about my future that many of them lacked.

I have discovered through the years that there are many ways in which individuals make fundamental human decisions, from what college to attend to what major to pursue to whether and whom to marry to what work of life to undertake to when to retire. Some muster all the facts and then try to arrive at a reasoned conclusion. Others act on hunches and instinct. Still others go with the flow and put off choices as long as possible. Even in religious terms, my vocational story is somewhat unique. I look back on Cristo Rey as the root and origin of my call. It seems to have been a moment of grace that continues to link me to my past and to call me forward in the same spirit of commitment and hope.

Las Vegas

Unlikely as it may seem, when our summer service project in Aguascalientes was over, I went with a fellow participant, John McGroarty, to Las Vegas to live with his family and work construction for his father. All this had been worked out during the spring semester when we were preparing for Mexico. When I broached the subject with my parents, I was a bit surprised that they were so enthusiastic about Las Vegas. I thought that they would want me back in D.C. for the last month of the summer. But I think my mother in particular was eager for me to have a wide range of experiences while I was young, something that she and my father never had the financial freedom to pursue at a comparable age.

In Vegas, John and I were joined by another Notre Dame undergraduate, Oscar Wong, who also was scheduled to live and work with the McGroarty's. But it soon became clear that Mr. McGroarty's construction business had room for only one summer worker in addition to John, so I was assigned instead to cook at Mrs. McGroarty's Broaster Haven fast food restaurant in one of the strip malls. My hours were eleven o'clock to seven in the evening, which was perfect in terms of our exploring the night life of one of the world's best-known gambling locales.

The McGroartys were wonderful hosts and made Oscar and me feel right at home. More importantly, they accepted our youthful interest in making the most of our time in Vegas, never expressing concern about the hours we kept as long as we were ready to fulfill our work responsibilities. Just about every night except Sunday, John, Oscar, and I went out to explore some aspect of the complex world of Las Vegas. Sometimes we began by playing basketball at an outdoor court or in a local gym. Other times we would go to a movie. Since Vegas is a city that never closes (and seldom sleeps), we were never in any rush.

At that time in its evolution, the Vegas gambling industry was divided into two large sections. In the heart of downtown were the smaller casinos that catered to the lower middle class and to the marginally poor. The centers of activity there were slot machines, blackjack and poker games, and craps and roulette tables with relatively low antes. At the other extreme were the full-scale casinos that offered live, high-quality entertainment and just about every game of chance, including sports gambling and elite betting formats like baccarat with roped off players' areas and dealers dressed in tuxedos and white gloves.

Although the three of us had little discretionary money, we learned to negotiate successfully both sides of the gambling spectrum. Mr McGroarty taught me a system for the nickel slots, which at that time were the heart and soul of the appeal of the downtown casinos. The system was simple but it required strict discipline. Like Pavlov's dogs, the downtown gamblers required the constant reinforcement of their conviction that they were just about to hit it big, and the management provided this by magnifying visual and oral stimulation. Every so often someone would win a jackpot and the house would proclaim the fact with flashing lights, falling coins, and the scooping of coins into a large receptacle. In truth, on a given evening only a small percentage of the slots were set to pay off at the top level, but the impression was just the opposite.

Using Mr. McGroarty's system, I finished the summer about $150 to the good, an excellent rate of return on nickel slots. The trick was never to play a machine where multiple jackpot signs were not visible in the nine spaces on the rotating discs. Then you had to look for re-occurrences of the jackpot images. If they were not manifest, you had to move on to another machine. The same judgment was required with small payouts, which could be seductive, so you had to be in the action for the big payout alone. I gambled only occasionally because I found it just as interesting to watch the other clientele. I saw poor women, clearly spending money from their welfare checks, playing five adjacent machines—a formula for a frustrating evening. I saw in-dividuals sit at one machine for hours. Scariest of all, I observed peo-ple with that glazed-over look which is one of the warning signs of the addicted gambler.

Downtown just about anyone of whatever social class could fit in. But out on the strip, where the major casinos were located, it was im-portant to look respectable and prosperous. On a couple of occasions we bought tickets to view one of the major shows. We saw a talented circus act and later a Vegas version of the songs from a Broadway mu-sical. With every show we saw elaborate chorus-girl routines. But we could find comparably good entertainment without spending a cent by hanging out on the periphery of one of the stages on the upper side of one of the bars in the center of the casino itself. One night we took in Don Rickles' routine as he insulted just about every person, one by one, along the length of the bar. I was amazed that no one got up to slug him or walk out. I guess they knew what they were in for when they sat down. Another night we watched the Harmonicats, a group of harmonica-playing midgets who sometimes showed up on TV vari-ety programs in those days.

The most startling discovery I made on the strip was how much money some people were prepared to lose. I observed tens of thou-sands of dollars being forked over in some of the high-roller games. Losing in gambling has a finality about it: one moment the money is yours and the next it is not. But the game goes on with new partici-pants and short memories. We found out that most casinos would

The Call

provide a nest egg to their star entertainers to gamble with so they would hobnob with casino patrons. One night a high-profile singer, who was clearly drunk, exceeded by far the provided funds and was deep into his own money when the pit boss decided to rein him in. The resulting scene was a classic Las Vegas encounter in the sense that all moral arguments were irrelevant and the only effective way to end the scene was to haul the singer away.

My Vegas summer had no effect on my resolve to pursue a priestly vocation. We went to mass every Sunday while we were there and otherwise preserved some of the fervor that John and I had experienced together in Mexico. I enjoyed the exposure to the hedonistic lifestyle of Vegas, if only because I saw how sad so many people seemed to be, particularly those for whom gambling appeared to be the main thrill in their lives. I also discovered the other Las Vegas, where people live normal lives, raise families, and go to work every day. My main concern for them was how they could pass their religious and personal values on to the next generation when they were surrounded by sensory stimulation that constantly promised that luck is more important than effort and one can have it all without sacrifice and self-discipline.

After Vegas I returned to D.C. for a short break before the start of school. I had many stories to tell about my time in Mexico and Las Vegas, but the time had not yet come to share where I saw myself headed.

Lima and Ilave, Peru

In the summer of 1963, after graduation from Notre Dame, I continued my participation in CILA by joining a group going to Peru with Father Larry Murphy, M.M., who had taken the first CILA contingent to Peru the previous summer and so had a firsthand knowledge of the logistics involved and of the people with whom we would be working.

Our stay in Peru went from June 10 until August 3, which was in the middle of winter in the southern hemisphere. Although Peru is relatively far north and snow is rare even in the mountains, both the Lima area, which is usually fogged in all year, and the *altiplano* (or highlands) are cool, especially in the shade.

The group I was assigned to spent the first week in Ciudad de Dios (City of God) outside of Lima, and then split up into twos and went to cities near Lake Titicaca about 12,500 feet above sea level. I was assigned to Ilave. We also traveled to Arequipa, Cuzco, and Machu Picchu. In most of our assigned areas we lived with Maryknoll priests; we ate meals with the priests but bought our food. Rather than taking on a large, restrictive project as we had done in Mexico, we performed a variety of tasks: teaching English and art in local high schools, coaching basketball, painting, building roofs, distributing surplus food, running a medical study, and so on. These jobs enabled us to have almost daily contact with schoolchildren, workers, and mothers and to have opportunities to be granted access into their homes. The biggest challenges were language (not only did we have varying levels of competence in Spanish, but the indigenous peoples did not always speak Spanish fluently); health (the availability of clean water and altitude problems); and separation (we spent most of our time in twos apart from the rest of the participants).

My time was divided about evenly between Ciudad de Dios in Lima and Ilave in the *altiplano*. I taught religion and English to local high school students, some of whom were in their twenties. Because my Spanish was limited, I learned on occasion to cope with teaching English in Spanish to Quechua Indians whose first language was Quechan, not Spanish. I made it through each day with good will and humor, but I would not want to guarantee how much the students comprehended.

Coaching basketball was easier since I could demonstrate as well as talk, but the rim of the basket was bent, there was no net, and the ball had seen better days. The kids preferred soccer but any exercise was fine with them. Once I adjusted to the high altitude my stamina improved, yet I never matched the students' ability to run endlessly.

I also helped out around the parish and school doing odd jobs of manual labor, but most exciting for me were the pastoral visits where I would accompany the Maryknoll priests in a four-wheel drive vehicle out to the distant reaches of the parish. There they would hear confessions, celebrate mass, and visit the sick. The Indian people lived in simple hut-like structures with reed roofs. Because of the pervasive cool, damp weather, the women wore many-layered hoop skirts and bowler hats and carried their babies papoose-style on their backs. The men wore pants, shirts, thick sweaters, and narrow-brimmed hats. Since the coca plant was widely grown in the region, many of the adults would chew coca leaves, which made their mouths green and was said to ease hunger and give them the ability to walk or work for long periods of time without stopping. The misuse of alcohol, especially a local concoction, was a big problem among the Quechua population. The men in particular seemed prone to alcohol abuse on the weekends. We saw them at night lying alongside the main highways.

On Saturday afternoons we visited the local markets where farmers and merchants had open air stalls. Raw meat hung from metal spikes, with flies and other bugs constantly sampling the bloody carcasses. Dolls and toys, usually simply constructed, were on sale for the children. The Saturday market was a great people-watching place and a source of community gossip. Police and soldiers were around but they had little to do. It was the sensory overload that I experienced there that remains most firmly planted in my memory.

The major part of our time in Peru was spent in the *altiplano* along Lake Titicaca, an area of the country that supported a small fishing industry, many small farms, a few plantations, and some ranches of cattle, sheep, llamas, and alpacas. The people were generally uneducated and spoke Aymra and Quechua, two Indian dialects. The town in which I worked, Ilave, had a population of 10,000. We sensed that because of the hard life in the region, the possibility for trouble of any kind, Communist or otherwise, was highest in our area. Most of the progressive outreach on behalf of the indigenous population was undertaken by Maryknoll priests, Papal Volunteers, and Peace Corps workers. Years later this region would become one of the centers of the guerrilla movement called *Sendero Luminoso*, or Shining Path.

When I accompanied the local priests to their outlying chapels, I observed the difficulties imposed by the language barrier (very few of the priests had become proficient in the native dialects), the infrequency of visits (often only once a year), and the value of the native catechists who were educated in Ilave and performed some of the pastoral functions of an absent priest. One of my most interesting discoveries was that once a year the priest would solemnize the marriages of all the couples in a village on the same day. Until he arrived, they had been living together after a native ritual. There was no alternative to this because of the shortage of priests and the difficulty of travel.

Ilave was the site of a big military training camp. One evening the commandant welcomed us for dinner, and later on we were prominent guests at his birthday celebration; we suspected that he was bored to death with his assignment in one of the more remote locations in the world. In our talks with him and his officers we gained insight into the thinking of the army leadership that has played such an important role in the history of Peru. Almost all of the officers were Caucasian and most of the soldiers were Indians who were recruited under coercion. The inauguration of President Belaude took place during our stay. He replaced a military junta which could move in again any time they did not like the new president's policies.

In Ilave, the glamour and excitement of the trip soon was replaced by my encounter with the hard realities of poverty, ignorance, and racial prejudice. Our work brought us in touch with the people, but it was still up to us to get to know them as individuals. The little kids always flocked to us as candy givers or hug providers or conveyers of affection, but it was the more restrained, suspicious teenagers whom we really hoped to impress. Many times we were forced to temper kindness with a word of admonition, lest we become the butt of jokes among the older kids.

I will always remember Peruvians like Ricardo and Alejo, the parish houseboys, who were in their twenties and still trying to get through high school. Alejo's ambition in life was to learn to drive so he would have a chance to get a chauffeur's job with some rich family. For him, this would be the pinnacle of success. Then there was Victor, a pudgy boy who constantly inquired about the price of a one-way ticket to Miami, the land of wealth and prosperity. And José, whose one ambition was to be a good basketball player—the only trouble was, he wanted to shoot long hook shots and throw behind-the-back passes before he could make a lay-up. Another volunteer and I took two kids to the circus one day and were delighted that they had the same spontaneous fun that we had when we were their age.

The thing that impressed me most in Peru was the outstanding job being done in very difficult circumstances by the priests, nuns, and Papal Volunteers. The radically different culture, the language differences, the barrenness of the terrain, the cold, the altitude all required a strong constitution and a deep faith. Some of the priests had been there as long as seventeen years. In the 1960s a new influx of missionaries from the States, Canada, and Belgium was giving some hope for revival, but the chronic and deeply rooted problems of the country meant the Church could be faced at any time with a hostile, anti-religious government.

My time in Peru was influential in shaping my view of the world and my interest in cultures different from my own. Building on what I had learned in Mexico, I became open to new experiences, adaptable in terms of living conditions and diet, appreciative of the rich diversity that constitutes the Catholic Church, reflective about America's role among nations, more aware of the culture of poverty and its malign effects, and confident that I could handle myself in facing the unexpected and the unknown. Although I developed great respect for the missionaries I met and worked with, I did not feel called to share in their type of apostolic engagement.

Tacambaro, Mexico

In the summer of 1964, after my first year in the seminary and before I went to the novitiate in Jordan, Minnesota, I returned to Mexico, not as a student participant in CILA but as a staff member. Father Hermie Reith, C.S.C., was the chaplain for our group of seventeen students. CILA was continuing to attract high-quality participants. The enthusiasm of those who had come back from the previous summers was contagious, and the spirit of the Peace Corps was very much a part of American campus life. America's culture was moving from its inward preoccupation of the post–World War II years to a new engagement with international awareness and with the obligations of an affluent society to share some of its blessings. In addition, the documents of the Second Vatican Council (1962–65) were appearing, with their upbeat orientation toward the obligations of the Church in the modern world. Many American- and European-based religious communities were sending significant numbers of missionaries to work in so-called Third World settings, especially in Latin America.

Father Reith was a philosopher by training but a tinkerer by vocation. He was fluent in several languages and his Spanish was passable. He loved to take things apart and put them together again, whether it was bicycles, motorcycles, or other mechanical devices. The problem was that he seldom completed a project, so his large work/storage room was always a mess. He also dabbled on occasion in art projects. His reputation in the community was that he was smart and well intentioned but somewhat quixotic. I wondered how he would do for a summer working with a bunch of talented but light-hearted Notre Dame undergraduates.

On our way to Mexico in an entourage of rented or donated vans and a red pickup truck, I remember urging all the participants to be especially aware of the risks of drinking tap water and consuming foods like unwashed lettuce and tomatoes. Father Reith, who had done a fair amount of international travel, pooh-poohed the notion that such caveats applied to him. It only took one more day of travel for him to be struck with the chronic diarrhea that is the bane of visitors to Mexico.

Our major work in Tacambaro was the construction of a house from the ground up for a poor family. A few Mexican construction bosses provided the expertise, and the students contributed most of the labor. Many smaller side projects were also undertaken: several of the students helped out at a local orphanage, others taught in the parish school or ran sports programs or visited homes. The group as a whole was actively involved in the worship life of the parish. The bishop of Tacambaro had invited us there, and he seemed to take great delight in our presence.

While I had to leave somewhat earlier than the rest to begin my year of novitiate, I did invest myself fully for the weeks I was there. Two experiences stand out. In the first, a group of us decided to take one of the station wagons for a brief trip to a small town on the Pacific Coast called Playa Azul (Blue Beach). The distance from Tacambaro to the Pacific was not that far as the bird flies, but it was a gut-wrenching, undercarriage-damaging journey on washboard roads. Our intention, in order to save money, was to sleep on the beach. We arrived later than we expected and the sun was already down, so we pulled in for the night to an area not far from the water. Since I was never a big camp-out guy, I decided to bed down in the back seat of the station wagon instead of outside in a sleeping bag. All of us were tired, and even though we had only a sketchy idea of where we were, we went to sleep quickly.

The next thing I knew the sun was up, and as I peered out I had a surreal sense. We were parked about 150 yards from the shoreline under a sprawling tree. The area between us and the beach was empty except at the far right corner of the waterline, where two men were walking along with long bolo knives in their right hands. They appeared to me to be serious about some business, and I began to fear they might have evil purposes in mind. As they got closer, I wondered what to do. If I yelled out to my compatriots who were still dozing, it might signal danger before they would be alert enough to defend themselves. When the men reached the spot directly across from the sleepers, I thought maybe this would be zero hour. But they continued on, oblivious to our presence, and my fears began to seem irrational. By the time everyone was awake, I barely had the courage to share my moments of anxiety with them. I learned later that men who cut bananas begin their day with the rising sun. The two men had just been peasant workers off to earn a living.

The second experience in Tacambara was an opportunity to attend my one and only cockfight. I had been having a discussion with one of the locals about the hidden side of the life of the town and he offered to take me and a couple of the others to the Friday cockfight. Without hesitation we agreed, having no idea what we might be getting into. After paying an admission fee, we walked into an enclosure with a dirt-covered floor and perhaps ten rows of stands on three sides. Guarding the entrance and standing watch inside were several soldiers in battle gear with rifles on their shoulders. Their boss, a lieutenant, sat on a raised platform with the owner of the facility; he was constantly supplied with free drinks and he became noticeably drunker as things progressed.

When the cockfighting began, we noticed that the owners went through their pre-fight rituals. Some kissed their bird or made the sign of the cross over it or sprinkled it with tequila. They placed sharp blades on the birds' claws so that the outcome would be decisive. There was a referee whose role was not entirely clear except to signal when the bout had concluded. After initial skirmishing, the birds would usually be bleeding, one more severely than the other. At this point, an owner would try to dab the bird's feathers with a wet sponge. If this did not revive it, the owner would place the bird's head in his mouth and then throw the cock back into the ring.

Some cocks won clear-cut victories and survived to fight another night. In some of the bloodier contests, neither bird was likely to have a future as a combatant and both were destroyed, even though, for betting purposes, one was declared the winner. By the end of the night I was growing increasingly restless as the spectators drank more and more beer or tequila and occasional fights broke out. I suggested to my mates that we had had our cultural experience and it was time to head home. By now it was around midnight and, as we walked through the neighborhoods, some of the local teenagers who were hanging out called us names in Spanish, insulting our mothers and suchlike. We pretended not to understand and kept walking. Like a lot of things I did when I was young, I enjoyed the raw reality of the small town cockfight for the insight it provided into facets of Mexican life that we would never have known otherwise, but I had no desire to return.

By the early 1980s, a group of CILA students had become advocates for establishing a new structure at the University—the Center for Social Concerns (CSC). By the time the CSC moved into the old WNDU building just west of the Hesburgh Library, the growth of CILA over two decades had led to a new level of service learning and social justice involvements by the University. It was a fitting climax for the dream of Father Larry Murphy and the student founders of CILA in the early 1960s.

CHAPTER 6

"SPES UNICA—THE CROSS OUR ONLY HOPE"

(THE SEMINARY YEARS)

IN AUGUST 1963 I ENTERED THE HOLY CROSS CANDIDATE program at Saint Joseph Hall—the first of my six years of preparation for final vows and ordination to the diaconate, and of the seven years until my ordination to the priesthood. I knew little about the nature of seminary life and even less about the Congregation of Holy Cross. However, I joined of my own free will, with the support of my family and friends, and with a strong sense of a calling from God.

I had enjoyed my years at Notre Dame and felt some attraction to working in higher education. Most of the Holy Cross priests and brothers I had come to know seemed like down-to-earth, happy, committed teachers, pastors, and administrators. I could imagine myself in their midst as a member of the order. I knew there was no guarantee that I would end up at Notre Dame, but serving as a diocesan priest seemed to offer fewer options and, except for the Augustinians, I did not have any firsthand experience of other religious communities. Holy Cross seemed my best option. The fact that my first stage of religious formation was to take place on the Notre Dame campus meant I would be on familiar terrain, even if I was now across Saint Joseph Lake from the heart of campus. We had been told that the candidate program was deliberately low key so that the participants would have the opportunity for vocational discernment and a smooth transition.

By the time I joined the candidate program, ninety years after the death of the order's founder, Father Basil Anthony Moreau, the community had over 2,000 members, a presence on four continents (soon to be five), and responsibilities for parishes, high schools, colleges and universities, formation programs and retreat houses in the United States and abroad. Holy Cross was actively involved in ministerial service in the United States, Canada, France, Chile, Haiti, and East Pakistan (later to be called Bangladesh). By the time I was ordained, we also had a presence in Peru, Brazil, India, Ghana, Uganda, and Kenya. I was preparing for service in a large family with a sweeping vision of its role in the Church, and I had a lot to learn.

Saint Joseph Hall (1963–64)

The candidate program for undergraduate college students and recent college graduates dated back to the closing years of World War II. The early candidates lived in undergraduate dormitories and took a regular college curriculum, supplemented by courses in Latin and philosophy. They also participated in weekend retreats and spiritual direction. Eventually, "Old College," the first building erected at Notre Dame, became the program's location, but as time went on that facility became crowded. In 1958, when the new Moreau Seminary was completed along Saint Joseph Lake, the old Moreau (its name changed to Saint Joseph Hall) became the site of the candidate program. From then on, although the number of candidates varied, the average was around forty.

As I soon discovered, the tone of a religious house, especially a house of formation, is set by the religious superior and his staff. I was fortunate to have as my first superior Father Joe Fey, C.S.C., an experienced parish priest who was strong on encouragement and inspiration and not preoccupied by rules and formal requirements. He was gentle of heart, a big baseball fan, and someone who instinctively projected the heart of the Gospel message. He treated those of us who were college graduates with respect and displayed an appropriate level of confidence in our judgment as young adults. The assistant superior was Father Len Banas, C.S.C., who taught classical languages at Notre Dame. Father Banas was a dedicated priest who regularly assisted at parishes on the weekends and who, while more reserved than Father Fey, was more familiar with the demands of higher education and more plugged into the culture of Notre Dame. Their personalities were nicely complementary.

Four other priests and two brothers also resided in the hall. The one who had the biggest influence on me during the course of the year was Father Tom Chambers, C.S.C., who became my first spiritual director. (We both became college presidents, he at Our Lady of Holy Cross in New Orleans.) The role of the spiritual director, especially for a new seminarian, is to help the candidate adjust to the rigors of a structured prayer life, to answer questions about the Church, the Congregation, and the seminary, and to assure that the directee dealt positively with the normal human emotions that go with major transitions in life. Tom Chambers has a characteristic hearty laugh and an upbeat attitude toward life, and we hit it off quickly. Generally men are wary of discussing their inner life, especially their emotions and their struggles, so the challenge for a spiritual director in a seminary is not to push too hard too fast. My relationship with Tom Chambers was helpful to me, and unlike some of my peers I did not dread the time set aside for our meetings.

As time went on, I became familiar with the two other Holy Cross formation programs on campus. The first was the minor seminary for high school students, called Holy Cross Seminary. The seniors from that house who were approved for the Novitiate would be joining those of us from Saint Joe. Some of them would have spent all four years of high school in a seminary setting. To be honest, I was never convinced that minor seminaries were a good thing. I felt they took teenagers away from normal social interactions prematurely and tended to foster immaturity and discomfort around females. Many of my peers at Saint Joe Hall had the same point of view, so we shared some trepidation about what the Novitiate would be like when we were joined by a cohort of high school seniors from Holy Cross Seminary. But the young men we would get to know a year later often were far from our stereotype of them. (Eventually, in the wake of the reforms of the Second Vatican Council, the Indiana Province elected to close the minor seminary.)

The other formation program was located in the new Moreau Seminary, a stone's throw from Saint Joe Hall on the same side of the Lake. The men in Moreau were college students who had been through the Novitiate and were under temporary vows. (In the formation period before final vows, each seminarian was approved for temporary vows of chastity, poverty, and obedience for one year at a time.) In 1963–64, there were approximately ninety seminarians at Moreau, along with a staff of thirteen. The seminarians, in addition to taking classes, dressed in habits and adhered to a fairly rigorous prayer schedule.

Most of my involvement with Moreau during that first year was through the use of its gymnasium, which was available to us when not otherwise reserved. In addition to the basketball courts, there were several handball courts and a small weight room. In the winter that was a real plus. The better athletes at Moreau knew that I had played on the Notre Dame basketball team, so they were eager to invite me and some of my colleagues to their intrahouse games. In general the Moreau seminarians, though younger than I was, seemed to consider themselves as more elite because they were under vows and had been through the Novitiate. It was as though that rigorous year of testing in Jordan, Minnesota, was tantamount to official approbation of one's vocation. If they were the Army Rangers or the Navy Seals, we were just regular grunts who were still learning the rudiments of religious life.

Our class at Saint Joseph Hall had about thirty-five participants, of whom eighteen would be approved to go to the Novitiate. Of the eighteen, seven of us were college graduates when we entered. In the social dynamics of the hall, there were no great barriers between the younger and the older among us; however, a core group of elders, all of whom were of age, used to get away to local establishments, particularly on weekends. We were accustomed to shooting the breeze over a few beers with our friends, a routine that carried over into our new circumstances. We never made a big deal about it or caused any disturbance, so the staff was tolerant of our desire to get away periodically.

When I moved to Saint Joe, I wondered if I would be drawn back to Badin Hall. As it turned out, most of my attention and interest were focused on the seminary and the new friends I was making, and on the responsibilities that went along with my new condition in life. At the same time, I and my fellow candidates participated selectively in events on the campus, where we took classes as well. At home football games we sat in the top row in the end zone above the student section. The interim coach, Hugh Devore, did not produce much of an improvement over Joe Kuharich. One of my peers at Saint Joe, Ollie Williams, knew Hugh Devore's son, so twice during that season the two of us went over to the Devore home on Friday evenings before home games, an experience that provided a more personal look at the life of a Notre Dame football coach, even a short-term one. At home basketball games it was an odd feeling not to be on the team myself. As it happened, that was Coach Jordan's last year as head coach.

Our time at Saint Joseph Hall began and ended with a retreat. The regular schedule included morning prayer before breakfast, mass in the late afternoon, and evening prayer after dinner. Compared to the later years of formation, it was a relatively light level of formal prayer, but for us it was far more than we were accustomed to. We also had times of special devotion: praying the rosary, doing the Stations of the Cross, and attending holy hour. Once a month we met with our spiritual director, and we went to confession regularly.

Periodically Father Fey or one of the staff led a conference on some pertinent topic about the Church, the Congregation, or the Novitiate. Several members of our group could play the guitar, so the music for our worship was better than it would have been otherwise. Nevertheless, in an era when Gregorian chant was still popular in community prayer, Father Bill McAuliffe, C.S.C., had the responsibility of teaching us the rudiments of chant and how to read the musical notation that goes with it. These exercises were the subject of endless humor and mockery. The seminary system we were preparing to enter after our candidate year had changed little since the reforms of the Council of Trent in the sixteenth century. The main intellectual development had been the adoption of scholastic philosophy as articulated by Saint Thomas Aquinas, which was intended as a synthesis of the best of human and divine wisdom. Mass and the other sacraments were celebrated in Latin, so we were expected to gain a competency in that language, and the college graduates among us took basic courses in Latin that year. Because philosophy was seen as a necessary preparation for the study of theology, the same group took courses in philosophy too. I was an earnest student, but I found both types of courses less than stimulating, and that judgment was shared by most of my peers. We were not learning the disciplines for their own sake but because someone had determined it was necessary.

Because of my low level of enthusiasm for a relatively light load of required courses, I read widely in other fields. One day I was carrying around a copy of Erich Fromm's *The Art of Loving*, which is a beautiful treatise on love by a Swiss psychoanalyst, when one of the staff members inquired whether I was reading salacious literature. He was embarrassed when he found out what the book was really about.

While changes were taking place gradually on campus during the 1963–64 academic year, developments were taking place externally that would revolutionize both the Church and the seminary system within it. When Pope John XXIII summoned the Second Vatican Council in 1962, few even of the Council fathers realized what their three years of meetings would lead to. Each year of my formation was progressively more shaped by the Council, its documents, and the ensuing debates about their implementation. Change was also happening in the sphere of American government and culture. The assassination of President John F. Kennedy on November 22, 1963, was the first of what would become a sequence of public killings that eventually included Malcolm X, Martin Luther King, Jr., and Robert Kennedy. The civil rights movement, the anti–Vietnam War movement, and other protests led to rioting in the streets and profound social changes.

I was in one of the house cars picking up another candidate, Tom Smith, at the dentist's when I heard the first radio reports of the shooting of President Kennedy. We rushed back to the hall and, like the rest of the country and the world, we watched events unfold on TV almost non-stop for days. The only times we broke away were for prayer and meals, since University classes had been cancelled for the mourning period. Since Kennedy was a Catholic, most of us had been deeply inspired by his leadership, eloquence, and charm. He was one of us. In a sense our decisions to enter the seminary were connected to his appeal to "ask what you can do for your country." Whether it was the Peace Corps or the inner city or the seminary, it was a time when the young were seeking to make a difference. The summers I had spent in Latin America were, for me, a concrete connection to the rhetoric of the Kennedy era. But now, after his shocking death, our generation was learning firsthand about the reality of evil and the capacity of human agents to thwart even the best-motivated plans. That

November, none of us recognized that a decisive change had taken place in American life. We simply mourned with the nation and the world, and admired Jackie and her two children for the way that they handled themselves right through to the burial in Arlington National Cemetery.

One of our members was an older candidate for the brothers who seemed to possess about every idiosyncrasy one could imagine. He was ascetic looking, wedded to strange forms of piety, prone to dress oddly, and utterly devoted to helping out in the sacristy. For me, he embodied everything I feared I might find in the seminary, and to my pleasant surprise it quickly became clear that the seminary staff had the same misgivings. Long before the end of the year, they let the young man know that his future lay elsewhere. It was my first lesson in the old saw of religious life: "Many may feel called, but not all are chosen." Next to this unfortunate candidate, the rest of us felt rather normal. Every seminary cohort can pray that at least one among them is manifestly unacceptable.

Every group needs a class wit and humorist as well. In Saint Joseph Hall, an insightful individual named Ray helped the rest of us keep our sense of perspective when times got tough (like February in northern Indiana). He was somewhat overweight and a master imitator; he could do knock-down impressions of the seminary staff. A passably good student, he had the courage to say publicly what most of us thought about the academic quality of classes designed especially for seminarians. Ray never made it to ordination, but he was a prized part of our social network during that first year.

Our group had a pretty good distribution of athletic talent. Among our informal activities in the fall were touch football games. Tom Stella had been a highly regarded quarterback in high school, so he usually ran one team and I led the other. Our main offensive strategy was to throw long bombs on just about every play. The final scores were high, but the competition was intense. For me, as for many of us, athletic participation was a key to surviving the seminary years. I had been accustomed to several hours of exercise daily all through my teen years; when deprived of it, I felt logy and antsy. Little things got exaggerated and my coping skills were diminished. The same was true of the group dynamic; when we exercised together we felt a closer bond and were more tolerant of each other's failings. And athletics provided something to look forward to that was not imposed upon us.

On December 14, 1963, the University announced that Ara Parseghian had been hired away from Northwestern as the new football coach. Because Northwestern under his leadership had beaten Notre Dame several times, there was a great enthusiasm for the appointment. At a spontaneous pep rally that took place immediately after the press conference, the Fieldhouse was crawling with students and media representatives. After Joe Kuharich's four years, hopes were high and everyone was dreaming that Ara would wake up the echoes. Handsome, well spoken, modest, enthusiastic, and full of energy, Ara immediately won the hearts of fans. Little did he realize how demanding his new responsibilities would be, and little did I realize how much my future life would be connected to the fortunes of the football program.

By the end of my first semester at Saint Joseph Hall, the Vatican Council had approved the *Constitution on Sacred Liturgy*, which began the process of liturgical changes that would be the most obvious result of the Council to the average parishioner. It also approved the *Dogmatic Constitution on the Church* (*Lumen Gentium*), which would begin a new phase of theological reflection about the very nature of the Church. As a seminarian, most of my access to the debates among the Council fathers was through the writing of Xavier Rynne (a pseudonym for Father Francis X. Murphy, a Redemptorist priest) in *The New Yorker* magazine. Rynne regaled his readers with behind-the-scenes information, with the good guys (the reformers) against the bad guys (the traditionalists). Because the outcome was always in doubt and I was clearly on the side of the reformers, the three years of Council deliberations were full of drama for me. By the time the work of the Council was done in 1964, I knew instinctively that the Church in which I was preparing to serve as a priest would be significantly different from the one I had grown up in. For me, this was a source of great hope and expectation. I wanted to be one of the agents of change. Yet I also knew that the transition would not take place in a year or two, and I suspected that seminary life might be among the last facets to feel the impact of the Council's new vision.

That year also saw the publication of Betty Friedan's *The Feminine Mystique*, which offered a critical interpretation of women's subordinate place in American society and became a rallying point for a sometimes harsh national debate about gender, domestic roles in the family, equality of opportunity in the workplace, and related matters. This secular discussion inevitably carried over into the life of the Church, where religious women were the bulwark of the Catholic school system as well as its health care systems and social service agencies. Yet women were excluded by gender from eligibility for the priesthood. Here too, ideas percolating in those years would influence both the world and the Church.

In our candidate year, we wore no distinctive dress. Most of the time we were indistinguishable from other students at the University. Since we were new to the Congregation, someone recommended for each of us to befriend one of the retired priests in Holy Cross House, the Indiana Province's health care and retirement home on campus. That seemed like a good idea, so I met about once a month with Father Matt Schumaker, C.S.C., who must have been in his eighties. He was a kind, gentle priest who enjoyed sharing stories about his ministry years and some of the humorous incidents he had experienced. He was a grandfather figure to me. Among the staff of Saint Joseph Hall were three Holy Cross brothers who normally were engaged in some form of manual labor. In 1948 when Holy Cross divided into two societies, one for priests and one for teaching brothers, some of the brothers asked to stay with the priest's society. This was a highly controversial matter among the teaching brothers, since they thought It relegated the coadjutor brothers to a subordinate status within the priests' society. But by the time I joined Holy Cross, the debate was a historical curiosity because the coadjutor brothers were held in high regard by the priests and even more so by the seminarians.

At Saint Joseph Hall one brother was responsible for the kitchen (the candidates helped out with meal preparation, serving, and cleanup); one oversaw the maintenance and cleanliness of the building; and one kept the grounds in good order, including snow removal. Each of us was expected to work on one of the crews under the supervision of the appropriate brother. Their word was final, but generally they were tolerant of our ineptness in domestic tasks and the use of mechanical equipment. Cleaning the bathrooms and doing the dishes were our least favorite tasks. One of my jobs was to clean the room of Father Ralph Fisher, C.S.C., the vocation director. He was a several-pack-a-day smoker, so the biggest challenge was removing all the cigarette butts. He was also a great storyteller (only a certain percentage of which turned out to be true), and when he was working in his room and I came by to clean up, I spent more time listening to his tales than wielding my rags and brushes. He did not seem to mind.

At the end the year I received approval to become a novice in August 1964 in Jordan, Minnesota. The feedback I had received during the year was generally positive. I really liked most of my peers who were approved to go to the Novitiate, and I looked forward to taking on the challenges of what some described as "religious life boot camp." As for those among us who had left of their own volition or were not approved to continue in Holy Cross, we wished one another well as we went our separate ways. I would eventually learn that saying goodbye to friends and peers is one of the hardest dimensions of community life. It was doubly painful in the Novitiate year when no announcement was made ahead of time and there was no opportunity to say goodbye.

Sacred Heart Novitiate, Jordan, Minnesota (1964–65)

All learned professions have some defined period of preparation during which a candidate learns the essential elements of the practice and is reviewed on a regular basis by those who have distinguished themselves through long service. At the end there is usually a formal evaluation and, if one is thought worthy of acceptance, some public ratification and certification. Thus it is in medicine, law, accounting, and education, as well as firefighting, police work, plumbing, and optometry. It should not be surprising that both religious life and priestly ministry in the Catholic Church require a period of structured formation.

The nature and length of this requirement has varied considerably in the history of the Church. At the time that I was admitted to the Indiana Province of Holy Cross, the expectation for a college graduate was a year of candidacy (Saint Joseph Hall), a year of Novitiate (Minnesota), a year of further preparation (Moreau Seminary), three years of theology (Holy Cross College in Washington, the Foreign Mission Seminary, or Rome), and a deacon year (same as the theology site). One would be eligible for final vows after the completion of the three years of theology, with the final-vows ceremony usually taking place the day before ordination to the diaconate. The effect of this sequence meant that for most college graduates there was a seven-year gap between admission and ordination to the priesthood. For those who entered the congregation at a younger age, the formation period would be even longer.

The Novitiate year was sometimes compared to the Jews wandering for forty years in the desert before reaching the Promised Land, or to Jesus going into the desert for forty days to prepare for his public ministry. The Novitiate, I was told, was intended to be a time of intense preparation for the religious life, with a rigorous prayer schedule, regular manual labor, a reduced study load, rather severe rules regulating the common life, and constant scrutiny by the Novitiate staff. While we would be part of a cohort, each of us would be evaluated as individuals for our capacity and readiness to live a vowed life. If everything went well, we would commit ourselves to living under the vows of poverty, chastity, and obedience for one year, with an opportunity to apply for renewal of temporary vows each year until we were eligible for final vows. Prior to taking the vows, we could leave the Novitiate of our own volition at any time or be asked to leave if we were thought unworthy or incapable of living the religious life.

When I became a novice I was twenty-three years old, 6'3½" tall, 190 pounds, with an undergraduate degree in English. I had a reasonably good grounding in catechism and basic Catholic theology, and I was familiar with various forms of Catholic piety, from recitation of the rosary to the Stations of the Cross, from the Miraculous Medal Novena to First Friday devotions. As an undergraduate at Notre Dame I attended mass daily and I went to confession with normal frequency. I believed in God, in the essential proclamations of the Creed, and in the Catholic Church as an instrument of God's grace active in the world. While I had my share of weaknesses and sins, I was excited to be responding to the sense of a call from Christ. My year at Saint Joseph Hall had gone quickly and my exposure to Holy Cross, to seminary life, and to my peer group had all been positive. I expected all of this to be characteristic of my Novitiate time as well.

In the middle of August 1964, I drove with my parents to Jordan, Minnesota. It took us two days to get there, but my parents and I knew it was a major point of transition in my life and in my relationship to them, so we relished the opportunity to talk in the car. We knew that during the Novitiate year there was no vacation time and no provision for visits home. We could write home and receive mail, but our letters would be read by the Novice Master before being passed along (a practice that I interpreted right from the start as medieval and offensive). Even telephone calls home were reserved for emergencies and only with permission. It was intended to be an entire year apart, free from such distractions of contemporary life as radio, television, movies, newspapers, trips to the mall, and even family.

We arrived at the Novitiate in time for a welcoming ceremony at which the Novice Master greeted the families, thanked them for giving their sons to Holy Cross, invited them to share a meal, and then explained the opening liturgy when each of us would receive our habit, office book, and other materials for the coming year. Since the Novitiate building was already overcrowded and there was no room for guests, after the opening mass we had to say goodbye to parents and family members. For me, after the long drive from D.C., the farewell was almost anticlimactic. One moment the Novitiate was full of guests, the next moment all that was left were two classes of novices and the staff. It would not be the last dramatic change I would experience that day, that week, or that year.

Thirty-one novices were professed the day after our arrival (twenty-seven clerical candidates and four brother candidates). In our class there were twenty-seven novices (twenty-six clerical candidates and one brother candidate). For a week, the two groups lived together so the departing group could acquaint the new contingent with the physical layout, the schedule of the common life, the manual labor responsibilities, and the insider details that create a culture and a distinctive manner of interaction. Then the newly professed went off to Land O'Lakes, Wisconsin, for a vacation period in the outdoor camp run by Notre Dame in the wilds along the Wisconsin-Michigan border.

The first reality of Novitiate life was wearing a habit from morning arrival in chapel until retiring to one's room after night prayer. The only exceptions were work details, recreation, and trips into town (usually for medical visits or to pick up supplies for the house). It was easier to wear a distinctive outfit in the hothouse environment of the Novitiate because everyone else did and no one else was around, but right from the start I found the collar uncomfortable, especially in the heat of summer, and I never got used to wearing this form of dress. I did what I was expected to do but never with enthusiasm. Years later,

"Spes Unica—The Cross Our Only Hope"

when the reforms of Vatican II began to click in, I was pleased to be able to abandon the habit, including the distinctive Holy Cross cape, cord, and cross, since I aspired to be closer in clothing and style to the people I was serving than the distinctive religious garb seemed to allow.

The second reality of Novitiate life that required a real adjustment was the rule of silence. This was not just silence in the chapel or after we retired for the evening, it was a pervasive dimension of much of daily life. We were expected to refrain from all conversation except when we were given permission to talk; this was true in the corridors, in our work assignments, and even for all or parts of meals. At breakfast one of the novices read from a book chosen by the Novice Master, and this reading continued through part of the evening meal, though at lunch we were free to talk. Since meals are normally times to share the events of the day, the imposition of silence during meals was particularly alien. We had to learn hand signals to ask our tablemates to pass the salt. Squeezing the hand like milking a cow was the sign for milk. Simulating pouring from a kettle was the sign for tea.

The rationale behind the rule of silence was connected to the monastic tradition that the individual should have time for personal prayer and reflection. We were supposed to develop skill in meditative and spiritual practices as well as in the public prayer of the Church. Many retreat houses and centers of prayer are known for their pervasive quiet. I have made retreats at Trappist monasteries and silence was part of the attraction in going there. But in the Novitiate context, the rule of silence was not freely chosen as a way to step away from the busyness of life; it was an expectation that affected, for better or worse, every aspect of the social dynamic, especially for a group of energetic young men between eighteen and thirty.

I did not have too much difficulty keeping silent for much of the prescribed time, but I found it counterproductive to have so many of my peers preoccupied with either scrupulously keeping the letter of the law or only observing it when the staff was around. One result of the rule was an unhealthy limitation on sharing the experiences of the year as they unfolded. One-on-one sharing with personal friends was discouraged under the guise of the threat of "particular friendships" (or the fear there might be a sexual component in such relationships).

A third feature of the Novitiate was the absence of intellectual and creative stimulation. As someone who had been going to school nonstop for seventeen years, I welcomed a change of pace. However I quickly discovered that it was not classroom learning and tests and papers that I missed, it was the exposure to new ideas, the joy of reading and movie-watching, and the exposure to the debates going on in society and the Church over civil rights, women's rights, social justice, and ecclesial reform. We had no access to newspapers, radio, or television (except if we happened to be cleaning the staff recreation room or taking out the trash, and then it was mainly headlines that we glimpsed). Occasionally the Novice Master would make reference to some major event in the world or in the Church, but usually with no context-setting commentary. It was as if we had moved to an alien planet. I did not then, and still do not, consider such extreme isolation as necessary.

The classes we took revolved around the religious life, the history and Constitutions of the Congregation of Holy Cross, various approaches to spirituality, and some of the mechanics of praying the Office or singing Gregorian chant. No tests were given and the expectation was that we would learn what we needed to because we had nowhere else to go. I was aware that I had much to absorb, yet I found the class sessions boring and mainly inconsequential. Much of it I could have grasped better by reading a couple of books.

There was a small library at the Novitiate that we were encouraged to use. Much of the collection was made up of books on spirituality and the lives of the saints, outdated church histories, and material connected to the history of Holy Cross. I had a difficult time finding anything of interest. Finally, I decided to read in order the circular letters of the Superior Generals of the Congregation, from Moreau on—a sign of my sense of intellectual deprivation. Yet I did learn quite a bit about the concerns and administrative styles of the top leaders of Holy Cross, and what issues they thought important enough to address in letters to the whole Congregation. I also wrote some poetry; it was one method of expressing my feelings and coming to grips with the daily life in a community of forty men. The poems tended to be highly introspective, convoluted, and fraught with a deep emotional tone that rendered them inaccessible to others.

Much of our time was taken up with manual labor, especially with work on the small farm that we sustained. Brother Clarence Breitenbach, C.S.C., was the manager of the farm and the overseer of most of our outside activity. He had been raised on a farm and quickly won our trust. He was salt of the earth, a friendly, manly, holy guy, and we saw him as personifying the best of religious life. The main problem he had with us was the fact that most of us were city slickers, or at best suburbanites who may have laid sod or operated a lawn mower. In other words, he had little raw talent to work with. We learned *en masse* how to plant and harvest crops, tend and pick strawberries, potatoes, cucumbers, and tomatoes, hoe weeds, oil machinery, clean out barns, bale hay, transport crops to market, and otherwise keep busy during an abbreviated workday, according to the agricultural weather cycle of central Minnesota.

For whatever reason, Brother Clarence put me in charge of one of the work crews. It was his wont to give general instructions and send you on your way. He figured you would either ask questions or learn the hard way. Most of the time that was well and good, especially on the smaller projects. It might be tedious and uncomfortable to pick strawberries when they are ripe, but almost anyone could figure out how to do it. But it was exceedingly difficult to plow a field in a straight line with a tractor. First of all, the ground is not as level as it appears, and second, it is a challenge to make the turn at the end of a row. I now have great admiration for farmers when I drive along interstates and see perfectly straight lines of corn or soybeans.

One embarrassing moment occurred because of Brother Clarence's confidence in me. On different occasions in the spring he sent me out to sow corn or soybeans, which was done by driving the tractor with appropriate seed dispensers along the plowed fields. Later when the crops emerged, Brother Clarence discovered to his consternation and mine that I had mistakenly planted corn and soybeans on top of each other in one large plot, and they were choking each other in their quest for water and nourishment. All I could say was "sorry," but I was sure that his opinion of my competence suffered a big setback.

Another major form of work was supervised by Brother Raymond Boudreaux, C.S.C., a Southerner from Louisiana who tended to the interior maintenance of the facility and the laundry room. He was a great storyteller, and since he had a ready audience he did not hesitate to share his philosophy of life, his insights into religious life, and details from his autobiography. He was our best source for digests of news from the outside world, which he passed on with idiosyncratic commentary.

Laundry work was basic and straightforward. There was a task, a method to attain a desirable outcome, and a finished product. Just like work on the farm, being part of the laundry crew made us feel like we were getting something worthwhile achieved. But it was the other main jobs under Brother Raymond's purview that represented the worst of Novitiate make-work experience. The first was tuck-pointing the exterior walls of the buildings. This involved using a file and a hammer to clear away the mortar between the bricks up to about two or three inches deep so new mortar could be applied. Sometimes it involved erecting scaffolding for access to the upper levels of the building. Tuck-pointing might have made sense if we had not discovered that previous generations of novices had worked on the same exterior surfaces. Like slave laborers everywhere, we soon realized there was no reason to rush our activity. With an infinite number of bits of mortar to be chiseled away, lollygagging became the order of the day. There was always tomorrow or the next day.

The other thankless job that Brother Raymond oversaw was the constant scrubbing and polishing of the linoleum floors in the corridors of the main building. By their nature these surfaces constantly absorbed dirt and mud and gum and other substances, which meant that the floor crew was constantly scraping and laying down wax and buffing with a large, unwieldy machine. It was the ultimate make-work engagement.

The third brother on the Novitiate staff was Brother Walter Henning, C.S.C., who was responsible for the preparation of meals and the upkeep of the kitchen and dining area. His crew of novices had limited experience with cooking or meal planning, which meant Brother Walter had a lot of gofers but not many reliable assistants. On the other hand, as in prisons, military messes, and other institutional settings, the expectations of the people being fed were not all that high. They wanted hearty, filling food and a lot of it, and that was what Brother Walter provided.

One of the disciplines at the Novitiate was not to eat between meals except on special occasions. That was when I first learned the term "carbona," which in Holy Cross speech meant goodies such as cakes, candies, and ice cream that were brought out for moments of celebration or sometimes simply to break the routine. Carbona included cigarettes (and sometimes cigars), which were still considered a reward for good behavior at that time. I was never a smoker, so this bonus had no impact on me.

Our Novice Master was Father Daniel Farley Curtin, C.S.C. He was a man of medium height and build with dark hair and a stern visage who was wedded to the Rule. Over the course of the year he seemed to me to be the ultimate organization man—I doubted that he ever had an independent thought. He was not tyrannical or sadistic, and he did not prowl the grounds looking for trouble, but he treated all matters brought to his attention with a maximum of legal conformity and a minimum of personal interpretation. He ran a tight ship. The three priests on the staff took turns celebrating mass and preaching, but Father Curtin had the superior's prerogative in leading all of the most important liturgies. He was a methodical rather than an inspirational preacher. His conferences were heavy on facts and instruction and low on context-setting and theological depth.

The role of the Novice Master in a religious community is a difficult one indeed. Because of the isolated setting and the mix of instructional and evaluative roles, it can be a lonely responsibility. No one who accepts it can know what issues will arise in a given year—how many will be part of the novice class, how many will persevere, or how they will do in their remaining years of formation and beyond. Father Curtin also had to deal with what, to his eyes, were cataclysmic changes in the Catholic Church. Of the twenty-seven novices we started with, twenty finished, not too far from what might have been predicted before the year began. In the following year, however, rapid change was coming in every area of Church life and all the taken-for-granted practices and traditions were being called into question. The novice class that year basically went into revolt, and Father Curtin did not make it through the year.

He never fully recovered from that trauma. For a while he was on sabbatical, then he helped out at a parish in Michigan. Eventually he left the community and the priesthood in order to marry—not because of any liberal advocacy of changes in Church teachings or ecclesial practice, but because, as he saw it, the Church that he knew had disappeared. It was a sad ending for a man who had done his best at what had become an impossible task.

The other two priests on the Novitiate staff were Father George Schidel, C.S.C., and Father Sal Fanelli, C.S.C. Father Schidel was my spiritual director, and in my meetings with him I felt I was in the company of a wise, experienced man of faith who could keep me focused on fundamental things. Father Fanelli was in his eighties, retired from parish work, and proud of his Italian heritage. Somehow or other he had kept a record of how many marriages, baptisms, confessions, and masses he had officiated during his priestly career. His main role at the Novitiate was to offer Christ's unconditional forgiveness no matter what kinds of sin one might have fallen into. I suspect that we could have told him that we had just murdered another novice and he would have told us that God loved us and we should say our penance and go be a good boy.

There were a number of reasons why Jordan, Minnesota, was a bad site for a novitiate. The first was the topography. In the back was a large swamp, a foul-smelling place full of mosquitoes during the rainy season and the cyclical presence of large black flies and other pesky insects. Adjacent to the front entrance was a single track for a railroad line that ran passenger trains several times a day, sometimes in the middle of prayer. A second liability was the weather. Minnesota has hot, humid, brief summers and brutally long, extremely cold winters. During our year in Jordan we experienced fifty below-zero days, and one day the thermometer bottomed out at minus 24 degrees. In the worst part of winter, the book *With God in Russia*, by Walter Ciszek, S J , was assigned to be read at meals. The book recounted Father Ciszek's experience as a religious prisoner in a Siberian gulag. His story is an inspiring one of faith and courage, but what we remembered was the day by day account of surviving on the outdoor chain gang, crushing large rocks while the temperatures sank to minus 20 or 30. It was as if we were with him in his quest for survival. In both Russia and Minnesota the weather was cold enough to crush the human spirit.

While the weather was bitter most of the winter, it usually did not snow as much as in northern Indiana. But in my Novitiate year, the whole Upper Midwest had unusual amounts of snow, and when the spring thaw came we were swamped by floods. The Mississippi River backed up into its tributaries and our property had to be evacuated, even though it was a mile and a half from the river. Most of the novices moved temporarily to a Jesuit novitiate about ten miles away. Brother Clarence and four novices, including me, stayed behind to keep the power plant sandbagged. We slept on the top floor of the residence building and had sufficient food and water supplies to make it until the water receded. In some ways it was a lark, since we gained semi-heroic status among our peers and it was a welcome break from Novitiate routine. Jordan, Minnesota, was not Egypt, but sometimes we felt like we were afflicted with the ten plagues of punishment.

One interesting twist at the end of the year was that all fifteen of the men who had come from Saint Joseph Hall were professed, but only five out of the twelve from Holy Cross Seminary. The withdrawal rate from the high school seminary cohort was always high, and our year was no exception. Of the twenty who made it through the Novitiate, eight would eventually be ordained—six from Saint Joseph Hall and two from Holy Cross Seminary.

The rhythm of Novitiate life was greatly determined by the prayer schedule. Rising was at five o'clock in the morning (an assigned person walked through the corridors ringing a bell and chanting a morning greeting in Latin, to which we were to respond *Deo Gratias*). At five twenty-five we had morning prayer followed by community mass. After silent breakfast and housework, we returned to the chapel for lauds. The rest of the morning was taken up with conferences, classes, or study.

Before lunch we had particular examen (a brief period of self-evaluation). Lunch was at noon, followed by recreation. Then we returned to the chapel for a visit to the Blessed Sacrament and the public chanting of the canonical hours—terce, sext, and none. We worked for two hours on one of the indoor or outdoor crews. After showering, there was a thirty-minute study period, then meditation in the chapel and the recitation of vespers and compline.

Supper took place at six o'clock and usually began with public reading of the assigned book until the Novice Master rang the bell.

"Spes Unica—The Cross Our Only Hope"

Then we could talk for the remainder of the meal. The novices took turns doing the meal readings and mistakes in pronunciation or understanding were not uncommon, usually to the amusement of the novices and a public chiding from the Master. After awhile, most of us paid hardly any attention to the readings, which tended to be either boring or excessively pious. After supper there was a recreation period followed by spiritual reading in the chapel, rosary, litany, and night prayer. We were expected to be in bed for sure by nine thirty.

This basic schedule had exceptions. On Tuesdays in the late afternoon, we had a half hour of singing practice (not one of my favorite events) followed by the opportunity for confession. Sundays brought a later rising time (five thirty instead of five), morning office in private, and hours of recreation in the afternoon. The recreation periods were much prized and provided something to look forward to. Our novice group was fairly athletic, so we organized competitions according to the season. We played touch football and softball in the fall and spring, and hockey on an outdoor rink in the winter. We had no basketball court, so my favorite endeavor was not available. The hockey games were the most physical since it was often quite cold and that was one way of keeping warm. I had not developed skating proficiency, and though I could propel myself from one end of the rink to the other with the puck in tow, I could not stop myself, which meant that I characteristically crashed into the snow banks behind the nets.

The recitation of the Office in Latin was a fairly large component of our daily prayer life. The Office was composed of a mix of psalms, readings from Scripture, hymns, and traditional prayers. The Office book itself was rather complicated to the uninitiated because its organization had to take into account the liturgical season and special feast days. One of the skills in using the book was figuring out where to place the different colored ribbons in order to flip easily from section to section. Some of the other prayer practices of the Novitiate were familiar to me—praying the rosary, reading spiritual texts, benediction, morning and night prayer. What I had never heard of before was the Chapter of Accusation.

This weekly period on Friday nights focused on violations of the Rule that guided our life as novices, not on matters that would be brought into confession. Violations were publicly acknowledged in the chapel before the Novice Master, the staff, and the novice community. Each Friday three or four novices were invited to come forward and participate. I always found this exercise particularly objectionable because it either promoted scrupulosity or it tempted us to go through the motions in rather trivial fashion. Some of the misbehavior that novices would acknowledge (including the number of times) included not cleaning our rooms on time, showing up late for prayer, work, or meals, talking in times of silence, walking too fast, custody of the eyes (for example, watching planes fly overhead while working outdoors), imitating the idiosyncrasies of the staff or fellow novices, and other such matters. After each novice had accused himself, the Novice Master assigned a penance.

My interactions with Father Curtin over the year were rather formal. Several times he gave me feedback and asked how I was doing. I tried to be honest but only up to a point. I am sure he knew that I did not find the overall structure of the Novitiate formation to my liking, but I was faithful to the essentials. What I refused to do was accept the minutiae the hothouse existence imposed on us—things I doubted had anything to do with what I aspired to become as an apostle and priest. My most disappointing encounter with Father Curtin had to do with the way he conducted business. His office was rather small and far from soundproof. This created a situation where private conversations were almost impossible. This was regrettable.

In the all-male environment of the Novitiate in that era, there was an overarching concern about structuring the common life to deal with potential manifestations of homosexual inclination. Sexuality as a topic was treated in our classes only in passing, and that included the

"Spes Unica—The Cross Our Only Hope"

discussion of celibacy. The fact that half of our novice class had come directly from a minor seminary meant that they had not dated or been in coeducational environments very much. Nevertheless, they were human beings and they had to deal in their own ways with their need for friendship, love, and affection. Although those of us who were college graduates were older and presumably more mature, most of us had attended Notre Dame when it was all male, and our social life tended to have been limited as well. At the Novitiate I first learned the term "particular friendship." This sort of relationship was frowned upon because it might lead to something untoward as, at times in the past, it may actually have done. But the opposite of "particular friendship" was not intended to be "no friendships" or "no close friendships," and unfortunately that was sometimes the consequence. So as a result of an overreaction to occasional problems, the formation system was fostering a style of community interaction that was either large-group oriented or inclined to an unusual degree of privacy and potential loneliness.

Unlike military boot camp or male locker rooms in high school and college, the novices were taught to fear male nudity even in the most harmless of situations. We were instructed to wear a robe in our rooms or in the shower area when we were dressing, so that no one who saw us would be tempted or vice-versa. This required a certain agility, not to mention some wonderment about the reason why it was necessary.

Except at the beginning of the year and at its completion, I do not remember any women whatsoever being present on the Novitiate property. It made us into a self-sufficient all-male community, affecting the daily dynamics among us and setting the tone for the style of life we expected to find in future religious community settings. It would be a few more years before this type of exclusivity would be called into question, not only in religious settings but in the broader life of the Catholic community.

At the end of our Novitiate we had a retreat to prepare for the taking of first vows. For me, this was one of the highlights of the year, since it was an opportunity for focused reflection on the essential elements of the religious life and the vows to which we were preparing to commit ourselves. I felt prepared to move on, and I was pleased that the majority of my novice class would be doing the same.

The new novices arrived the day before we were to take first vows. The incoming class had forty-three members, and we recognized from the start that it was not only large in size but also full of expectations that the debates of theory and practice underway in the wake of Vatican II would have a quick impact on the structure of Novitiate life. For them, the Novitiate year would be full of such turmoil that the Province had to rethink the whole nature of the Novitiate before the following class began its formation. Of the forty-three who entered, eight would go on to be ordained and one would take final vows as a brother.

Moreau Seminary (1965–66)

One of the members of our successor class was Al Goodrich, a good friend with whom I had spent time in Latin America. Before my class left for vacation camp at Land O'Lakes, Wisconsin, I promised Al I would write him periodically, and toward the end of the first week at camp I wrote a long letter that included some comments about being an agent for change and not taking the petty things too seriously. Unfortunately, Father John Burke, C.S.C., the assistant superior at Moreau Seminary and the director of the camp, decided to open my letter and read it—something I had no idea he would do. He informed me that he had sent the letter to the Provincial, Father Howard Kenna, C.S.C., with whom I would have to meet when we returned to Notre Dame. The whole second week at camp I shared my dilemma and concern with my best friends and we were all worried about the potential outcome. After surviving Jordan, I did not want to get kicked out of the community for something stupid like a letter.

When I arrived at Moreau Seminary, I had a note informing me of an appointment with Father Kenna at the Provincial House. I dutifully drove there and was ushered into his office. Father Kenna had an odd body type—a long torso and short legs—and he was about the same height sitting down as he was standing up. His nickname was "Yahweh," since he evoked the same admiration and response as God did. He welcomed me, made reference to the letter, and told me he had not looked at it since he did not like the practice of intercepting personal mail. He added that he heard I was of a reformist disposition when it came to religious life. He acknowledged that after Vatican II many changes would be coming but stressed that it was important that change be done the right way. He encouraged me to be thoughtful about being an advocate and not to get too far ahead of the curve. With that he congratulated me for receiving first vows and bid me adieu. On my drive back, I was grateful for Father Kenna's understanding and even more eager to have a good year at Moreau.

Through the years that Father Kenna was Provincial, many members of Holy Cross left the community and/or the priesthood (it was happening everywhere in the Church), and that was a source of great pain for him. Yet he remained a compassionate and understanding man who was much beloved. After I was ordained and had finished graduate school, I was invited to be a member of the Provincial Council. Father Kenna was also appointed to the Council and we used to sit next to each other at meetings. We felt a special bond, and he knew how appreciative I was that he had treated me so kindly after the incident at Land O'Lakes. When Father Kenna died and was buried in the community cemetery, the turnout was large, including many who had left the Congregation. I thought it was a great testimony to the man who looked like God and who learned during his priestly career to treat everyone with respect and tenderness.

If I had entered the seminary in college and thereby lived under vows before graduation, I most likely would have gone directly from the Novitiate to one of our theologates. Instead, I was now back on the Notre Dame campus at Moreau Seminary. But because Moreau was primarily a college seminary, the course of studies I was to take was largely designed from scratch. I was told I had to take another course in Latin to better prepare for the study of theology the following year. I had taken four philosophy classes as an undergraduate (the Notre Dame norm at the time) and six philosophy classes at Saint Joseph Hall, so I was relatively well prepared in that area. All the philosophy courses that I took at Notre Dame, however, were Thomist in orientation; other approaches to philosophy only appeared in order to be exposed as inadequate or subjected to extensive critique. It was still a time when Catholic intellectual life was seen as an integrated synthesis, with philosophy as propaedeutic to theology (i.e., as a foundation for but subordinate to theology—the study of God).

In Latin class, motivation was even lower than in philosophy. Since Latin was still the language of liturgy, and in some places in the study of theology, priests were expected to have a basic reading competence in it. But all of us knew that the Mass and the other sacraments would soon be celebrated in the vernacular, and that all theology in the States was taught in English. The one remaining argument was that those who wanted to do doctoral work in theology or canon law needed to read Latin well. However, the quality of the language courses available to us were far from that kind of long-range ministerial self-awareness.

The Indiana Province academic advisor that year was Father Ed O'Connor, C.S.C., a theologian of decidedly conservative orientation. His religious worldview was unchanging and he was inclined to have the seminarians receive the same kind of formation that he had received. I was honored that he saw me as someone with potential for doctoral work, as I had been hoping to begin possible graduate work in English. Nevertheless, he recommended that I and some of my postgrad peers sit in on a graduate course in philosophy offered by Charles De Koninck, a Canadian scholastic philosopher. Professor De Koninck operated at the blackboard in four languages as he expounded on Aristotle's *De Anima*, and most of the time I had no idea what he was talking about. Furthermore, I was not sure I was interested enough to try to figure it out. In the second semester I was coerced into auditing a course by Charles De Koninck's son, Thomas, a class which was equally arcane.

Eventually, Father O'Connor agreed to allow me to sign up for graduate English courses. Meanwhile, my intellectual life at Moreau was sustained by everything I was reading on my own initiative. The Novitiate had been such a vacuum in terms of mental stimulation that I was excited to catch up with national, world, and Church events. I began to read fiction again on my own, and to explore theological materials that were relevant to the debates about how the Council should be implemented. There was hardly any area of Church life or practice where a theologian, or theological grouping, was not proposing some rethinking or reorientation, and to me it was quite exciting. I felt like I was on the cusp of some major breakthrough that would radically transform the Church that I was preparing to serve.

Being back on campus was a real plus in the sense of exposure to the intellectual, social, and athletic events that I had been accustomed to before my year in the Novitiate. However, my circumstances had changed now that I was a professed religious. The house schedule and the general orientation at Moreau, while much less rigid than the Novitiate, still reflected the form of seminary formation that had prevailed more or less unchanged since the First Vatican Council: early rising, meditation and prayer, spiritual reading, classes and study, and bed at ten thirty. Seminarians were expected to wear the habit at Moreau; when we left the property to visit the doctor or engage in an apostolate, we would normally wear black shoes and pants with a white shirt and a black tie. If it were a more formal occasion, we would also wear a black suit coat. As for events on campus, it all depended. We were in informal black for football games, lectures, and other such occasions, but in habits for worship, First Sunday devotions, and funerals.

Moreau Seminary was intended to be a self-sustaining living, studying, and recreating unit. While we were on land adjacent to the University, the Indiana Province owned the seminary property. Generally, the spirit of cooperation between Notre Dame and Moreau Seminary was good since Holy Cross priests were responsible for both entities. The Moreau faculty and staff were twelve Holy Cross priests and nine Holy Cross brothers. The superior was Ray Cour, C.S.C., a faculty member in political science. His most celebrated trait was that he was always super organized with a propensity to plan every activity down to the second. He knew precisely how long it took to walk from Moreau to Sacred Heart Church or from his room to the dining room. His presentations to the seminarians and his homilies were always read off of 3 x 5 note cards. By temperament he was rather unemotional and straightforward in dealing with people. He was well educated but not inclined to questioning. The view of the Church and the Holy Cross community he offered us was only thinly affected by the deliberations and documents of Vatican II. If and when the Church authorized a change in practice, such as vernacular in the Mass, he would obediently embrace it, but he did not see it as his place to foster speculation about what was coming or how quickly.

The assistant superior, John Burke, C.S.C., was a member of the Notre Dame mathematics department. He was a superb teacher of introductory courses to first-year undergraduates. The rest of the priests were an interesting mix. Father John Cavanaugh, C.S.C., who preceded Father Hesburgh as Notre Dame's president, helped out in campus ministry and was a great raconteur. I especially enjoyed hearing him describe the challenges that he faced during his presidential years and his warm friendship with Joe Kennedy, the patriarch of the Massachusetts Kennedy clan. Father Hermie Reith, C.S.C., was a

"Spes Unica—The Cross Our Only Hope"

member of the Notre Dame philosophy department. Father Tony Lauck, C.S.C., was a member of the Notre Dame art department and the original collector of materials for what eventually became the Snite Museum of Art. He was a prolific sculptor.

One of the most enjoyable outlets for me was inviting groups from campus to come over to the Moreau gym to play basketball against our seminarian team. Usually they would expect to have an easy time, but we were never beaten. Eventually we were able to attract some of the better campus competitors and our margins of victory were substantially reduced. The gym was an excellent place to play since the court had a good floor and soft rims, a real advantage to a shooter. Games against campus teams were a way to break down the stereotype that seminarians were all wimps or unable to hold their own in circumstances of vigorous physical engagement.

When Ara Parseghian became head football coach, he sought permission to use Moreau Seminary as a residence for the members of the team on Friday nights before home games. After the pep rally, the team would show up *en masse*, move into their rooms, and come down to the auditorium to watch a commercial film. We were invited to join them for the movie. The consensus among us was that the team did better when the movie was a war epic or an upbeat sports story or a gangster movie than when it was a love story or a comedy. Coach Parseghian believed the seminary would be a safe place to sequester his team; he wanted to limit outside distractions and assure a good night's sleep. However, those of us who were alert to the rhythm of seminary life became aware that a few of the players found ways to escape through one of the many building exits and, even more importantly, how to get back in undiscovered.

In the social dynamic among the seminarians, I often found myself watching how the younger seminarians interacted. There were some who seemed to me to be excessively prudish, afraid of any variance from the norm of religious life as espoused in the Rule—I wondered how they would do in the give and take of student life on campus. Some others seemed close to recognizing that religious life was not for them; these tended to have few friends or to be snarly when they did not get their way. They went through the motions but their hearts did not appear to be in it. I had the sense that some of the seminarians may have practiced mass when they were little boys and always looked forward to dressing up in priestly garments. Others came from rough and ready backgrounds and found life in the seminary an oasis of order and tranquility. Still others struggled with academics or social acceptance or celibacy. Beneath all the seeming uniformity, Moreau Seminary was not unlike any other group of nineteen- to twenty-four-year-old men. Some were happy, some were on the way out, and some were struggling with basic vocational decisions.

My pursuit of a graduate degree in English happened almost by accident. When Father O'Connor allowed me to sign up for two courses in English in the fall semester of my transition year at Moreau, there was no formal agreement that I could continue on to a master's degree. As long as I took the other courses he specified, he did not seem to care one way or the other. But I knew I needed to identify a possible area of doctoral study if I wanted to qualify myself to teach at a place like Notre Dame. Since my undergraduate degree had been in English and I knew the faculty, I figured that was the most convenient direction to pursue. In the first semester I registered for classes in eighteenth-century literature and Romantic poetry. By the end of the term I had decided to complete as many of the English department requirements for the masters' as I could, so I took four more courses. When I received permission to take two more courses in English in the summer of 1966, the Province had effectively given the go-ahead for me to finish the degree the following summer. In the summer of 1967 I took two more courses and received my M.A.

More and more I had come to see myself as a scholar, someone committed to the life of learning. I felt I had a particular strength in organizing diverse materials into coherent structures of understanding.

As I would learn later in my doctoral studies, I was by instinct a typologist. I developed the habit of reducing fifty pages of text down to one side of a loose-leaf page, with major emphases and significant names highlighted in different colors of ink. I was then able to synthesize from these outlines an even more compact summary. Finally, I would do a summary of the summaries so that I could, for example, identify the major figures in the Victorian period and capture their distinctive characteristics.

I also began to be interested in the historical development of the different forms of creative expression such as novels, theater, film, or poetry. At the end of my undergraduate degree, I figured I knew isolated periods and particular authors reasonably well, but I had no feel for how one school of thought or literary form connected to another. It was as if I were familiar with Boston, New York City, and Washington but had no idea what lay between.

Even in the pre–Vatican II era, the dropout rate among seminarians was relatively high, especially when high school seminary programs were taken into account. The question was asked then, and with even greater urgency after Vatican II, whether the investment of resources was worth it. Sociological studies were conducted, priests and bishops were consulted, and ex-seminarians were asked their opinions of the experience. One result was the move to close many high school seminaries; another was to reexamine the nature of college seminaries and the age of first admission to candidacy status. From the other end of the potential pipeline, vocation directors were seeking more mature candidates who had graduated from college and worked for a number of years or earned an advanced degree. Gradually, from the time I entered Holy Cross through the first decade of the 2000s, the size of seminary classes grew smaller, the admissions approval process became more rigorous, and the persistence rate to final vows and priestly ordination grew higher.

Questions about the kind of seminary formation I received in my first three years in Holy Cross were not easy to answer. In its essence, the formation was intended to promote a good Christian life in the world through regular habits of prayer, a familiarity with Scripture and theological tradition, and acts of service. Even if only by osmosis, it was hard for the seminarians not to get the message. Second, seminary formation fostered a level of spiritual and vocational discernment that was not available to peers in the broader society. Third, the system was substantially increasing the pool of those interested in and motivated toward lay ministry in the wake of the Council which had highlighted the inclusion of lay people in just about every area of Church life. Ex-seminarians were often the best prepared to take these roles.

On the negative side, the inbreeding of seminary life and the relatively young age of applicants tended to foster personal immaturity. It was especially difficult for those of tender conscience who, in a sense, identified keeping the Rule with being right with God. When adjusting to living on their own, they sometimes found the real world much more complex and murky than their seminary experience prepared them for. Exposure to the human side of religion, to the personal weaknesses and inconsistencies of some of those responsible for the formation process, led to some becoming disenchanted with the Church and with organized religion in general. All in all, I was convinced early on that the traditional seminary system was incompatible with the reforms of Vatican II. Yet it had its saving features, and many who survived its rigors went on to lives of generous, committed, holy service as priests and brothers in Holy Cross.

Holy Cross College (1966–68)

Holy Cross College was an independent entity adjacent to the campus of the Catholic University of America in Washington. It was a four-story building surrounded by other religious-community theologates. About two blocks away was the Holy Cross Foreign Mission building, where those preparing for service in other parts of the world lived together. The Foreign Mission Seminary, as it happened, was directly across the street from my old high school, Archbishop John Carroll.

Nearly all classes at the college were taught by Holy Cross priests, which leads to the question, why was the theologate established at Catholic U if none of the seminarians took advantage of the professors and courses there? The answer can be found in historical decisions that made sense when they were approved. By the time I arrived, however, the challenge of finding sufficient numbers of credentialed clergy to teach the required courses—and still staff the Holy Cross high schools, colleges, and universities—was becoming problematic. The issue would eventually lead to a decision to close down the College and move the whole program to Notre Dame.

I loved being back in my hometown. Although my parents lived only about a mile away, I visited them only occasionally since I was very much preoccupied with my studies and my pastoral commitments as well as with the community life of the seminary. I did, however, take full advantage of my knowledge of the city to give tours to my compatriots and to participate in some of the activities that inevitably gravitate to the center of national government.

The daily schedule at Holy Cross College preserved many of the traditional elements from the previous standard, but it was beginning to change at the edges. Every day we had meditation, mass, particular examen, and night prayer in the chapel. But there was no assigned time for retiring and there was much greater leeway in regard to travel into the city. A spirit of silence was to be kept in the house at large, especially during class and study times, but in the individual rooms, the recreation room, and outside, these expectations did not apply. Since all of us were twenty-one, we were allowed to have beer for our parties and there was no prohibition against going out on weekends. We were expected to be sober and discreet but we were treated as adults.

The Superior of the College was Father George Bernard, C.S.C., who had earned a doctorate in Catholic moral theology and had done his dissertation on the morality of prize fighting. He was a good priest, open to change (though not too quickly) and to going in new directions if he found the arguments persuasive. I think in retrospect that Father Bernard was an excellent choice for superior in what would turn out to be a volatile time in seminary formation and the Church. The assistant Superior was Father Joseph Rehage, C.S.C., a canon lawyer from Louisiana. He was replaced in our second year by Father Bill Toohey, C.S.C., who taught preaching and was a very charismatic figure. Bill would later serve as director of campus ministry at Notre Dame and we would become good friends. The faculty was small and quite disparate in their levels of preparation and teaching skills. Even when supplemented by an occasional faculty member from one of the other area houses of formation, they had almost no time for research (or publication) and they were often expected to cover courses outside their areas of expertise. Thus the content of the classes tended to be directed toward the middle range of student ability, which meant that just about everybody passed. For those interested in going on for a doctorate in theology or some related discipline, however, supplementary reading and reflection had to be undertaken independently.

In my first semester I took courses in dogma, moral theology, Scripture, canon law, liturgy, and church history. In the second semester, I had a similar curriculum with a few additions, such as prophetic literature and Pentateuch. At face value, these were all important areas of study but the problem was in the execution. For example, the teacher in the introduction to Scripture class, while a nice person, was hopelessly incompetent as a teacher. The dogma teacher was a first-class instructor, but he also taught church history and he rendered that course into a kind of trivia contest to prove that the students had done the reading. The teacher for moral theology, perhaps the most challenging field in the wake of the Council, was ill prepared to interpret what was going on and seemed to be only a book or two ahead of the students. Liturgy was a field changing before our eyes, and it was impossible for anyone to be sure what new approaches would be ap-

"Spes Unica—The Cross Our Only Hope"

proved or how quickly. Canon law as a discipline received scant attention except in those areas that had obvious pastoral application, like marriage annulments.

Despite the academic limitations I loved my first year of theology. I read widely both in the religious journals and the burgeoning number of books trying to root the reforms of the Council in Scripture and in theological history, as well as those exploring new methodologies and ways of interpreting the rich heritage of Catholic intellectual life. The Church was becoming more ecumenical and more open to developments in the modern world, so it was desirable to learn more about the Protestant and Jewish traditions as well as the other world religions.

In the second year of theology I added two semesters of preaching and one of Hebrew to the familiar mix. The preaching courses combined theory with practice. Very quickly I found that I enjoyed preaching, both the preparation that goes into it and the effort to find a comfortable and effective manner of delivery. Our teacher, Father Toohey, was a master preacher himself and I relished the chance to work toward a similar level of competence.

All of us were expected to have a regular apostolic commitment in the D.C. area. The first semester I started teaching a theology course part time at Holy Cross Academy, an all-girls high school run by the Holy Cross sisters in suburban Maryland. It was a comfortable setting and I found that I could keep the students' attention reasonably well. However, I did not think it was sufficiently different from what I was accustomed to, having spent my entire academic career as a student in Catholic institutions. So when I learned that some seminarians were volunteering at Saint Elizabeth's Mental Hospital, I decided to accompany them to see if I would like it better. From my first visit, I knew that Saint Elizabeth's was the place for me. In the second semester I switched over and stayed there the following year as well.

Saint Elizabeth's had a large, sweeping campus atop a hill looking down on the Anacostia River and beyond to downtown Washington and northern Virginia. At the time it had over 7,000 patients—a scale that resembled a junior college or a major military encampment. To be approved for the chaplain corps of visitors we had to be briefed about the risks in dealing with some of the patients, the need for confidentiality, and the importance of following hospital procedure in gaining access to the buildings and informing the staff of our whereabouts. I readily signed off on all of this but did not really know why it was necessary. I would soon learn.

There were wards for people with different mental problems and physical limitations. One building, for example, was for patients with Alzheimer's or other forms of dementia who could still participate in a form of community life. The seminary volunteers took turns organizing Sunday mass and leading the singing in that building, and one Sunday I ended up there all by myself. I had to sing four songs and the common parts of the Mass without any accompaniment, since the patients were out of it and the staff was busy taking care of them. At the end of mass I received a round of applause from the patients. I thought it was very nice of them until I looked at the staff and saw in their eyes the truth about the quality of my singing.

I soon decided that I wanted to be in a more interactive environment than the Alzheimer's ward. Eventually I settled in at John Howard Pavilion, a six-story building reserved for prisoners who had been certified as criminally insane. There were bars on all the windows, armed security guards at the entrance and around the periphery, and a rather elaborate method for gaining entry. I once took a fellow seminarian for a visit to see if he wanted to assist our small group of visitors and he was so traumatized that he never returned.

On each floor, from the first to the sixth, the patients were progressively more dangerous. I decided to take on the challenge of regularly visiting wards eleven and twelve on the sixth floor. I would come dressed in my black outfit with white shirt and black tie. I would show my credentials at the main entrance, receive a large identification tag to wear around my neck, and be given a key for the elevator. To reach the elevator I would go inside one of those areas with sliding doors on each end, both of which could not be opened simultaneously, so that the guards could verify who I was—especially on the way out. Once I made it to the elevator and opened the door with the key, it was a straight shot to the sixth floor. When I exited and locked the door behind me, I was entirely on my own except for some unarmed staff present to supervise the patients. It was a lot like *One Flew over the Cuckoo's Nest*. Each visit was unique.

On the first floor of the pavilion, one ward was given over to the psychiatric testing of people who made threats against the president or his family or other national officials. John Hinckley, the man who shot President Ronald Reagan, is still housed there. What attracted me to the sixth floor was the fact that most of the patients were long term, and despite the severity of their crimes they were interesting to be with and appreciative of my time with them. Because the eleventh and twelfth wards were open, it was relatively easy to come off the elevator, survey the scene, and decide whom to spend time with on a given day.

One of my favorite patients was an African-American man in his late forties or early fifties. Joe was a professional boxer who had found himself confronted in a social setting by a man who charged at him. Joe delivered such a blow that the attacker fell back, hit his head against a solid object, and died. Joe was convicted of manslaughter and sent to federal prison, but while there he had a mental episode and was moved to Saint Elizabeth's. Joe was a gentle giant, and he assured me that no one would mess with me on the ward as long as he was around. I found this quite assuring. Joe did not expect a lot of face time but he was always hovering in the background in case his protection skills were needed.

Another patient was a white weight lifter of solid build who had been convicted of multiple bank robberies. When he was coherent, he was okay to be around, but he had a violent temper and it did not take much to set it off. One day as I made my way off the elevator he was yelling at me that he had been attacked by the guards and I should be his witness in court. I quickly learned he had flipped out and the guards had just put him in a straightjacket and were about to confine him to his cell. After they did, I let them know how much I admired the work they did under difficult circumstances. In other words, they should not fear that I would back the man's claims of staff abuse. It was tough enough in the ward as an occasional visitor without the staff suspecting my motives.

Perhaps the most perplexing patient was Ramon, a relatively young, light-complected African American who had attended a Holy Cross–run high school in inner-city Washington. At sixteen he had been charged with multiple counts of housebreaking and rape. At the end of a long trial he had been declared not guilty by reason of insanity on the rape charges, but given ninety-nine years on housebreaking. Around the time I began meeting with him, his appeal of the obviously excessive sentence for housebreaking had made its way to the United States Supreme Court. A *Washington Post* article on him went back and interviewed the women he had raped. They all were afraid he would be released and put the safety of the community in jeopardy.

I had a chance to read his file and to interact with Ramon on a regular basis. He was smart, good looking, seemingly repentant, and on the basis of his terrible upbringing one could at least understand what may have been behind his psychotic behavior. He was also an outstanding basketball player and I was convinced that he had the ability to play Division I-A basketball on a scholarship. His charm and youth were persuasive arguments that he be given another chance, provided that his psychological evaluation found that he would not be a risk to others. On the other hand, I could clearly understand the counter-arguments.

It was easier to decide how to deal with another class of patients that included a man named Willie. He was an African-American man in his mid-thirties who had been convicted of multiple crimes of aggression. One of his favorite tricks was to drive a car and run down police officers who were directing traffic in the middle of the street. Since he was sent to John Howard Pavilion he had developed a reputation for unprovoked attacks on other patients and guards. One time he had pulled a steel coil out of a mattress and came up behind a guard and attempted to poke his eye out. People like Willie were going to be lifers either at Saint Elizabeth's or somewhere in the federal prison system.

A patient who was harder to figure out was Sweet Lou, an African American from a poor background who had murdered someone in a gang fight when he was relatively young. Since then he had generally been a model prisoner with occasional bouts of delusionary behavior. He was the best player on the Pavilion basketball team, even better than Ramon. Sweet Lou reminded me of George Gervin in that he was an offensive threat from anywhere on the floor. He was about 6'6" and had great leaping ability. He could hang in the air like Gervin or Elgin Baylor. When I was with him Sweet Lou seemed normal enough and there was some talk about his eventual release and the possible opportunity to play college and professional basketball.

Many years later, I noticed an article in the *Washington Post* about how the police had solved a murder on the grounds of Saint Elizabeth's Hospital. It turned out that Sweet Lou had been released from John Howard and assigned to a transition building where patients had the freedom to walk around the grounds as they were preparing for their parole back into society. One night Sweet Lou was walking outside when he encountered a woman worker whom he mistakenly took to be his old girlfriend. He thought she had been two-timing him. In revenge he killed her and then made his way back to his residence. It was fortunate that the police figured out who committed the crime but it was a reminder to me about how hard it is to extrapolate from the behavior of patient-prisoners behind bars to their potential state of mind after release.

John Howard had a nice gymnasium that provided a great way for the patients to let off steam. When the group on the sixth floor learned about my basketball history, they encouraged me to recruit a team of my friends to come play against them. Twice I was able to arrange the logistics and get the approval of the hospital staff for a game. The first time the team I assembled was reasonably good but not in the best of shape so we were handily defeated. The second time I decided to up the ante and I convinced George Leftwich, John Thompson, and some of my old classmates to make the trek out to Saint Elizabeth's. This time around we were comfortably ahead at halftime. All the players on the John Howard team were African American and the in-house referees were white. Most of the players on my team were black, as were the spectators. As the second half began, the atmosphere in the gym got more raucous and it appeared that the referees were being intimidated into making questionable calls in favor of the home team. With a couple of minutes to go, we called time out to assess our situation. We arrived at a quick consensus that it was more important for us to protect our bodies and to make a quick exit than it was to win the game. Besides we did not really care that much, but if the John Howard team won they would feel better about themselves. I would not say that we threw the game but we did not compete quite as hard as we had. After that I was never able to muster another team to come out to John Howard.

While I was volunteering I read books on psychological counseling and pastoral practice. One popular approach at the time was Carl Rogers' non-directive counseling, where the counselor tries to get the patient to do all the talking. My visits seemed to be a good opportunity to test out this method. One time I was having a one-on-one session with a patient when he said out of the blue, "You must have read Carl Rogers. You're using a non-directive style on me." I was flabbergasted, though I should not have been. Many of the men were well read in psychology and spent a lot of time in sessions with psychologists. They knew the only way out of John Howard was to have their counselors give a good report, so it was important to figure out what the counselors were looking for (a strange kind of transference).

Another time I was invited to a session of psychodrama in a building other than John Howard. The experimental technique was designed to have a patient act out events from the past and have volunteers, including other patients, play assigned roles. The patient-playwright developed the story line, determined the cast of characters, then focused on the central emotional issue at stake. The other participants surrounded the actors as a kind of interested audience and the play began. Initially, the targeted patient played himself or herself. The other characters, having been told the personal characteristics of the person they were playing, usually rendered the part with great effectiveness. But the secret of the technique was to have the central person in the story switch roles—for example, become his mother while someone else played him. Another move was to have the targeted person join the audience to watch the dynamic among the characters unfold from a cool distance. On the day I watched a psychodrama as part of the audience I was impressed with the acting skills of the patients. I guess I should not have been, since many of them had survived emotional deprivation and traumas that I could only imagine.

Saint Elizabeth's Hospital, especially John Howard Pavilion, was an outstanding place to volunteer during my theological training. It regularly put me in touch with people who were living on the margins of society and dealing with issues of which I had only a textbook knowledge. I learned to muster the courage to face all the unknowns of life on wards eleven and twelve when I left the elevator and walked in there by myself. I was physically big and strong enough to defend myself until help came if I had had to, but fortunately I never had to. I accepted the patients I worked with on their own terms and figured out what being a minister of the Gospel might mean in my time with them. I learned instinctively that it was more important to listen than to advise, and that establishing a relationship was of higher value than whatever outcome the relationship might lead to.

The men in John Howard Pavilion had committed every type of violent crime, some multiple times, yet when I was with them they did not seem all that different from other people I knew. But there was always tension in the wards, a kind of emotional discomfort and stress that could have broken out into something worse at any time. I always felt it. After adapting to the rhythm of John Howard—an imposed order amid widespread mental illnesses and potential chaos—I figured I could handle myself in other challenging contexts.

At Holy Cross College, meal preparation and the laundry chores were entrusted to a group of religious sisters based in Mexico. Mother Oliva was the Superior and the primary go-between for the seminarians and the house staff. Most of the sisters did not speak English and most seminarians knew only a few words in Spanish. The sisters had their own prayer schedule and lived a relatively cloistered life except for the soirees on big feasts when they would join the rest of us for the festivities. The big joke among the seminarians, who considered the cuisine acceptable but not great, was that we had olives in one form or another with every meal—in honor of Madre Oliva.

One of our favorite extracurricular activities was inter-seminary competition in touch football and basketball. We had a rather talented group of athletes in both sports. The football games took place on one of the Catholic University fields. We had more depth than most programs and were able to win the championship two years in a row. In basketball we were also victorious, primarily because I and a fellow seminarian, Jim O'Donnell, who had played for the University of Portland, were both accomplished scorers and the other players had complementary skills. Jim was a very intimidating type of player who, after we returned to Moreau Seminary in 1968–69, would often frighten the campus teams who played against us in the Moreau gym.

Jim and I and an African-American seminarian from Theological College who was 6'9" and a great leaper all decided to participate in a citywide league run by the D.C. public schools. The remaining players on our team were neither as good nor as experienced as the three of

"Spes Unica—The Cross Our Only Hope"

us, but we generally held our own. The games were played in public high school gyms. Normally, our team had the only white players; that was no big deal to me, but we used to get stares from some of the hangers-on. The opposing players were cool and treated us like any other team they faced. I was glad that the games were over by eight-thirty or so because the neighborhoods we were playing in got progressively more dangerous as the night went on.

My potential ordination class at Holy Cross College in 1966–67 had twenty members. By my second year of theology in 1967–68, the class size had been reduced to fourteen. In a sense, it was a good sign that individuals were making firm vocational decisions before they took final vows or were ordained. The system was designed for such ongoing vocational discernment. Still, it was sad to see friends decide to move on. Some of us had lived together for four years and had become good friends. For some, the largest issue was a lifetime commitment to celibacy. Others discovered that they either did not enjoy the things that priests were called to do or they felt they lacked the talent to do them. While most decisions were self-generated, in a couple of cases the feedback from the College staff or spiritual directors was probably decisive. Of the fourteen who were part of my second-year theology group, nine would be ordained.

One of the most distressing things that happened during my second year of theology was the suicide of one of the college seminarians at Moreau. When the news reached us, Father Bernard sent five of us to represent the College at the funeral. We drove to Notre Dame and arrived at Moreau in the early evening. We could sense almost immediately that the place was in a state of distress. Suicide is always traumatic for those left behind, but when it takes place in a college or seminary setting, it shatters the myth that most American young people live by—the belief that they will live forever. Friends and family members instinctively feel that there is something they could or should have done, and they begin to blame themselves. Over the course of our two days at Moreau, we were able to some degree to help the college seminarians share their emotional reactions and support one another. It was not that the other theologians or I were immune from our own sense of grief, but in microcosm it was the kind of pastoral situation that all of us would face many times in the future.

It was somewhat odd to spend two years in the neighborhood I grew up in. Saint Anthony Grade School was about a mile from the College. Archbishop John Carroll High School was no more than three blocks away. We were on the Catholic University campus where I spent many hours in my youth wandering around. The Shrine of the Immaculate Conception was two blocks straight ahead out our front door. Almost every building or street in the neighborhood had some memory attached to it.

The College had a limited number of cars that the seminarians could use in the daytime for apostolic assignments, classes, medical visits, and the like. They were less available at night and on weekends, so most of the time we ended up going out in groups. The other, and cheaper, alternative was to use streetcars or buses. Since the seminarians lived on limited budgets, there were always schemes for how to get somewhere in town cheaply and have enough money left over for a meal and a beer. One of our favorite haunts was the Washington Zoo, which had free entry and was a great place to while away a pleasant afternoon. A couple of seminarians found the outdoor cafes on the Connecticut Avenue side of the Zoo that were popular with retired people. The seminarians' ploy was to start up a conversation with a retiree who, when he or she found out who they were, would end up treating them to a snack and a beer or two. The rest of us, while envious, tried to convince them that such false posturing must be immoral.

Most of the seminarians got to know Washington rather well. They had visited the museums, federal buildings, and public parks and could find their way around. The location of the seminary in the city was a real asset. Some worked in poor black parishes, some volunteered at the National Training School for Boys (a kind of reform school), some visited the city jail, and some taught in Catholic grade schools and high schools. In a sense, being immersed in the rhythms of big city life in the late 1960s was a great preparation for ministry in the 1970s and beyond. A special ministry that evolved ahead of its time was the campus ministry at Gallaudet College, the national school of the deaf. Several seminarians became proficient in sign language and brought this skill with them when they moved on to later assignments.

Time of Turmoil

As I began my second year of theology, it was clear that the combination of racial tension in U.S. cities, disenchantment with the Vietnam War, and radicalized college campuses meant that our generation was facing a huge challenge. By 1967 the seminarians as a group, but with nuanced differences of opinion, were opposed to the Vietnam War and interested in joining their voices to those who were seeking to gain American disengagement from the conflict in a peaceful fashion. We were convinced that prolonging the war made no sense, and we were waiting for the right opportunity to join the anti-war chorus. When we heard about the protest planned for October 21, 1967—the "Levitate the Pentagon" rally—it seemed the ideal moment to get involved. The so-called March on the Pentagon was organized by the National Mobilization Committee to End the War in Vietnam, but the publicity that preceded the day was rather light-hearted and good spirited. It seemed more Haight-Ashbury than Weathermen-oriented. Those of us who were planning to participate were convinced it would be peaceful.

That day ten or twelve of us made our way to the Lincoln Memorial where we joined an estimated 70,000 marchers. What was striking was the large presence of police and security forces from the city and from multiple federal agencies. Helicopters constantly flew overhead, surveying the scene. Long before the speeches began, we were convinced that we were part of a major event in American history.

In the early afternoon, as the crowds swelled, representatives from anti-war groups began to address the assemblage. David Dellinger, a radical pacifist, advocated direct resistance as a strategy. Dr. Benjamin Spock, the famous baby expert, spoke of his disenchantment with the policies of the Johnson administration. Other speakers spoke from a wide variety of perspectives. Eventually, as planned, about 50,000 people began the trek across Memorial Bridge toward the Pentagon. It took roughly an hour and a half for the whole entourage to complete the trip.

The Pentagon was ringed by soldiers in battle gear with rifles at the ready. Early on a group of hippies began to chant in order to "exorcize" the military establishment. Some of them, in a famous photograph, placed flowers in the ends of the soldiers' rifles. Others in the crowd sought to enter the building and were arrested. Some tear-gas was used and a few demonstrators were hit by rifles, but overall the damage was minor. After the attempt at entry was thwarted, most people left except for a group that spent the night surrounding the building before marching off to the White House the next morning.

Norman Mailer's book about the March, *Armies of the Night*, expanded the influence of the day of protest on public attitude. But for me the most noteworthy outcome of my participation was a decision to forsake rally going as a way to make my voice heard. During our march across the Potomac, I looked around me at the other protestors and saw people carrying obscene signs or espousing positions that I found abhorrent. I saw countercultural families with little children who were clearly undernourished and maybe even a bit high. I began to recognize that while everyone in the March was anti-war, their reasons varied across the spectrum from Quaker pacifist to radical anarchist. I determined that from then on I would find other means of expressing my opinion about important public policy issues. For years afterward, when I observed rallies in my hometown or anywhere, I was more interested in how police handled crowd control than in the actual content of the rally.

While the turmoil over Vietnam was divisive, it did not compare in immediacy with the assassination of Martin Luther King, Jr., on April 4, 1968, in Memphis, Tennessee. I was shocked when I heard the news. Like most Americans, I hunkered down in front of the television. That evening, rioting broke out in several D.C. neighborhoods, but the burning and looting and violent encounters with police, while frightening to behold, appeared to be contained to a few hotspots in poor neighborhoods.

The next morning, the city seemed peaceful. As a longtime Washington resident, my curiosity got the better of me and I talked another seminarian, who had been a combat veteran in the Korean War, to accompany me into the trouble areas to see how much damage had been done. The only available car was a brand new Pontiac that the seminary had picked up from the dealer a week before. We drove from the College down North Capital Street to the center of town, passing a few areas of damage but no crowds, though the police were out in force. Gradually we made our way over to the 16th Street, N.W., and headed north, intending to return to the College. For some reason I decided to turn east on Florida Avenue to go up 14th Street. I was a bit surprised when the cars in front of us made such slow progress, but finally I was able to turn north on 14th Street. Then all hell broke loose.

A riot had been under way for quite some time on 14th Street. I got only a block or two when I had to slam on the brakes, at which point the motor conked out. On both sides of us mobs were smashing plate glass windows and looting stores. Fires burned to the side of us and in front. Soon some people in the crowd began hurling stones and bottles at us, and before long all the car windows were shattered. A large rock hit the windshield head-on, directly in front of me; fortunately, the safety glass prevented it from smashing all the way through. Meanwhile, my companion was urging me to be calm and to try to restart the motor. Thank God, I was finally able to do so; the newspapers reported the next day that around that time on 14th Street several people had been dragged from their cars and beaten.

Putting the car into drive, I raced due north on 14th Street. There were other pockets of rioters along the way but I kept going. Finally I made it to Harvard Street, where I turned east. We were fine until we hit Georgia Avenue, where another riot was underway. Our progress was impeded for a spell but we made it through, primarily because the rioters saw that we had already been hit. I drove directly to the 12th Precinct House in my old neighborhood and went inside to report the incident and the damage. A single police officer was on duty and I described what had happened. He looked at me with incredulity and asked if anyone had been hurt. When I answered that we were both okay, he suggested in no uncertain terms that I leave promptly, since the city was up for grabs and he was utterly preoccupied with redirecting the squad cars under his command.

My companion and I made it back to the College where the seminarians listened with great interest to our tale. Father Jim Denn, the acting superior, seemed grateful that we had not been harmed and simply requested that I take the car back to the dealership to be repaired. The dealership was located on 14th Street, two or three blocks away from where we had been attacked. I told Father Denn it would be prudent to wait a few days.

That evening we kept hearing that more and more neighborhoods were out of control, and there were rumors about armed gangs on the rampage. Late in the evening we went to the roof of the College building and saw fires burning in just about every direction. It felt like wartime. Since no one knew what might happen next, we were pleased to learn that the Catholic University security force was patrolling the perimeter of the campus.

It took several days for life to get back to normal. Meanwhile, we were encouraged by Father Bernard to venture out only for necessities and only in the daytime. Several days later, after the National Guard had been mobilized and the city locked down under curfew, it

"Spes Unica—The Cross Our Only Hope"

was possible to return to 14th Street, not with the damaged car but to observe the aftermath of the riots. There were soldiers and police on foot and in jeeps and halftracks. My hometown was under occupation, and it was a sad sight to see. Washington took decades to recover from the physical and psychological impact of the riots. The 14th Street and H Street corridors were particularly hard hit. If it had not been for the presence of the federal government, the tourist sites, the higher education institutions, and the government-related industries, Washington could easily have become a ghost town, like Detroit and Newark.

At the same time that American civil society was going through dramatic and sometimes bloody social change, the Catholic Church in the U.S. and around the world was continuing the process of implementing the Vatican II renewal. That fall the National Conference of Catholic Bishops indicated that they would propose further liturgical changes to Rome but that priests lobbying for rethinking the celibacy requirement should not expect a change. It was around this time that a large exodus from the priesthood and from religious life began, with one of the volatile issues being celibacy. What really precipitated a sea change for Church life in this country, however, was Pope Paul VI's 1968 encyclical *Humanae Vitae*. For the first time, large numbers of laypeople began to question the Church's moral teaching in their personal lives, not only the morality of various forms of birth regulation but many other moral issues as well. Bishops' conferences around the world disagreed with one another about how to respond. Local ordinaries and their diocesan clergy came at the matter from much different perspectives, and on occasion some clergy who spoke out were censured by a local ordinary. Catholic theologians signed petitions protesting the appropriateness and/or legitimacy of the encyclical. Many Catholic couples started confessor-shopping and eventually began to fashion their practices according to their own consciences.

No sub-discipline of theology was more regularly at the center of the Church's debates in the late 1960s than Catholic moral theology.

Not only would that eventually be my field of study, but the controversies made it impossible for our teachers to act as though nothing had happened. Intense questioning, openness to multiple points of view, and an interest in the perspective of the other Christian and non-Christian churches became hallmarks of how we learned to think. No longer could we presume that the priest had all the answers or that a distinctive Catholic perspective was the only legitimate approach to a debated topic. On the other hand, I was a deeply formed Catholic who loved the Church, chose to pursue ministry within it, and wanted to be well prepared in both my intellectual and pastoral formation. For me it was exciting and stimulating to be nearing ordination at a time when a broader frame of reference, including the life experience of ordinary Catholics, was being brought into theological reflection. I was confident that the spirit of *aggiornamento* of the Council would prevail in the end.

In the summer of 1967, I had some vacation time with my family and spent the rest of the summer at Moreau Seminary completing my M.A. degree. Although it was not required, I attended the summer graduation ceremony at the Grotto. The following summer, 1968, I went with a group of seminarians to work in inner-city parishes in Detroit. Tom Stella and I were assigned to Blessed Sacrament Cathedral Parish in a neighborhood that at one time had been rather exclusive but was now in decline. The pastor was Bishop Joe Schoenherr, a wonderful man who did everything he could to make us feel at home.

Our job was to oversee various outreach programs to the children and young people in the neighborhood, most of them African American and not Catholic. The parish grade school had a gymnasium that was available in the afternoons and on the weekends for basketball games. That gave us a nice point of contact with the teenagers, mainly the boys. We both were familiar with the macho style of free-flowing inner-city basketball contests, with its posturing, braggadocio, and use of foul language. For the younger kids, the parish ran a storefront center on a major city street not far from the parish; it included a pool table, some Ping-Pong tables, a play area, some indestructible chairs, and a lot of donated equipment, from books to coloring sets to dolls and different types of toys.

I liked to work on reading and spelling with kids who had started school. I quickly found out how important environment is when I realized they could spell billiard, ambulance, and salon more easily than tennis, maid, and redbird. The center was always on the edge of chaos, but somehow we kept it functioning with the help of a couple of older neighborhood women who had been hired for the summer. These women knew by sight and reputation just about everyone who might start trouble. Sometimes the police would stop by, although I never saw that as a plus since the relationship between police and the inner-city community was problematic.

One day I took a carload of kids to the Detroit Zoo. That went well, but on the way back and forth they kept spotting unlocked bicycles and other items that they could steal. They wanted me to stop, and I had a hard time convincing them that this was a bad idea. Then at the Zoo itself they went back to being young innocents as they oohed and aahed when they saw the lions, tigers, elephants, and seals.

The parish had a school bus and both Tom and I had chauffeur's licenses. Periodically, we would drive groups to some of the city sights or one of the nature parks in the suburbs. When we arrived, especially outside the city limits, we attracted a lot of attention. Beyond an occasional glare or muttered comment, there were no unpleasant moments, yet it was a constant reminder of how much America was divided into two cultures, black and white, at least in the Detroit area.

Separate from the parish but sometimes using its school facilities was a fairly radicalized group of black college students who were also working with the youth of the neighborhood. When Tom and I saw them around we were friendly, but they were dismissive of our presence. About midway through the summer we learned that a Methodist youth camp in the Upper Peninsula had been made available to this black-led youth group. The only way they could get there was on the school bus, so Tom and I agreed to alternate driving on the long trip to the camp.

The college students were big into Black Power rhetoric. We took off early on the assigned day, and when we stopped at rest areas for gas, our passengers went into the convenience store and the kids proceeded to shoplift as much as they could. The cashiers refused to complain because they were afraid of being attacked. When the group got back on the bus, the counselors complimented the youth for asserting their rights in the face of centuries of injustice. We stopped twice more along the way and the same thing happened. Tom and I were appalled but by then we were just hoping to make it to the camp.

When we arrived, Tom and I expected to stay overnight to rest up for the drive back, but we were told that we were not welcome because we were white, and we would have to leave immediately. In a sense, we were happy to get out of there. We figured by alternating the driving we could make it to the Motor City by midnight or so. On the return we studiously avoided the places we had stopped at on the way up, lest we get thrown in some small-town Michigan jail. The irony of the story was that after one week at the camp (out of a scheduled two), the youth group revolted and kicked out the counselors. I have no idea how they got back, but Tom and I had no interest in picking them up.

We also oversaw the Friday night dances in the gym. These events were major security risks, since members of several gangs attended. We required them to leave weapons at the check-in area during the dance. This included guns, knives, or whatever. When the dance was over, they could pick up what they had checked in. The main punishment we could dispense for misbehavior was to bar the offenders from the following Friday's dance. That was well and good until the last Friday rolled around. We had a black Catholic sister who assisted us on Friday nights and who was streetwise and had good rapport with the kids. Before the last Friday dance, she asked the police to be present outside the school around the time that the dance let out. When the dance ended the police were nowhere to be found. Into the gap came the sister and the two of us, who stood in the middle of the street between the gangs and, with firmness of voice (and much nervousness), sent them on their way. Fortunately, it worked.

One night that summer I was alone in the parish rectory. About ten o'clock I heard a series of gunshots and went out on the porch to see police cars with sirens and flashing red lights rush to a corner about a block away. A cab driver had dropped off a fare who then ran off without paying. The cabdriver pulled a gun from under his seat and shot at the passenger, who ran inside, found his own weapon and got off a few shots in return.

Another time Tom and I were driving in the neighborhood when two undercover police pulled ahead of us, stopped, came out with their guns drawn, and made the passengers in the car right in front of us get out with their hands in their air. The police thought they might be connected to an armed robbery at a nearby liquor store.

In the wake of the Vatican Council, the Indiana Province of Holy Cross was rethinking (for some reluctantly) the whole structure and sequence of religious and professional formation. In 1967, at the Indiana Provincial Chapter, the decision was made to close Holy Cross College as of the summer of 1968. It was also determined that the Foreign Mission Seminary would remain open and that students who lived there would take classes at Catholic University. Faculty from Holy Cross College who had a doctorate or its equivalent and were interested in teaching at Notre Dame would be given full consideration for available faculty positions at the University. The only faculty members who ended up going to Notre Dame in the fall of 1968 were Fathers Bill Toohey, Jim Sullivan, Maury Amen, Jim Denn, and Lenny Paul. Father John Ford chose instead to join the Catholic University faculty, and Father Charlie Schleck remained in Washington and continued his writing and consultation work with religious communities.

In retrospect, it seems unlikely that Holy Cross College could have been sustained much longer. Yet the confluence of events in the Province meant that, once the formal decision had been made, further thinking could go into the shape of the Master of Theology program at Notre Dame and to the role of Moreau Seminary as a combined house for both undergraduate seminarians and theologians.

"Spes Unica—The Cross Our Only Hope"

CHAPTER 7

FINAL VOWS

Moreau Seminary (1968–69)

Father Louis Putz, C.S.C., became rector in 1966 when Moreau was still a college seminary. His appointment represented a radical break from the model of seminary education that had prevailed in the Holy Cross community and in the American Catholic Church throughout the twentieth century.

Father Putz was born in Germany in 1909. In 1922, his aunt, who was a Holy Cross sister, arranged for him to enroll at Holy Cross Seminary at Notre Dame. He arrived at age fourteen, did well in his studies, and graduated with a bachelor's degree. After ordination, he did pastoral work in France where he became familiar with the Catholic Action movement, which placed a heavy emphasis on lay involvement in the Church and on outreach to the broader society. In 1939, as Hitler's armies attacked Poland, he returned to Notre Dame to become a professor in the department of religion. In the 1940s he was involved in the initiation of the Young Christian Students (YCS) on campus, and then became chaplain for the Christian Family Movement (CFM), which would become particularly strong in the Midwest. Somewhat later he helped found Fides Publishers, which published the best European theological writings in translation, a critical step for preparing American receptivity to Vatican II.

Louis Putz was by instinct an organizer, a cultivator of other peoples' talents, and an activist more than a theoretician. He was somewhat suspicious of authority and was used to acting first and asking permission later. He was a friendly maverick whom his Holy Cross colleagues generally admired, but it was considered unlikely that he would ever be given any formal authority in the life of the community or the University. In a fortuitous bit of timing, however, in 1965 Fides Press published a book titled *Seminary Education in a Time of Change*, co-edited by Father Putz and a lay colleague, James Michael Lee. It came out just as Vatican II was drawing to a close, and it offered a fund of ideas for the future shape of seminary education.

The book reminded readers that many models of seminary education existed at different periods of church history. The chapters that focused on academic concerns were uniformly critical of the intellectual preparation of clergy and endorsed seminary education in a university setting. When it came to the selection of seminary candidates, the book argued for psychological testing. Louis Putz's own chapter in the book focused on "The Layman in Seminary Education." The initial reaction of seminary rectors to the book was hostile, as was to be expected. They objected to the emphasis on education more than formation, to the description of the priesthood as a profession rather than a vocation, to the proposal that minor seminaries be closed, and to the assertion that smaller major seminaries should be amalgamated into larger ones.

What Father Putz was thinking when Father Kenna invited him to become Superior of Moreau Seminary in 1966, no one will ever know. Some in the Indiana Province saw the selection as a tragic mistake. I and my peers, on the other hand, interpreted the move as a great sign of hope for us: finally things were starting to change in seminary formation, and even if it did not affect us directly at Holy Cross College, we were delighted that our younger peers would be living under the new dispensation. The first thing Father Putz did was recruit to the seminary staff priests who were sympathetic to the need for change. Among the newcomers the first year were Chet Soleta, Bill Lewers, and Tom Chambers. The following year, Joe Simons and John Dunne joined the staff. The new blood was much more involved in the lives of the seminarians than those who had been carried over from the past.

One of the most noticeable early changes was that the college seminarians took classes on campus and dressed like other students. Just as importantly, the total group of seminarians was broken into teams of around ten students, each with a chaplain who had special responsibility for their spiritual and personal formation. The Sunday morning mass in Moreau soon became well known to people on campus and in the surrounding community as an opportunity to experience excellent contemporary church music and well-prepared homilies.

Louis Putz was pious and rather traditional in his own spirituality. For all his reputation for leadership in liberal or progressive movements, he prized the priesthood, loved Holy Cross, and wanted to turn out priests and brothers who were not only well trained and highly professional, but also men of prayer and deep commitment to the Church. This meant that the changes he implemented in the college seminary program at Moreau were not undertaken for their own sake but in order to better prepare young men for their future service. What he was not so ready to deal with was the relative immaturity of the men who were in formation. Not unlike their peers on campus, they were sometimes suspicious of authority figures (even well-intentioned ones), somewhat baffled by all the changes they had been through, still struggling with fundamental issues about vocational discernment, and fully capable of disappointing their mentors in matters large and small. Given the new freedoms of seminary life, it was more obvious when things went wrong—for instance, when someone came back from a party drunk or decided to go on a quasi-date or failed to fulfill an academic or apostolic responsibility. Disagreements between seminarians and staff were more public. Some seminarians inevitably took to testing the limits of acceptable behavior.

After two years of the new regime, Father Putz must have welcomed the news that Holy Cross College would be closed and the theologians in Washington who had not finished their degree work would be moving to Moreau. Almost overnight the makeup of the house became older and presumably more mature. For the first time in the recent history of the Indiana Province, collegiate professed seminarians and professed theologians lived together and shared a common life.

For me, returning to Notre Dame for my third year of theology gave me an opportunity to find out whether the quality of the courses and the overall learning environment would be superior to what we had at Holy Cross College. And in fact, it was. The Master of Theology (later changed to Master of Divinity) degree was newly offered at Notre Dame in 1968–69. The guiding philosophy was to combine four content courses each semester, divided according to the major branches of theology, with pastorally oriented courses which were intended to develop specific priestly skills such as preaching, liturgical leadership, and counseling, and to foster diverse practical experiences—working with particular groups and reflecting about it in an organized way. The first obvious advantage of Notre Dame was that the faculty in the theology department were more numerous and much better prepared. They also had a research orientation and were writing some of the books we were reading. On the other hand, some of them had never taught seminarians and they had to adjust to a new mix of expectations. For example, in Scripture classes we were interested not only in the theoretical debates about interpretation, but also in how to preach about specific passages.

Final Vows

At the end of our coursework that year, we took written and oral exams. All members of my third-year class passed our requirements and were awarded the Master of Theology degree in June 1969. Later, after I joined the Notre Dame faculty and became director of the Master in Theology program, the curriculum and structure I inherited were not too different from what I took myself as a student in the program.

The new Moreau Seminary in 1968–69 was transformed significantly from the year before, both in composition and in style. In 1967–68, the student body was made up of twenty-eight college clerical seminarians and five brother candidates. One year later, it had twenty-two college seminarians, two brothers in formation, and fifty-three theology students. Furthermore, the theology students included members of the Indiana, Eastern, Southern, and Anglo-Canadian provinces. Additional diversity was achieved when Father Hesburgh invited Monsignor Jack Egan, the inner-city pastor and social activist from Chicago, to come to the campus as a Senior Fellow. When Louis Putz heard about Jack Egan's availability, he offered him room and board at Moreau if he would serve as chaplain to the newly constituted group of diocesan seminarians being recruited to study in the Master of Theology program. Monsignor Egan quickly became a valued member of the Moreau staff, and his contacts in Chicago and around the country were invaluable for future seminarian pastoral placements.

Another non–Holy Cross priest in residence at Moreau in 1968–69 was Father Henri Nouwen, a Dutch-born psychologist in Notre Dame's psychology department. Subsequently he became a popular teacher and lecturer in the United States, Europe, and Canada, and one of the most prolific and best-selling spiritual authors of the post–Vatican II period.

Change and experimentation were in the air at Moreau Seminary under Father Putz. In house masses, concelebration became the norm. Liturgical music went in the direction of the guitar more than the organ, and new compositions appeared with great regularity. Some secular songs were occasionally introduced, especially in the reflective period after communion, because of their seeming profundity or fit. Those with musical talent in the house organized themselves into groups that sometimes included guitars, bass, drums, piano (or keyboard), and horn. Some of the music stirred our souls and some was tedious or banal from the first hearing. It was also an era of banners and flowing vestments and greater incorporation of non-clerics in liturgical roles. For the canon of the Mass we usually gathered around the altar rather than remaining in the pews.

Moreau became a place of regular hospitality, not only for the Holy Cross community but also for laypeople, male and female, family members, and other invited guests. Not only did the Notre Dame football team stay overnight before home games, we also put up fathers, brothers, uncles, and male cousins of the seminarians. For meals and special celebrations we were free to invite faculty members or fellow students or visitors. The Thursday night social gatherings that followed a prayer service called *Lucenarium* became especially popular.

We had much readier access to the campus. It was a year of great ferment nationally and internationally, and Notre Dame was not spared some of the manifestations of these tensions. When Senator Strom Thurmond spoke on campus, members of the Notre Dame Afro-American Society walked out chanting "I'm black and I'm proud." The same organization demanded scholarship support for blacks, black admission recruiters, black counselors, black faculty members, tutorial programs for black freshmen, and a goal that 10 percent of the student body be black by 1972. Father Hesburgh met with them but made no specific promises. In March, the Afro-American Society and Student Government's Civil Rights Commission sponsored a Black Arts Festival, and later in the year the Black Power Forum heard from James Farner and Adam Clayton Powell.

A second campus issue revolved around the CIA and Dow Chemical recruiting on campus, both strongly opposed by anti–Vietnam War groups. The third issue was frivolous. The Student Union organized a conference on Pornography and Censorship, part of which was a display of controversial pieces of art on the second floor of La Fortune (material that was thought risqué at the time but would generate no interest today) and the showing of X-rated movies. The first turned out to be boring. The film portion led to the involvement of the county prosecutor and a short chase around the campus. It was a madcap scene made more absurd by the disconnect between a rational discussion about censorship and the actual events.

My third year of theology experience was affected by the realities of the Roman Catholic Church and American society. The encyclical *Humanae Vitae* precipitated debate about the status of papal teaching (including encyclicals), about theological dissent, and about the freedom of the individual conscience to make decisions about such matters as contraception. Most informed Catholics knew a Papal Birth Control Commission had been meeting for several years before the issuance of the encyclical, and there had been continued speculation that a nuanced change in Church teaching would be forthcoming. It also was known that a large majority of the commission had recommended such a change. On campus, the theology department chairman, Father James Burtchaell, C.S.C., wrote that he considered the encyclical "grossly inadequate and largely fallacious." He was not alone, either in the theology department or among the overall faculty, in expressing a critical opinion. Father Hesburgh defended the right of faculty to speak publicly from their professional competence, even if they disagreed with the pope. Neither on the Notre Dame campus nor in the larger Church community would this controversy disappear in my remaining years of formation or thereafter.

One of the most emotionally distressing realities of Catholic Church life was the growing number of clergy who were leaving the priesthood, many to get married. The explanations for this exodus were numerous, but it meant that I was preparing to be ordained in a Church where many were making a decision to leave, including some who had been priests and religious for decades. I had already come to know priests who left. Some of them had seemed characteristically unhappy, with maturity levels suggesting they may have been naive when they chose to be ordained. Others had simply fallen in love, perhaps for the first time. In the face of this trend, our generation tried to focus on fundamental things—good community life, close friendships, first-rate professional training, and an effective personal spirituality. We hoped that the Church that was coming into existence would be more amenable to what we expected in the wake of the Council. We wanted to be *with* and *of* the people rather than *above* them. We were not interested in preserving priestly privilege or clerical status.

In the wider Church, the revised rite of the Mass was promulgated to become effective on the First Sunday of Advent in 1969. It took more time, however, for a full vernacular translation to appear. Because of the timing of all this, I never, as a deacon or as a priest, played a liturgical role in a Latin mass. All of my priestly experience would be with the new mass in English or some comparable vernacular language.

At the end of the year, my classmates and I took final vows and were ordained to the diaconate. My parents and my sisters and their husbands were all able to attend the ceremonies in the Moreau Seminary Chapel. Louis Putz was his gracious best over the weekend, and everyone was taken by the spirit of hospitality that prevailed at Moreau. The rituals of the Church, simple but profound, are especially impressive in these ceremonies. We received a cross as a sign of our permanent membership in the Congregation and in response to the profession of vows of poverty, chastity, and obedience. I was delighted and inspired to have been approved for this step and was fully committed to doing my best to be faithful to the vows. The ordination to the transitional deaconate was less significant, since our goal was ordination to the priesthood, but we did from that point on have official approbation to function in sacramental contexts.

Because a number of us were going into graduate study after ordination, we engaged in the language preparation required by most doctoral programs. I decided to study Intensive German at Stanford University along with classmate Tom Oddo. We were provided a car and drove from South Bend to San Francisco, stopping at interesting points along the way. Several college seminarians who also had summer placements in California rode with us. Tom and I arrived a week ahead of Stanford's summer school. I had arranged for us to stay with Oscar and Alma Wong, who lived in the middle of the city; Oscar and I were undergraduate classmates and we had lived with the Mc-Groarty family in Las Vegas in the summer of 1962. This visit was my first exposure to the beauty and cultural diversity of San Francisco, and even though we had a car at our disposal, we spent most of our time on foot or in public transportation. We walked all around the downtown area, we rode cable cars, we drove through the Presidio and visited the Sunset District and the zoo and Twin Peaks and the Castro. We were amazed by the mix of sun and clouds and fog and how the same vista changed dramatically depending on the time of day and the weather.

Among the places we visited, none was more engaging than the Haight-Ashbury district of San Francisco and the People's Park section of Berkeley. The first ramification of an urban countercultural movement in the post-WWII era was centered in the North Beach neighborhood of San Francisco in the mid-1950s and early 1960s. It revolved around such figures as Jack Kerouac, Allen Ginsberg, Lawrence Ferlinghetti, and William Burroughs. The Beats, as they were called, were supplanted in the mid- to late 1960s by the so-called Hippie Movement. Like the Beats, the Hippies were seen as representatives of youthful alienation, a rock-and-roll lifestyle, and the open use of marijuana, LSD, and other hallucinogenic drugs.

By the summer of 1969, Haight-Ashbury had lost some of its bloom. The drug problems were more severe, crime had become endemic, and many of the people on the streets in the daytime were tourists, like us. Nevertheless, it was my first personal exposure to a Bohemian, libertarian settlement, and I was fascinated. Most striking for me was that most of the participants in the Hippie Movement were Caucasian teenagers and young adults, relatively well educated, who had grown disenchanted with their families' aspirations and had come to San Francisco to be liberated, to kick back, to smell the flowers and listen to music. It would soon become obvious to Tom and me that there was much sadness and personal dysfunction in Haight-Ashbury. But having read about it and seen the images on television and listened to the songs of the psychedelic generation, I was excited to have firsthand exposure.

In April 1969, the *Berkeley Barb*, an underground newspaper, called for the creation of a "People's Park" on land owned by the university. Hundreds of people cleared and planted the land, set up playground equipment, and provided food. For several weeks, there were no problems, but then Governor Ronald Reagan sent in 250 police and highway patrol officers who cleared the park, put up a chain-link fence, and took back control. Reagan pictured it as a confrontation with leftist sympathizers. Later that day, a protest began at Sproul Plaza on the campus and moved to the park, where a violent confrontation took place. There was one death and 129 protestors were injured. Governor Reagan then declared a state of emergency and sent in 2,700 National Guard troops. A week later, after a memorial service at Sproul Plaza, another violent encounter took place.

By the time Tom and I had a chance to see the Cal Berkeley campus and People's Park, things had quieted down somewhat, but there was still electricity in the air. The Guard had left, and security for the park had been taken over by the Berkeley police. Yet Sproul Plaza was still full of hippies and wannabees as well as regular students, international tourists, undiscovered singers, mimes, and other entertainers—plus the mentally ill, the down and out, and representatives of various groups with a message. Marijuana was smoked openly, but without fanfare. For all its songs and proclamations about peace and brotherhood, there was a fundamental anger and sadness about the Berkeley scene. A kind of disenchantment had begun, and it was palpable. As summer went on, we returned to Berkeley several times, both because we were intrigued by what we saw there and because it was a kind of barometer of the radical subculture in American life.

When our week in San Francisco was up, Tom and I drove to the Stanford campus in Palo Alto. We lived in a regular undergraduate student dorm, with separate single rooms in different parts of the hall. We made contact with the pastor of a Catholic church in Palo Alto who supplied chaplaincy services for Catholics on the campus; he was quite willing to have us preach at some of the parish daily liturgies. Each day we attended mass at the parish and, either on Saturday evening or Sunday morning, at the large campus chapel. That way we had a religious support system and also could exercise our diaconal skills on occasion. The Catholic community at Stanford was active, enthusiastic, and participative in the music. We felt lucky to be part of a well-established Catholic subculture amid the generally secular ambience of Stanford.

In my intensive German class there were about twenty students. The intent of the course was to enable us to pass the written qualification test for doctoral programs. I had taken no previous German, so I had a lot of learning to do. The reactions I got when some heard I was preparing to become a Roman Catholic priest were approximately the same as if I said I was Amish or a Hassidic Jew or Bahai. In the spirit of openness that characterized such campuses, one way of life was as good as another. Whatever I felt called to do was just fine with them. However, there was that celibacy thing.

Flanner Hall (1969–70)

At the end of my third year of theology at Moreau I received approval for placement as a resident assistant in Flanner Hall for my deacon year. I was to live on the fourth floor of Flanner (it had eleven floors in two connected towers), even though I was still formally a member of the Moreau community. Tom Oddo and I were the two deacons assigned to Flanner. Ollie Williams and Jack Lahey were in Grace Hall, right next door.

Because we had to get back to campus in time to start a training program for assistant rectors, several of us who were vacationing at Deer Creek, a summer recreational area for students and faculty of Holy Cross College in western Maryland, left for South Bend a couple of days early. Seven of us, including Tom Oddo and Jack Lahey, got up before sunrise that morning and piled into a station wagon with a rack on top for extra luggage. Tom Oddo drove, with two others in the front seat, three in the back, and one facing the rear surrounded by luggage. It was raining hard with substantial pools of water on the road.

Our route took us across a one-lane bridge that had to be entered at almost a 90-degree angle. As we approached the bridge and Tom began to brake, we all sensed that the vehicle was fishtailing. The turn was approaching fast and Tom had to make a decision—risk going directly into the water or hitting the inside metal guardrails of the bridge deliberately in an effort to bring the car to a stop. He chose the guard rails.

The left side of the station wagon collided with the metal support beams of the bridge. Our bodies were thrown around, some hitting the roof, others the windshield, and still others being pinned by the vehicle's caved-in door frames. All this took place almost in slow motion. When the metallic screeching of the collision ended, there was utter silence.

I turned out to be the only one not seriously hurt; I was seated on the far side from the point of impact and had been able to brace myself. I knew I had to get out and go for help but I was not sure I could open the door. After I managed that with a little effort, I saw a large semi-truck coming in our direction. In the dark and misty rain, I worried that the trucker would not see us, so I moved in front of our vehicle, whose headlights were still working, and waved my arms. The truck kept coming, but at last I heard air brakes begin to click in.

It came to a full stop about five yards from us. The driver jumped out and I gave him a quick summary of the crash. He agreed to stay with the station wagon while I ran to a nearby farmhouse whose occupants, having heard the crash, answered the door readily and allowed me to use their phone. It took twenty minutes for the first police car to arrive and forty-five minutes for the first ambulance. Tom Oddo had a broken wrist and cuts and abrasions; Jack Lahey had a broken hip; Father Jim Sullivan, C.S.C., who had already survived two surgeries for brain tumors, had hit his head against the windshield. He was bleeding from a cut on his forehead. The rest had cuts, abrasions, and potential neck and back injuries.

Surprisingly, everyone was calm and focused on how the others were doing. By the time we all made it to the hospital, a couple of hours had passed and Father Putz had joined us with several of his staff. I returned to Deer Park to give a report of the accident to everyone there.

Eventually I called my parents to assure them I was okay. The main advice I got from my father was to get behind the wheel of a car and take a drive as soon as possible. When I finally got to bed, it was twenty-four hours before I woke up. Even though I had not been physically injured, my emotional system had been profoundly affected. I did heed Dad's advice and took a test drive; I was quite uneasy and even shook a bit behind the wheel, but that reaction passed quickly. Yet even today under certain highway conditions I can feel myself tensing up as though I were reliving the crash, and although I am a calm airplane passenger, I dislike driving in heavy rain, snow, ice, or fog.

It was several days before Jack Lahey and Tom Oddo were released from the hospital. Tom sometimes would be apologetic about what happened, but I never blamed him. If he had tried going into the water, I doubt I would have made it, since I am a confirmed non-swimmer.

Back on campus we settled into our dorm roles. Both Flanner and Grace Halls were brand new and similarly laid out, and the logistical challenges for the staffs were comparable. The buildings were state-of-the-art in some senses. The basements were given over to student common space. On the first floors were a huge study lounge, offices, a small chapel, and a large lounge with a pit area in the middle that was used for informal gatherings or Sunday liturgies.

One of the buildings' design flaws was that on each floor, in each tower, all the bathroom and shower facilities were in the middle and the student rooms were on the periphery. This was a major disincentive for interaction among residents of the same section. My challenge as a resident assistant was to make sure I got to know by name and face each of the fourth-floor residents and as many men in the rest of the dorm as I could manage. I had a number of strategies. At the beginning of the year I spent considerable time wandering from room to room in order to fix the identities of the occupants in my mind, and also to observe the dynamics among roommates and next-door neighbors. I also invited individuals and small groups to my room for casual chats, usually with some light refreshment. I knew that most men would not be inclined to share their inner lives with me until I gained their trust. They knew, and I also recognized, that I was an agent of the hall administration, so there could develop circumstances where I might have to confront them for violating regulations. I was interested neither in establishing a reputation as a heavy enforcer nor in being taken advantage of.

One advantage I shared with the men on the fourth floor was my access to the gym at Moreau. That year in Flanner I began hosting groups of undergraduate students for basketball at Moreau at ten o'clock one evening a week, a practice that later came to be known as "Monk Hoops." I also played basketball with students on the Stepan Center outdoor courts across the street from Flanner.

The rector of Flanner was Father Maurice Amen, C.S.C., who taught in the theology department. He was a popular teacher who generally had large classes. Maurie had been on the faculty at Holy

Cross College when I was there, teaching canon law and moral theol
ogy. In the transition to Notre Dame, he was hired as an adjunct faculty member, which meant that he was not on tenure track and not
under pressure to publish. Maurie had responsibility for a large group
of resident assistants and two assistant rectors. Our weekly staff meetings were free flowing, a mix of necessary business and discussions
about particular students or problem areas. Notre Dame had never
had a high-rise dorm before, and we learned as we went along how to
function in that environment. Because the building had been certified
by the builders just before we moved in, it was inevitable that not
everything would work well. One of our first problems was with the
three elevators: to bring some rationality into their usage, especially at
peak hours, we issued an edict that residents living on the first four
floors had to take the stairways and leave the elevators for those on
the upper floors.

Another person in the dorm was Father Ernie Bartell, C.S.C., my
mentor when I was thinking about the priesthood. We were periodically invited to join the Holy Cross community at Corby Hall, which
the four deacons did with some trepidation. The superior at Corby, Father Tom McDonagh, C.S.C., was reputed not to be particularly happy
with the changes at Moreau under Father Putz. Corby Hall in those
days was a somewhat daunting environment at the evening meal for
those of us accustomed to a more relaxed style of community gatherings. Admittedly, much of our aversion was in our own heads.

In addition to serving as a resident assistant in Flanner Hall, I was
to teach as an adjunct instructor. The theology department was offering a seminar on "The Problem of Evil," a course designed to have a
common set of readings. Before the semester began, all of us who had
been recruited to teach gathered to discuss the course goals and how
we might make it into a true seminar. I figured it would be exciting to
test out my pedagogical skills, but in my pre-class enthusiasm I imagined myself with something like fifteen to twenty students, just about

right for a lively, truly participative seminar. To my chagrin, I found I had been assigned more than fifty students in both of two sections. I decided, as only someone young and eager might do, to divide each class into three groups, which meant that I taught six three-credit sections each semester—the highest teaching load in the University, I am sure.

At the first session I gave the class three time options. Then I had to make sure we had places to meet. Many of my sections met in the lounges of student dorms, a few met in the seminar rooms in the Hesburgh Library, and one met in my room in Flanner. My most bizarre decision (since each group met once a week for two and a half hours) was to schedule a class from midnight to two-thirty in my room. I usually stayed up that late anyway, so it was not a problem for me, but it took all my energy to keep a few of the students awake during the last hour of class.

"The Problem of Evil" was a rich topic, full of many examples that students were struggling with—the Vietnam War, racial prejudice, urban unrest, female subordination, persistent crime. Our texts were a mix of classical and contemporary, from the Book of Job to Camus' *The Plague*. I was surprised, once they learned to be candid, to discover how many had been touched by profound encounters with evil in the world: the death of a loved one, involvement in the aftermath of an accident or a natural disaster, betrayal by a supposed friend, sexual abuse, being a crime victim. Even at their age, there were plenty of relevant examples to explore.

I found that students sought me outside of the class for counsel and advice or just a friendly ear. I was old enough not to be a peer but young enough to seem comfortable with their culture. Sometimes the issues that they brought up were beyond my competence and I encouraged them to seek professional help, much of which was available on campus. I found that it was important for me to act as a go-between in such situations, since many students feared making an appointment. In retrospect, I developed confidence about my capacities

Final Vows

as a professor-to-be, and I found my identity as a priest-to-be fully compatible with the vocation of teaching, and even reinforced by it.

By 1969–70 Notre Dame dorm life had morphed a long way from my undergraduate days. It was still all male, with parietal hours, but otherwise the social world had opened up considerably. Alcohol could be possessed on campus but not openly in corridors or other specified places. It was acceptable to schedule parties in the designated student lounges in each dorm, and it was tolerated to have alcohol at parties in student rooms if the participants avoided excessively loud music or disruptive behavior. Marijuana use and the possession and/or use of other illegal drugs were prohibited.

In a large dorm like Flanner, staff patrolling of parties and other social gatherings was a complicated matter. First of all, there was no place where I could hang out and get a feel for the mood of the hall on a given night. Everything could be relatively serene on the first floor while a huge mob of students was assembled on the sixth. I could take the elevator to the tenth floor and walk down the whole building, section by section, at eleven o'clock, and by eleven-thirty nothing would be the same. When an advertised band played in the basement it was easier to pay a periodic visit and feel confident that I was doing my job than when the basement area was relatively dead and all the action was on the upper floors.

We had to adjust our expectations as the year went on. A pulled fire alarm was always bad and we had zero tolerance for such behavior. Public drunkenness, fighting, and disrespectful encounters between students and staff were equally unacceptable. When it came to parties on the edge of acceptability, or periodic violations of alcohol in public places, or student antics like water fights or Frisbee tossing in the lounge, we were constantly called to use our best prudential judgment. Any inconsistency from one group or day to the next would leave us open to accusations of unfairness or ill will. Yet the vast majority of the time it was enjoyable to be residing with the students and to be playing a positive role in their lives.

Perhaps, the trickiest disciplinary case we had to deal with involved a student who was suspected of dealing drugs from his room and was said to carry a gun. The first step was to discuss the situation with campus security and make sure we had our facts straight. Once the evidence was clear, we had to figure the safest and surest way to intervene. By reputation, the young man stayed up quite late and slept late in the morning. The police and the rector arranged to arrive at his room while he was asleep and when most of the students on the floor were off at class. Because they had a warrant, they could barge in unannounced and make the arrest without any resistance. The student did, in fact, possess a gun and illegal drugs, and we were pleased to be able to safely and swiftly extricate him from the dorm.

Worship in Flanner Hall took two forms. The weekday masses were held in the small chapel at ten o'clock in the evening with a congregation of anywhere from ten to twenty students. We took turns preaching and it was a good opportunity to get accustomed to preparing a three- or four-minute homily intended to touch the students' everyday interests, concerns, and experiences. There were two masses for the weekend; the main one was in the Pit at midnight Saturday, and there was a smaller one at eleven o'clock Sunday morning. The Saturday night congregation had to be shoe-horned in. There was always a folk band and singing that drew upon the new liturgical music. Some of it was solid theologically and relatively singable, and some of it was trivial or saccharine and a few years later would be abandoned. As a new hall with no traditions, our first year was a challenge in terms of the common prayer life. The space was configured in such a way that many of the worshipers were around corners and could not see the celebrant. It was difficult to establish eye contact and hard to get active participation. When preaching, I had to walk around in order to assure that a good cross section was really engaged in the homily. It was also logistically difficult to distribute communion, which was by then regularly dispensed under both species.

We were delighted with the huge congregations we drew, but there was not room for everyone. In addition, the midnight hour on Saturday did not satisfy everyone. On some Saturdays there was a live band in the social space directly below us, and the syncopated bass guitar and drums were distracting. Sometimes students who had been out drinking would walk in one of the side doors without realizing mass was going on. By the end of the year, however, the men of Flanner were proud of their liturgical tradition which, despite its deficiencies, was student-oriented, hospitable, and well prepared. I was able to preach often enough to refine my skills with a largely student congregation.

The most public manifestation of sentiment against the Vietnam War on campus took place on October 14, 1969, the eve of a nationwide moratorium protesting the war. Father Hesburgh had announced the day before that he had joined a group of college and university presidents who signed a letter urging a stepped-up withdrawal of troops. This was a major change from his previous public stances, which had been more nuanced and noncommittal. It also signaled the change going on throughout the country, not just in higher education. The central event on October 14 was a mass celebrated in the area between the Library pool and the football stadium. Father Ted was the celebrant, and an estimated 2,500 students were present, including a couple who placed their draft cards in the offertory basket. I remember the tone of the mass as pensive and reflective. Many in the congregation were struggling not only with their own political views but with how they should respond if drafted. There was talk on other campuses about more covert forms of civil disobedience or the option of fleeing to Canada. At Notre Dame it seemed fitting that a liturgy should be the signal movement that brought us all together.

That same day a smaller group with lighted candles marched around campus placing small wooden crosses in the ground to represent those killed in Vietnam. There had been some threats made to burn down the ROTC building, so the security police instituted a 24-hour watch detail. Despite all the powerful rhetoric and deep emotion on campus, there was no violence that day nor thereafter.

I learned in that year of turmoil that the residential tradition of Notre Dame, with its priests and brothers in residence in the halls, is a great resource for facing big issues and for empowering students to think, to converse, and to pray. They could never claim there was no one to turn to for clarification, counsel, or consolation. I also discovered that there is nothing like teaching certain materials to someone else (such as the Catholic approach to violence) for entering into it more fully yourself.

Ordination

I was ordained to the priesthood on Saturday, April 4, 1970, in Sacred Heart Church, by Bishop Leo Pursley. Seven years after entering the Holy Cross formation program, I had finally made it. I was accompanied in the ceremony by five classmates from the Indiana Province. Three other classmates who had been part of our group at Moreau were ordained at North Easton, Massachusetts, a week later. Two Indiana Province theologians who had been studying in Chile were ordained there earlier in the year, and two who had been studying in Europe later in the year. Two others, who were preparing to work in the foreign missions, were ordained subsequently.

Overall, this was a large contingent of new priests in Holy Cross and a group blessed with a diversity of gifts. From my ordination class of April 4, there were Michael Glockner (who would spend most of his priestly service in parishes and chaplaincies), Jack Lahey (now deceased, who would teach and serve as a seminary rector and canonical advisor), Tom Oddo (now deceased, theology professor and president of the University of Portland), Frank Quinlivan (parish priest, novice master, foreign missionary, provincial in Bangladesh), and Ollie Williams (professor of theology, professor of business ethics, University administrator). My three Eastern Province ordination colleagues all worked in parishes, either in the U.S. or Peru. Dave Schlaver served in a variety of roles, from university administration to foreign mission work to religious publishing. Paul Marceau engaged in teaching, counseling, formation work, and Province administration. Both Steve Gibson and Duane Bulcerski served for significant periods in East Africa and subsequently worked in the U.S. in hall rectoring, retreat work, media services, formation, and parish ministry. John Connor served in Chile before joining the Holy Cross Ministry to Mexican Americans in the Coachella Valley area of Southern California. More than thirty-five years after our ordinations, of the total group of thirteen who became priests in 1970 two have died and three have left the active ministry. The other eight are still involved in a wide variety of ministries. God has been good to us overall.

Present for my ordination were my mother and father; my sister Joanne and her husband, Bob Rorapaugh, and their son, John; my sister Mary and her husband, John Long; Sister Elizabeth Malloy, I.H.M.; and various members of both sides of the extended Malloy clan. Also in attendance were some college and high school friends. The ordination ceremony lasted about one and a half hours and was characterized by the solemnity and symbolism that are such a rich part of the Catholic sacramental tradition. For anyone who had never been present for an ordination before—the vast majority of family members and visitors present—it was an impressive manifestation of the Church renewing itself in service to the people of God. At the heart of the ceremony were an instruction from the bishop, the certification of worthiness by the serving rector Father Putz, the laying on of hands by the bishop and then by all the priests present, the conveying of the Scriptures and the sacred vessels as a sign of the duties to be undertaken, and the vesting in stole and chasuble for the concelebration of the mass.

Family members brought the gifts up and were the first to receive at communion time, each going to the area where their son was standing. At the conclusion, the newly ordained were invited to give their first blessing along with the bishop. Outside the church, semi-pandemonium broke loose as large groups of family and friends cheered the ordained and asked for blessings. In the sacristy afterward, Bishop Pursley, who was an older man whom none of us really knew, congratulated us and told us not to get used to the applause—the implicit message being that our priestly lives would not be all roses and honey.

After the ceremony, there was a reception and dinner at Moreau Seminary. As usual, the staff at the Seminary were perfect hosts. For the assembled families, the dinner was also a feast that recognized their roles in preparing the way for their sons. My parents were good examples of how faith-filled lives, regular religious practice, support for education in Catholic schools, and emotional encouragement are crucial to the road to the priesthood. I knew that my parents and sisters would have loved me and supported me no matter what I chose to do. In being present for my ordination they were displaying their pride in what I had chosen to do with my life, and I was given a chance to thank them publicly for always being there for me.

The party carried on long into Saturday night. Then at eleven o'clock on Sunday morning I had my first post-ordination mass in the Pit area of Flanner Hall. Most of those present were part of my entourage, and in my homily I was able to thank everyone for being part of a special weekend. We spent the rest of Sunday wandering around the campus, sharing meals together, and otherwise enjoying each other's company. The odd thing about the weekend was that it snowed on Friday evening, even though it was April. The snow melted quickly but it reminded the visitors of the stories they had heard about South Bend weather.

The week after my ordination I celebrated my official "First Mass" at Saint Anthony's Church, my home parish in Washington. Six Holy Cross priests concelebrated with me, and it was a great thrill to celebrate mass in the church where I worshiped as a child, was an altar boy, went to confession, received my First Communion, and attended retreats and other celebrations. This was the church community that had nurtured me, helped my parents pass on their faith, and made me proud to be a Catholic. It was here where I had first come to know priests on a personal basis and discovered that they were real human beings, full of the same range of likable and off-putting qualities as everyone else.

After mass there was a reception and buffet-style dinner in the parish hall. Later that evening the faithful remnant gathered at the Malloy household where stories were told, a few beers were drunk, and everyone debriefed on the excitement of the day.

As I reflected about priesthood in the wake of my ordination, I knew that my faith life had been nourished by regular (and often daily) participation in the Eucharist. My recognition of the special place the Mass holds in my personal piety was not simply a function of seminary training or the expectation that priests should celebrate mass daily; by 1970 I had had the opportunity to be present for the sacrament in every possible kind of setting, from basilicas and cathedrals to beach fronts, from mountaintops to kitchen tables and hotel rooms. For me the people present and the inspiration for the gathering were always more important than the splendor of the backdrop or the formality of the ritual. While I could appreciate the special parts of the liturgical calendar like Christmas and Holy Week and Easter, most of the time I preferred simplicity and ease of celebration over fancy vestments, long processions, and polyphonic song.

In interaction with the people I was called to serve I was never big on the use of titles or other formal signs of deference. I introduce myself to students, faculty, and staff as "Monk," not as "Father Malloy" or "Reverend Malloy." As a young priest, that was relatively easy to pull off, but even years later it is my established manner of presenting myself. And I still find myself uncomfortable in certain ecclesiastical circles (like the Vatican and East Coast Catholicism) where even life-long friends who are clerics or bishops address each other as if they were titled royalty from the Middle Ages.

I looked forward to my doctoral work in theology as a necessary next step toward teaching in a university setting. In my deacon year, as much as I relished the six sections I taught each semester, I also discovered my limitations as a thinker and expositor of the Catholic Christian tradition. I knew I had much to learn and I was eager to get about it.

By the time I was ordained I had come to the firm conclusion that I was fortunate indeed to be a part of a religious community of men. I enjoyed community life, even if on occasion the dynamics became complicated. It seemed clear that diocesan priests would more and more end up living with one other person, often with a big age and ex-perience gap, or else by themselves in large rectories designed for a different era in church history. It looked to me to be an inherently lonely way to live. My years in the seminary and as a staff member in Flanner Hall had convinced me that I would do a lot better with friends and colleagues as regular parts of my residence and work situ-ations. Even in graduate school, that is how it turned out to be.

Theoretically, I was what might be called, at the time of my ordi-nation and today, a progressive Vatican II Catholic. My experiences in Latin America, in Saint Elizabeth's Mental Hospital, and in inner-city Detroit, as well as my exposure to the American counterculture in San Francisco and Berkeley, all disposed me to be an advocate for social justice and to be open to the rethinking of complicated social issues. I did not feel comfortable with fanatics of either the left or the right. I was a centrist by temperament and disposition who was convinced that positive change could be effected by good analysis, persuasive ar-guments, group mobilization, and hard work. I felt that the Catholic theological tradition, which had been slow to take on certain issues like slavery, torture, capital punishment, and the status and treatment of women, was a great resource that needed to be plumbed anew in the aftermath of the Vatican Council. I was delighted that the Catholic Church was displaying a new ecumenical and interfaith openness. I considered myself to be a patriotic American who saluted the flag and enthusiastically sang the National Anthem, but I looked to political leadership to offer a more responsible vision when it came to both domestic and international priorities.

The real issue in my deacon year had been what I would study for the doctorate. English was one possibility, but I became quite interested in theology while pursuing my M.Th. degree. For a while, I thought it made the most sense to apply to schools that had a combined degree, sometimes called theology and literature. The University of Chicago was one distinguished institution that offered that alternative. Before committing myself, I consulted widely with people in the Holy Cross community who knew the ways of the academy better than I did. Their unanimous advice was not to do a combined program, since it would be hard to find a disciplinary home after receiving the doctorate, and it would be too easy to become marginalized. They thought that I should choose either English or theology.

I decided that as a priest, I would be inherently more interested in and committed to the issues we would take up in theology. (The ironic side of all of this uncertainty is that after I became president, having already taught for over a decade in Notre Dame's theology department, I ended up teaching seminars in literature and film which drew upon my earlier training in English.) Next I needed to determine which area of theology would be closest to my native gifts and preoccupations. Once I phrased it that way, I quickly chose Catholic moral theology or Christian ethics.

Once I had a clear notion of what area I wanted to pursue and had taken the requisite GRE exams I applied to five schools—Boston University, Chicago, Princeton, Vanderbilt, and Yale. I was eventually accepted at Boston, Chicago, and Vanderbilt, and I received attractive financial offers from all three. In the end I chose Vanderbilt because it was ranked in the top five in my field, it was in a part of the country that I hardly knew, and they really seemed to want me. As it turned out, I was the first Roman Catholic priest Vanderbilt had ever had in the Christian ethics area.

It was only after I said yes to Vanderbilt that I learned that my ordination classmate and friend, Ollie Williams, was also planning to attend Vanderbilt. That meant that the two of us would be able to share a common life, including an automobile. I have never regretted my decision to enroll at Vanderbilt. It was a university on the move, and the Divinity School had attracted outstanding faculty talent. It would be my first experience of studying outside of an explicitly Catholic environment—that was a special part of the lure.

For the summer of 1970 I needed to stay around Notre Dame to take a course in French. I lived that summer in Moreau Seminary, which was an interesting place to be even though most of the seminarian students were gone. John Dunne, C.S.C., was writing his first book, *The City of God.* He used to come to the faculty recreation room in the evening and brag that it was a good day because he had written a paragraph. Father Henri Nouwen was also living at Moreau and writing his first book. Other members of the staff or the priests in residence were also involved in various projects. It was a small but compatible group, and in addition to the common prayer, we enjoyed each other's company at meals and late at night in the recreation area. It reminded me of the kind of intellectual-pastoral community that Saint Augustine of Hippo tried to establish after he became a bishop.

One of the members of the Moreau community was Monsignor Jack Egan, who used the summer for meetings of clergy and laypeople involved in urban ministry from around the country. It was always interesting to talk to him about the trends he saw and to meet the guests he brought by. In so many cases, Catholic inner-city parishes were great centers of outreach but underfinanced and subject to all kinds of pressure and tensions from external forces in the neighborhoods. My one major involvement that summer was as a non-voting delegate to the Indiana Province Chapter, which was held at Notre Dame. It was my first direct experience of the basic every-three-year governance structure of the provinces of the Congregation of Holy Cross. The only higher authority is the General Chapter, which takes place every six years and governs the affairs of the whole Congregation, but the Provincial Chapters have a more direct impact on the everyday life of the members.

The Provincial Chapter of 1970 lasted for two weeks and was full of impassioned discussions as the members tried to come to grips with the same sources of tension and disagreement that were then present in the broader Church. The implementation of Vatican II, the role of Holy Cross in our various apostolates (including Notre Dame and Portland), the nature of lay collaboration, and the appropriate approach to seminary formation were all on the docket. Tom Oddo and I, although only recently ordained, helped with the logistics and hospitality. For both of us it was a great opportunity to meet a diverse cross section of the Province and to become aware of the different points of view they reflected. Some of the delegates from mission areas I had never encountered before. The elected delegate from the seminarian group was our classmate Frank Quinlivan, a great choice as far as we were concerned.

Father Howard Kenna, the Provincial, in his November 1970 *Circular Letter* describing the nature of the Chapter had this to say. "We met at a critical moment in our history. . . . We wrestled with deep differences of opinion in the Province. . . . They emerge from varieties of experience and from different perceptions of effectiveness in responding to the anguished society we seek to serve in the Lord." It was my judgment after watching the Chapter unfold that only when the 1973 Chapter came around and a new provincial elected that a real mandate for change would be built into the governance structure of the Province. The 1970 Chapter achieved a good degree of clarification about what the unresolved areas were, and it put in place some transitional mechanisms. As I prepared to go off to study at Vanderbilt, I could sense real signs of hope for my generation.

What had begun in the seminary under Louis Putz was beginning to have an impact on the life of the local communities throughout the Province. No one was sure exactly what shape the future would take, yet the direction my generation advocated seemed closer to being embraced by the Province at large.

CHAPTER 8

VANDERBILT (1970–1973)

SINCE I NEVER VISITED VANDERBILT UNIVERSITY prior to enrolling, I had to learn everything from scratch. It was my first experience living in the South and I was eager to encounter the richness and diversity of one more of America's regional cultures.

Ollie Williams and I drove down to Nashville from Notre Dame in a red Ford that contained most of our worldly possessions. The trip took about eight hours, which meant that Vanderbilt was close enough to allow for an occasional trip to Notre Dame but far enough to deter us from returning for non-essential purposes. Both of us were living on a budget and we sought to husband our resources effectively.

We settled into an apartment in a development two or three miles from the campus. Our commute was a straight shot back and forth on one of the main thoroughfares. An important step on our part was to get plugged into the local Catholic community and to make our services available to area parishes. Before our arrival we had contacted Monsignor George Rohling, the chancellor of the diocese, who was also the pastor of Saint Henry's Church. He made us feel welcome right from the start and soon gained credibility for us with the local diocesan priests. George was charming and gracious, the personification of Southern hospitality. He had been born and raised in Nashville and had great pride in the city. He also possessed a perfect Tennessee accent, a mid-level drawl with extra syllables added to many words.

On weekends Ollie and I alternated celebrating mass at four or five different parishes. I often ended up preaching at five masses at Saint Henry's from late Saturday afternoon to late Sunday morning; it was the tradition for one priest to preach at all the masses on a weekend. I was exhausted by the end of the last mass but I enjoyed getting a feel for parish life and meeting the parishioners, some of whom had either Notre Dame or Vanderbilt connections. Before we left the area three years later, Ollie and I had been in most of the parishes at least once, given retreats and helped out with substitute work as chaplains for the sisters at the big Catholic hospital, celebrated daily children's masses for periods of time at one of the parishes, and regularly attended the biweekly priest get-togethers, in which Bishop Joe Durick sometimes participated as well. We became well known in diocesan circles and we both thought highly of the quality of the diocesan clergy we met. In addition to the liturgical and spiritual involvements with Catholic institutions in Nashville, I also gave a commencement address at Saint Cecilia High School and later returned to Nashville to speak at the dedication ceremony for the new Bishop Ryan High School.

The Catholic community in Nashville was relatively small in size but quite fervent. Unlike some Southern dioceses that were dependent on FBI's (foreign-born Irish clergy), Nashville's diocesan priests were almost all born and raised in Tennessee. Some of the older priests had memories of Klan crosses burning on their rectory lawns, but by the time we arrived relations between Catholics and Protestants were civil, and in some cases quite good.

My most embarrassing incident in Nashville occurred as the result of rearranging our apartment furniture. It was summer and I was scheduled to substitute at an ex urban parish for three weeks while the pastor took a vacation. It was a small parish with two masses on Sunday. I had been there once before and had enjoyed the talented music group that led the liturgical singing. In any case, one Saturday afternoon Ollie and I moved our dressers around and, by mistake, attached the electric alarm clock to an outlet that turned off and on along with the overhead light. That night when I flicked off the light, I also shut off the alarm clock. On Sunday morning I was awakened by the phone and discovered to my horror that I was already late for the first mass and the parish was at least forty-five minutes away. I dressed quickly and sped off to the parish. When I arrived about ninety minutes late, the church was full and the congregation was staring at me with a mixture of compassion and ire. The late start of that mass meant that those arriving for the second mass had a problem finding parking places. The parishioners were good about it, but for the next two weeks I took every precaution to arrive early so there would be no doubts about my reliability. By the third week, even their gentle jibes about promptness had dissipated.

Ollie and I were two of the first Catholics in our respective programs in the Vanderbilt Divinity School, and I was the first priest to study for a doctorate in Christian Ethics. At first, we were curiosity pieces, but since most of the graduate students spent so much time together in courses, in the school cafeteria, and in the student lounge we quickly got to know each other rather well. Once mutual confidence began to develop, some of the students would come up spontaneously to tell me that when they were growing up, they had been taught to be suspicious of Catholics and even to connect the pope with the Anti-Christ. Now that I was the first Catholic they knew, they wanted to pledge an openness of mind and a desire for friendship. Such moments were a bit awkward, even though I myself had grown up in something of a Catholic ghetto. I deliberately chose to attend a Protestant divinity school to round out my familiarity with the breadth of the Christian ethical tradition.

One day one of my friends in the program who was a Methodist minister told me he thought his denomination needed a private, anonymous, confidential way for ministers to interact with their flock, perhaps a dark room with a screen. I looked at him kind of quizzically and said that my tradition and his were like ships passing in the night. Catholics for decades had been going to confession to a priest who was sitting in a dark room while the parishioners knelt anonymously behind screens. Now, after Vatican II, many were going to confession face-to-face in comfortable, well-lighted rooms, a change designed to make the sacrament more comfortable and more personal. We agreed that there may be room for both forms of pastoral outreach.

At one point there was a report that Ian Paisley, the curmudgeonly arch-conservative Protestant minister from Belfast, Northern Ireland, was going to preach at a tent revival near Nashville. At first, I contemplated paying a clandestine visit to hear a person known as one of the world's prime examples of anti-Catholicism. Then my wiser self took over and I considered what I would say if someone at the rally asked me where I was from. My northern accent would give me away and I would not know any of the code words or secret signs. I had seen too many movies of Klan gatherings not to have second thoughts. Even though I ended up not going to the tent meeting, I have always wondered what it would have been like.

Twice during my time in Nashville I made retreats at the Gethsemani Trappist Monastery in Kentucky. Gethsemani was famous as the residence of Thomas Merton, whose *Seven Story Mountain* had been a huge bestseller. In the 1960s Merton published extensively on matters of social justice and inter-church relations, as well as on spirituality and monasticism. By the time I visited Gethsemani, he had died tragically in a hotel room accident in Thailand while on his way to meet with Buddhist monks.

The monastery was regulated by the rhythm of prayer and work that had characterized the Trappist community since its foundation, although Merton had forced certain changes in the quality of theological formation and in the monks' outreach to the broader society. I was able to attend the common prayer and to walk through the surrounding fields. The lay cemetery right outside the main entrance had tombstones that went back to the early period of the settlement of Kentucky. The monastic cemetery inside the gates had rows of crosses, each with a simple notation of name, birth date, date of first profession, and year of death. Merton's plot was a carbon copy of the rest. In one of the farm fields I found a large stone marker commemorating the death of three civil rights workers who were killed in Philadelphia, Mississippi, during the protest movements in the South. I found Gethsemani a prayerful place in which to make a retreat. Even though I have never felt any personal attraction to the monastic life, I admire those who do and recognize how powerful their collective witness can be.

In my second year in Nashville, Ollie and I were joined by two other Holy Cross priests—Jack Lahey and Terry Lally—who were to be enrolled in the doctor of ministry program, which was somewhat less than a Ph.D. but a serviceable credential nonetheless. Since there were four of us, we were able to find a house owned by a faculty member on leave. In many ways, we were ideal house-sitters since we were older, had no children, and were unlikely to hold wild parties. At first, we decided to cook for ourselves, something Ollie and I had only undertaken a couple of times in our first year together. The first two meals went reasonably well, since Ollie and Jack had some experience. Then it was Terry's turn. His idea of a good meal was one that had a maximum number of carbs. That did not go over very well. But the *coup de grace* was my attempt. The potatoes were lumpy, the meat was burnt, and the vegetables were only cooked on one end.

That night we had a heart-to-heart meeting and decided to gather each evening for a half-hour social and then go out to eat. One of our favorite haunts was an all-you-can-eat cafeteria. Unfortunately, Terry, who was a long distance runner and an exercise freak who looked like Charles Atlas, was capable of eroding the restaurant's profits in a couple of meals. Eventually the manager politely disinvited us.

Jack and Terry brought a second car to our household, but Jack had never learned to drive. It became my responsibility to teach him and he was not a quick learner. He was so afraid of making a mistake that sometimes he just sat there. He feared two things above all— parallel parking on a downhill slope and driving on the interstate. After several weeks of inconsistent performance, I convinced Jack to take the Tennessee driver's test. At the courthouse he filled out the appropriate forms, took the eye test and written exam, and then drove off with the state inspector. He passed—possibly because the tester was impressed by his sense of caution. On the way home I had him turn onto the interstate, at which point he started sweating profusely. He almost got a ticket for going under the minimum speed.

Once Jack had his license, Ollie and I figured everything would be alright. How wrong we were. Every morning Terry and Jack would race for the keys to their car, since neither could stand riding with the other at the wheel. To Jack, Terry was an irresponsible daredevil who pulled into oncoming traffic without looking. To Terry, Jack was catatonic, scared of his own shadow, the kind of driver who sat at intersections until there were no cars in sight and who rode the brakes instead of the gas pedal. Ironically, it was Jack the slowpoke who ended up denting the car more than once. On one occasion, he hit the cars of two other priests on the semicircular driveway outside the rectory that was hosting one of the priests' get-togethers.

That year all four of us helped out at parishes on weekends. Both Terry and Jack were excellent preachers, so our collective impact on the Catholic community in Nashville was rather significant. Jack, who knew next to nothing about Notre Dame football, was worried at first about what to say after a fall mass when a Notre Dame fan might ask his opinion about yesterday's game. He developed a kind of Rorschach Test approach that allowed for multiple possible responses. Thus he would say, "It all depended on the second half" or "It was a classic case of the offense against the defense" or "What a coach!" or "Whoever would have thought?" Usually, the fan then took five minutes to deliver his own opinion of the game, which was what he really wanted to do anyway.

In my third year in Nashville, Terry and Jack decided to move onto other programs, and Ollie and I were joined by a Jesuit priest and a Jesuit seminarian. Additionally, another Holy Cross priest, Father John Chaplin, had moved to the area to become the Catholic chaplain at the Tennessee State Prison. After John established himself there he invited us to come out for a visit. The prison was old and dilapidated; it reminded me of the movies I had seen that were set at Alcatraz or Sing Sing. In many ways it was a scary place. Its population was about half white and half black, and when we went into the eating area, it became obvious that it was self-segregated. The same was true in the exercise yard. There seemed to be a consensus that it was safer to stay with one's own, even though white and black guards had responsibility for the whole prisoner group. We also visited death row and sat in the electric chair, not something I needed to do more than once. John stayed as chaplain in Nashville for several years. I admired him for his perseverance since it was difficult pastoral work indeed.

One day I was cutting the grass at our house when an older gentleman walked up and asked if I was one of the priests that he heard were living there. When I acknowledged that I was, he told me he had never met any priests before. He asked if he could use our bathroom and I said sure, pointed to the restroom just inside the door, and went back to my mowing. After a few minutes the man came out and told me that he never would have believed it; he had gone to the upstairs bathroom and looked in the medicine cabinet. To his surprise he found no evidence that any women were sequestered there. I had to laugh at his gall and his honesty.

Perhaps the best-known institution in Nashville was the Grand Ole Opry, with the Ryman Auditorium downtown serving as the stage for the live radio show that had been broadcast since WWII. Ollie and I went to the Opry four or five times, usually with visitors from out of town. It was an interesting cultural shift from the music I had grown up with. I liked some of the milder forms of country, but I did not have an ear for most bluegrass or Texas cowboy songs. The best lyrics often reminded me of soul music and traditional Irish songs, with their continual lament about promises broken, relationships ended, jobs lost, and hard times.

Vanderbilt is an urban campus with a student population close to Notre Dame's 12,000, but given its large medical complex it has a smaller undergraduate student body and a larger professional and graduate student base. The Divinity School is a fairly modern structure with its own chapel, dining hall, classrooms, offices, and lounges. The presence of a separate dining facility meant that it was possible, particularly at lunch, to interact on a fairly regular basis with my classmates and faculty in a relaxed setting. Right next door to the Divinity School was the main library, which made research quite convenient. I had always been a big reader, but never before in my life had I steadily worked my way through so much challenging and stimulating material. The classes were helpful, as were the discussions in the seminars or informally in the lounge or over a beer in a local pub. We took the pivotal comprehensive exams one by one and not as part of a group.

I knew when I arrived at Vanderbilt that I needed some place to work out regularly. I soon discovered a group that gathered for basketball every afternoon on the main court of the university gymnasium. The talent level was good and the style of play was to my liking. A man named Sam oversaw the student recreation programs at the gym and we soon became good friends. Sam gave me instant credibility with the long-time gym regulars, an important consideration when seeking to break into an established set of competitors. I played two days a week on average.

Within the Divinity School in my first year, I became a player-coach in the intramural league for graduate programs. Despite the fact that our depth was limited, we had enough front-line players to hold our own. In my three years we always made the playoffs, something the Divinity School had never done before. Playing on the team was another way to help break down barriers. When people asked me how I liked being a player-coach, I told them the great thing was that I never had to come out of the game unless I wanted to.

My peer group in the degree program was a mix of men and women, predominantly Protestant, many of whom were ordained ministers in mainstream denominations; the only other Catholic was Sister Aquin O'Neill. As I soon discovered, doctoral work was heavily dependent on extensive reading by the individual students. Course grades were often dependent on a final paper. Very seldom did students miss class and, especially in the seminar classes, participation was expected. As a graduate of a Catholic seminary, I knew quite a bit about topics that the courses did not cover and that no one seemed particularly interested in, but I had much to learn about Luther, Calvin, and the Anabaptists, about H. Richard Niebuhr, Reinhold Niebuhr, and Paul Tillich. Over time I learned to distinguish among the subtle theological distinctions that had led to the gradual proliferation of Protestant denominations. While Anglicans (Episcopalians), Presbyterians, and Baptists all had their origin in post-Reformation England, their present ecclesiastical and theological commitments continued to divide them.

At the end of my first semester all of us in the first-year group felt that we were lacking a historical sense of the evolution of Christian ethics. We knew a lot about specific authors or definable movements of thought. What we wanted was a course that moved beyond a particular faculty member's present research agenda to one that looked at the whole. At the initial meeting with the faculty, a fair amount of emotion was expressed about this lacuna in our training. Tom Ogletree later taught a course that had us reading many of the most significant and influential works in Christian ethics, from authors like Augustine of Hippo and Thomas Aquinas to H. Richard Niebuhr and John Courtney Murray. In my own later teaching career, I would take this lesson to heart and assume responsibility for providing a sweeping historical overview for new graduate students.

Over time I became interested in the ecumenical dimension of Christian ethics manifest in the United States. My presence in the ethics section of a historically Protestant divinity school was one sign of this development. I knew a growing number of lay and clerical Catholic scholars were studying at Harvard, Princeton, Yale, Chicago, Duke, and Baylor and that in some cases a Catholic professor had been hired in recent years. One reason why schools like Vanderbilt were so attractive to Catholics, especially in the area of social ethics, was that much of Catholic moral theology had been seminary-based. In addition, the best scholarship was being produced not in the United States but in Europe, and Catholic universities like Notre Dame, Boston College, and Georgetown had only recently begun doctoral programs in theology. Furthermore, Catholic moral theology had lost its scriptural roots and become preoccupied with canon law, penitential practice, and a catechetical approach to moral decision making. Young Catholics interested in graduate study considered the best Protestant divinity schools more solidly rooted in research and farther along in methodological sophistication. These schools also constituted an interesting change of direction and perspective that nicely complemented the education that students had already received under Catholic auspices.

What the Protestant churches lacked then, and still do, was a definitive teaching office within the church governance structure. I discovered at Vanderbilt that Episcopalians, Presbyterians, Lutherans, Methodists, and Baptists, among others, did not expect their top authorities to play a role comparable to the pope or to the bishop in the Catholic Church. As a result, a given theologian could gain a wide readership and a fair amount of personal influence among students, but this would not necessarily translate into an acceptance by the church itself of positions taken or reforms advocated by the scholar.

Ironically, as much as I enjoyed the debates and the free-flowing conversations during my Vanderbilt years, I found that I was a Roman Catholic through and through. I prized the sacramental sense of reality, the respect for tradition as well as Scripture, the concern for the Church as a community of learning and prayer and service. Whatever disagreements I might have had with particular popes or bishops, I still saw their teaching office as an asset. The Catholic instinct was to spawn reform movements, like new religious communities or lay confederations, while remaining bound to the center as represented by the papacy. Contrariwise, the Protestant way was to create new denominations and sects that were divided by doctrine, region, race, or ecclesial structure. Catholics were inherently centripetal, Protestants centrifugal.

Intellectually, one of the amazing parts of my experience at Vanderbilt was that I read the Protestant reformers' major works at a time when the Catholic Church was rethinking many things. I was especially taken by the writings of Martin Luther, many of the issues that he considered problematic were again under debate in the 1970s, with four centuries of religious experience behind us. Luther started out with no master plan but was led from topic to topic by the events of the moment and by the counter-arguments of his opponents. His antagonists in the discussion were not only the Catholic representatives of the Counter-Reformation but also other Protestant leaders. Luther quickly discovered that he had unleashed forces in European Christianity that would not necessarily reflect his views theologically or ecclesiastically. I found John Calvin's writings more systematic and less introspective. Luther and Augustine of Hippo resembled each other as did Calvin and Thomas Aquinas. The latter two were more reserved and orderly, yet I found Augustine and Luther inherently more interesting.

After successfully completing two years of classes I was eligible to take the comprehensive examination. First I had to submit an extensive reading list and indicate the subfields I wished to be tested on. Then I was pretty much on my own until the exam. Although I had confidence that I was up to the task, it was daunting to realize that the examiners could quiz me about almost any dimension of Christian ethics, from methodology to historical figures to major debates to contemporary applications.

The time passed quickly. With no more classes to take, I accepted a one-course teaching assignment at Aquinas College, a junior college in Nashville run by Dominican sisters. My course was designed to be a general overview of Christian ethics, and I figured that my comprehensive exam preparation would dovetail nicely with my teaching responsibilities. The students in the class were very different from the ones I had taught during my deacon year at Notre Dame. They were mostly older. Some were women going back to school after having raised their children. Some were full-time employees in hospitals or restaurants or small businesses who needed a college degree to be eligible for promotion. My most memorable student was a guard at the Tennessee State Prison who had grown up in rural Tennessee; he wrote an excellent paper on the state of the prison system and the need for reform. In his analysis he was acutely aware of how the ravages of society (family dysfunction, racial prejudice, violent subcultures) were largely responsible for perpetuating the types of criminal behavior that put the men he supervised in prison.

My two semesters at Aquinas were a good lesson for me. I learned firsthand that some of the best education and some of the most motivated students are to be found outside of the elite institutions of higher education. There is no substitute for life experience, and adult learners usually have a lot more of it than traditional age students. That is why service learning and study abroad and internships have become so important for the talented young students we normally deal with.

The next thing I knew, it was time for my written exams, which covered the gamut of readings in my major and minor areas. After succeeding in the written phase, I moved on to the orals. I know now, having given many oral exams myself as a professor, that the face-to-face nature of the second phase of comprehensives is designed to allow the faculty to probe the student's verbal facility, logical processes, and ability to be calm under pressure. Having read the written exams, the faculty would have identified areas of potential weakness in my answers or would want to push me to be clearer in particular areas of inquiry.

My oral exam was administered by three faculty members. Their tone was respectful and humane, yet energetic and probing. I had taken courses from all of them, so I felt I had already established myself. Even if the proceedings were not quite verbal sparring among equals, they were more than a formal grilling by the hierarchically superior. I stepped out of the room while my examination panel deliberated. When I was informed a few minutes later that I had passed, I knew that I was two thirds of the way to completing my Ph.D. What remained was to craft a dissertation proposal, gain approval for it, and then complete the writing in a reasonable amount of time. I set myself the goal of being well into my dissertation by the end of the 1972–73 academic year, at which point I hoped to return to Notre Dame, probably to Moreau Seminary where I felt I could keep committed to my dissertation writing before pursuing a faculty position.

In November 1972, during fall break at Vanderbilt, Ollie and I took a celebratory trip to the Smoky Mountains to experience the beauty of the mountains as the leaves changed. For me, it was a perfect time to relax a bit and forget about reading and boning up and memorizing and fretting about papers and tests. The section of the Great Smoky Mountains National Park that Ollie and I explored in eastern Tennessee and western North Carolina abuts other national forests along the

Appalachian chain. We stayed for two nights in a motel in the middle of the park and spent most of the daylight hours exploring the scenic vistas and the hidden nooks and crannies. We were particularly taken by Cade's Cove, a small, isolated community that was advertised as the last place within the continental United States where genuine Shakespearean English was spoken. This was a function of the residents' cocoon-like existence, hidden away from the outside world. By the time we returned to campus, I felt re-energized and ready for the next stage of my pursuit of the doctorate.

From mid-fall of 1972 to mid-spring of 1973, I was busy refining my dissertation proposal. I wanted to undertake a topic centered in the American context. In my reading of certain American Catholic moral theologians I noticed that the "ethics of responsibility" motif, as articulated in the writings of H. Richard Niebuhr, was beginning to show up with some regularity. This Protestant-Catholic interplay seemed a good example of how ecumenical influence in the diverse world of American religion was taking place. Niebuhr taught for many years at Yale, and his orientation was more theoretical and methodological than that of his brother Reinhold. On the Catholic side, many moral theologians were beginning to explore the writings of Protestants who helped define the field of Christian Ethics. A second motivation for choosing an ecumenical topic was that it would allow me to draw upon my previous study in a Catholic setting in addition to my exposure to the Protestant corpus in ethics at Vanderbilt.

Professor Howard Harrod expressed a willingness to be my dissertation director. As anyone who has done doctoral work can testify, the dynamic between the director and the dissertation writer is crucial for the eventual completion of the degree. The term ABD (all but dissertation) describes the dilemma of some graduate students who successfully pass the comprehensive exams but never quite complete the writing component, sometimes because they get burned out or they prematurely take a full-time teaching position or they run out of money. But just as often it is due to poor advising or too slow a response time to chapter drafts. Good dissertation direction is a time-intensive activity, especially at critical points in the writing. Some faculty members, unfortunately, give it low priority compared to teaching and their own research and writing.

My experience was generally good. The feedback Howard Harrod provided was helpful and kept me on track. My main complaint was the lag time between submission of new material and critical reaction, but I kept working and was able to defend my dissertation in the spring of 1975, five years after I had enrolled at Vanderbilt.

My dissertation was titled "Contemporary Catholic Appropriation of H. Richard Niebuhr's Ethics of Responsibility." I defended it before my director, my four other readers, and a cross section of my peers. The appropriate formality was preserved, yet there was a strongly supportive spirit among those present. By then, all my readers had given their tentative approval to the document, so it was mainly a matter of not doing anything that might come across as tentative or lacking in confidence. In fact, I was by that time the leading expert in the world on my precise topic (more so than my faculty readers, who had only read some of the literature). My defense ended with the happy news that I would receive my Ph.D. officially at the May 1975 commencement exercises. Since I had no real reason to actually attend commencement, I received my diploma *in absentia*.

The mechanics of dissertation production in the 1970s, before the advent of word processors, spell checking, and computer-generated final copies, were tedious. Although I was a reasonably good typist and personally produced the original drafts that I sent to my director, once re-drafts became close-to-final versions I turned to the commercial market and employed a professional typist. The problem was that each change toward the end required considerable retyping and repagination. The final copy had 242 pages of text and 16 pages of bibliography. I received one bound copy and the Vanderbilt Library was given the other. Eventually, like all American doctoral dissertations, it was microfilmed and made available on call to any interested party.

The rumor mill had it that in the time between the completion of a dissertation and its defense, anxious doctoral candidates were subject to periodic nightmares about losing their only copy. Stories were told about tragic fires, thefts, and lost luggage. I knew some of those fears. I made sure on my flights to Nashville that I never let the dissertation out of my sight; no way was I going to put it with checked luggage. The funny thing is that after I defended the dissertation, it shrank considerably in its significance in my life. Like Lancelot looking for the Holy Grail, once I had found it I was ready for the next quest.

In graduate school, I had to keep my personal relationships to a minimum, not accept invitations very often to have dinner in parishioners' homes or enter into their lives the way their parish priests could. Graduate study is inherently tedious and requires constant recommitment to the task. I saw some of my graduate cohort drop out of the program, not because they lacked the intelligence but because, for whatever reason, their heart's desire led them elsewhere. I came to appreciate that the reward went to the persistent—stick-to-itiveness was more important than mental genius.

AFTERWORD

As I look back on my life from birth to the completion of my doctorate and the beginning of my full-time ministerial engagement at Notre Dame, I feel a sense of amazement and thankfulness. I came from relatively humble roots yet with certain God-given talents, and the opportunities that accrued to my education in Catholic schools and at Vanderbilt prepared me well for the challenges to come during my professional career. My schooling was first rate, and both my curricular and extracurricular activities were instrumental in teaching me how to think, how to research a problem, and how to build a consensus. My athletic involvements opened me up to negotiating the country's growing racial and ethnic diversity. I also became comfortable as a public speaker, as a group leader, and as an advocate for positions and causes. My Catholic faith was nurtured at home, in my local parish, and in the schools I attended. I discovered that the older I got, the more I wanted to live out my Christian faith in a way that drew the connections among reflection, prayer, and service.

Almost all my education was paid for by others—my family and the institutions and benefactors that enabled me to pursue the degrees necessary to work in a university setting. As I returned to Notre Dame, I felt a great sense of indebtedness. It was time for me to give myself back in service to others and to prove that their confidence in me was not misguided. I was full of enthusiasm and energy and resolve. I hoped and prayed that the God who had so dramatically given me the gift of a call to the priesthood in the summer of 1962 would assist me in keeping focused on the mission and in joining my efforts to my Holy Cross and lay colleagues.

In many ways, at that point I felt like the luckiest guy in the world.

INDEX

Edward A. "Monk" Malloy, C.S.C.,

served from 1987 to 2005 as the sixteenth president of the University of
Notre Dame, where he is currently professor of theology. He serves on the
board of directors of a number of universities and national organizations
and is the recipient of twenty-two honorary degrees. Father Malloy is the
author of five books, including *Monk's Notre Dame* (University of Notre
Dame Press, 2005).